Manifesting

Lightworker's Log

Sam

Cover image (PIA16884:Taken Under the 'Wing' of the Small Magellanic Cloud) courtesy NASA/JPL-Caltech.

This book is dedicated to those lightworkers who have yet to find their way. Have faith; although physical appearances may not seem so, all is coming into focus, allowing a greater expansion of Self for all humanity.

Contents

HOW TO CREATE

No form can come into creation,
Without a thought as a picture.
For every thought contains an idea
That is the criteria of expression.

Let us look at the process
That brings access
To creation...

What is it your wish to create?
Is it worthy of your time and energy?
What is your reason to bring this into existence?
Is it to satisfy an addiction or comfort zone
Or get you arrested on the way home?

Make sure what you wish to create
Has no motive or need to do harm to another,
But has an intention of a loving brother.

Write down your plan in your own words,
As clearly and consciously as you can,
Then you have a starting plan...

Know you have the ability to create,
See it like a picture on a plate,
The seeing and the power to create
Are the gifts of God-state within?

Seeing and feeling within yourself
Allows you to lift creation off the shelf.

The heart already knows,
But keep reminding the mind
Creation is the ability
To see the God within all the time.
For God is the doer, the doing, and the deed,
And you through Him can create, and proceed with,

Whatever you need.

Read your written plan again and again
At the beginning and end of each day.
This way your creation is downloaded in your heart
That is the best part and start.
Keep your intention to yourself,
Hold its power inside you,
So only you know its view.

When you are ready,
Steady yourself and allow
You inner vision to come through,
Consciously connecting to the Law of Making
And the God-within you to come fully come through...

Cast out all doubts and fear
And know in your heart
Your creation is near.

Have no set moment for results,
Just know you and God are issuing
The picturing of results,
With no wishing.

Allow yourself to be surprised and delighted,
And filled with gratitude
When your multitude, comes forth.

"HOW TO CREATE" is used with permission from
*SACRED POETRY & MYSTICAL MESSAGES To Change
Your Life & The World by* Phillip Elton Collins. Visit
theangelnewsnetwork.com for book information and a
wealth of resources.

Author's Note

There are no mistakes. Those that cross our path brighten the way to true awareness. Of this, I am certain. Unseen guides continue to assure that this physical host is in the right place at the right time, always delivering the appropriate message to the right person. But even as I finalize this fourth book in the series, of a lightworker finding her way back to Oneness, I'm not certain it will make it to the printer. As things continue to change, I often wonder if it's necessary. Surely, the whole of humanity will reach unheard of heights of awareness very soon.

Manifesting is not as difficult as one would imagine. It is all a matter of deciding desires and focusing on the feeling of having them. Most people long for riches beyond comprehension but I've found that focusing on the little things of life often leads to something much better than imagined. The trick to manifesting is to feel gratefulness for what you already have. It's the feeling that drives the manifestation of all desires. This feeling springs forward easily by focusing on what is good in your life.

At one time, I found it difficult to manifest anything of value. It was then that I began the journey back to Wholeness by starting very, very small. I envisioned the joy of reaching the door and when that goal was met continued on to placing my hand upon the shining knob, turning it and opening the door to look outside. It took a week before I actually stepped out onto the porch but with each step into the neighborhood, I realized that reaching desires meant taking that first step into another reality.

This book is all about taking a step into another reality, learning how to change thoughts and create a better life. Although it often focuses on ego-based desires, it leads the way for one to manifest on other levels of reality for each difference in awareness helps us to reach the heights desired by soul. Each change in thought brings us closer to a new reality of Wholeness, Truth, Love and Light. We need only open our minds to the reality that this life is not the only life to live. There is so much more to experience!

Manifesting shows how it's possible to grow in awareness of the Oneness in which we reside. It's useful for anyone seeking to create a better life for it offers tools and resources to evolve consciously and notes many instances of being in the flow of Spirit. *Manifesting* also notes physical, mental, and metaphysical signs of an increasing vibrational rate.

As previous books in this series, *Manifesting* uses a unique method of comparison and expresses new ideas and valuable insights. It outlines daily practices leading to abundance, joy and peace, documents the power of thought, displays what it's like to be in the flow of Spirit, notes tools for self-mastery and increasing vibrational rate, and offers examples of Spirit's subtle guiding energy. It also relates what it's like to be connected to the God Network as an unknowing lightworker.

Italics identify messages received in 2007 and while writing the book. They also note beliefs while refining the book, lessons learned, and revelations after certain experiences.

Yet, when it's all said and done, everything is illusion, a virtual-reality game in time and space. I am grateful to report that humanity changed the game to expand beyond the original end-point. We are awaking to our true potential at an astounding rate, learning all we need to know by tapping into the Truth of our BEing, an eternal unnamed void of all that ever was, is, or will be. Enjoy the experience!

Chapter One

Down to the Essence

"It is only on this earth that separation appears to exist." SAM – Book of One :-) Volume 1

Messages mark my awakening to the Divine Essence within. Odd words, between midnight and sunrise, sometimes the tail end of sentences, wake me. It's hard to document them all. Knowing they're significant for spiritual growth, they eventually end up in the computer. Familiar words come on this New Year's Day 2007 as dawn breaks on the horizon.

"For the entire Kingdom of God is to be."

Sleep beckons after placing the yellow, legal pad under my now very, uncomfortable futon. More words encourage me.

"I will make every effort possible to see that your business is a success."

Daniel's essence breaks through the veil. He speaks of "more than one temporary lapse of judgment." Drinking and taking drugs, and then driving a motorcycle, certainly qualifies as a temporary lapse of judgment. Daniel passed this way. Yet, as souls, Daniel and I chose to help one another return to Oneness. He fulfilled his promise after physical death by alerting me of our immortality. I continue to do my part.

Spiritual practices, based on *The Science of Mind* by Ernest Holmes, continue. Love and joy, directed by *Cause*, overwhelm while giving thanks for steadfast faith. Immense gratitude fills me upon repeating daily prayers, treatments, affirmations, and meditation. Meditation helps to assure a well-balanced mental and emotional life. It offers a pleasurable way to merge with the infinite, indwelling Spirit within. True healing occurs in this place of perfect Wholeness that knows nothing but Itself. Tuning into *All That Is* helps to unify the ordinary mind making it easier to connect with True Self (a higher vibrating energy beyond the mind).

Meditation offers an expanded glimpse of the illusion. Sogyal Rinpoche tells us greater possibilities arise when one ventures beyond ordinary mind to tap into the vastly different real nature of Mind itself. Mind represents the activating agent of Spirit, supplying its creative energy. Spirit, *A Course In Miracles* (Course) notes, is the Thought of God. It retains the potential for creating, but its Will, which is Gods, seems imprisoned while the ordinary mind dwells in separation.

Either sleep claims me or I'm in 'the gap' during meditation time. Conscious awareness returns as Isaiah speaks of sending the Light. I so love to consciously spread Light throughout space, time, and beyond!

A refined visioning board offers reminders to thank *All That Is* for the ability to create and share with everyone while traveling worldwide. Conscious mind recognizes the truth of this daily visioning despite physical evidence to back it up. What a sweet life it is to have everything needed while awakening humanity to its spiritual magnificence! I'm ever so grateful to heal through relationships, filled with wonder, for I am rich in all things good. Joy and abundance fills my life as I play all day, remaining positive and wise, always approachable. A great professional, I heal everything as God flows through me.

Intuition guides while drawing a picture of my new home amid beautiful mountains. It features a small pond and a large rooftop area where I calmly watch the sun rise and set amid a pyramid-shaped object. The home overflows with love, peace, joy and prosperity.

It's been a rough two days, full of aches, pains, and extreme tiredness, as rains pummel Fort Lauderdale during another cold front in January 2011. Messages increase while drafting this book.

"You think there is no direction, no guides to help you along the way. But the truth is – you don't stop to take the time to document. It is, after all, the Higher Self in which you live that does the talking.

2

"Don't be concerned about the so-called little guy that you think helps to guide the other masses of people who seem to be around you in your dream world. It is all God and you know that in the very core of your being. Yes, as souls, you have made up a delightful game for most humans to play and yet you forget that it is only one game in a realm of many dimensions to play.

"Things are a hotbed of drama for many people right now but you need to stay clear of this drama and concentrate on the Whole. Be careful to focus only on that which brings more Light to earth, more Wholeness, more Beauty, more Truth and most of all more Love.

"Do not be dissuaded by the false reports of woe for they are just that, false. You must remember that everything here on earth is false but many are awakening to that truth now, if only in their dreams. The wait is almost over and you must strive to stay serene in this world of false woe. Do not be pulled into the drama. Recognize it for what it is, bless it with Love knowing elsewise and move on to your quiet sanctuary, the Mind of One.

"Truth be told, it is just a smoke and mirrors effect to keep you in the dream. Do not be dissuaded by those who try to pull you back to their world of bondage and limitation. The limitation is only in your mind, the small mind of one within the larger Mind.

"These times are wrought with unnecessary desire for things. Go with the flow of Spirit. Know that the Truth abides in you and never leaves.

"Do you know who I am? I am the one in which you live, and move, and breathe, the very heart of you.

"The disdainful past goes quickly away as we merge with the One. One great, total One abides in you. Abide in the one of Protection and Truth. One source of truth lies within."

Much time unfolds with my now fourteen-year-old grandson, Samuel. We both welcome these last few days of school vacation. Books entertain me on Rebecca's large, back porch while Samuel and his friend play video games. Positive energy surrounds the house permeating every cell of my being while watching beautiful, multicolored butterflies float beyond screens.

Experience taught me change is the only thing we can count on. Earth is merely a projection of ordinary mind and only the glorious state of Truth remains unchanged. Some people cling to beliefs keeping them in limitation. Clearly, belief has nothing to do with *Reality*. These past few years of study taught me that beliefs change quickly, if one views circumstances in different ways. A strong urge to sell the old business continues so I can further evolve, contribute to humanity, and live the life of prosperity that God intends. This life is a 'rags to riches' story, to bring hope and increase faith, for many others and myself.

Today would have been Daniel's forty-fourth birthday. As I write listening to Daniel Namod sing "One Power" in the background, the music begins to waver. The spirit of my last-born son fills the air as words enter my head. I type furiously to capture them all.

"I love you Mom, even when I know you don't believe I am here. I am always with you, always. Don't forget that as we move forward in time to its end. All is well in your world and will become increasingly so. So don't sweat the small stuff. I knew you'd like that. It was a favorite saying of mine right before I went Home to rest a bit. It is so awesome over there in Mind, the big Mind, not the little one that we seem to relish in.

"Stay clear of the drama Ma for you know it will only pull you back into the maze. Stay out of the drama and know that all is well as we move forward through this time of great change. All is well and will continue to be. Don't fret. It does not serve you well. Smile more, go out more, move more, be more. Continue to strive for more of the real you, that one that does not want material things but just to BE. Just to BE is the only thing worthy of your time. Don't forget that it will always be there for you to play with.

"I know things may not appear wholesome at times but you must move forward out of the maze to the true Reality of One. It is an everlasting place of wholeness and truth, the only place of consequence. BE, just be for the sake of BEing and know that all is well.

"You ask about the books now. It is your charge to write them, your souls charge. But you know there is no soul, no body,

no impermance. So now, you do what occupies your time. But yet, it seems to serve the masses, which seem outside you. Remember, nothing is outside, you or anyone, for there is in Reality only One. That is the key to living. There is only One in which all reside. Living that truth by just BEing is crucial in other realms of Reality, which you shall soon see for yourself. Take everything in stride and know that all is very, very, well in your world and your world is the only world there is."

The CD player operates normally as a new disk begins to play. Years ago, I would have sunk to the floor in tears, over the impermanent body of my last-born son. Those days are gone. Now I know, with great certainty, this world in which I seem to live is illusion. I'm grateful to move more fluidly towards the state of simply "BEing," remaining loving and compassionate, despite appearances. Ignorance of True BEing lifts more with each passing day, along with the urge to stop adding to this book series. Yet, part of little me thinks my past saga and continuing journey is useful to help others move from this dream.

It's time to create a life filled with positive interactions by maintaining only positive thoughts. Today's goal is to remember that all judgment is within. This little self decides what is good or bad, appropriate or inappropriate. And here on earth, artificial concepts, devised by the little mind, keep it entrapped within a limited field of possibility.

This world is temporary and the power of thought changes circumstances. Rinpoche tells us in *The Tibetan Book of Living and Dying*, "Always recognize the dream-like quality of life and reduce attachment and aversion." When appearances cause us to react, we need to change our perception.

Thought is energy formed by consciousness. As noted by Gary Renard in *The Disappearance of the Universe*, consciousness is the level of perception, ego's domain. It's not of God but an experience of individuality. Consciousness, the first split (from *All That Is*), initiated into the mind after the separation, makes the mind a perceiver rather than a creator.

The essence of *All That Is* connects everything and attracts our innermost thoughts. Effortless empowerment of the little self comes through tapping into the nature of this Authentic

Power. A profound transformation occurs in collective consciousness as we break mind patterns to recognize our divinity, as parts of this massive Force. We awaken from the dream of matter, form, and separation. This rebirth, the ending of time, is a change of mind about the meaning of the world. There's no need to struggle or to stay in situations that no longer serve. We need only be true to our Self, that one lovely Self of *All That Is*, the only existing Truth.

Chapter Two

Changing Ordinary Mind

"Once we realize the Law of Attraction, the power of thought, we can rest safely and calmly unaffected by the turmoil around us." SAM – Bits of Wisdom

Time fills with prayer and wise words from recommended teachers. "Is Authentic Power truly within us?" I wonder while reading. Of course, conscious intention is important for increased awareness comes from believing new ideas! We are much more powerful than consciously imagined and must become aware of our different aspects. Appearances always change to match our state of awareness.

Invitations to family gatherings continue to decrease but it's increasingly clear; I'm not alone. There's good reason for what occurs as insights, intuitions, and messages continue. Today I scrutinize my attitude, choosing to act only with love and reverence. Will this change affect family interactions even more?

It's time to be more sensitive to energy fields and to develop the kind of psychic energy that comes from the super conscious mind, True Self. Sonia Choquette's tapes greatly help to allow myself the pleasure of being physic. Frequent gut feelings, what Sonia refers to as "vibes" guide me more each day. This very subtle and non-coercive guidance is unlike other experiences. I'm now grateful to recognize when it comes.

The cassette player unexpectedly switches to the reverse side of the tape while I listen in 2011. It repeats what sounds like "freak realities," reminding me that we live in an illusionary world. Everything we think and see, everything we hear and touch, is all a part of consciousness made by human thought and souls. Love is the only eternal thing existing between souls.

*Only **All That Is**, whatever name one chooses to describe before the beginning of separation, is real. This knowing makes writing about past beliefs more difficult. Is there still a part of me* *lost in the dream? Are there people within this false reality unaware of their true nature and living in undesirable conditions? I would prefer to believe there is not, and yet, something spurs me to continue writing in the event that this information makes a positive difference.*

The cassette player again reverses sides when I push the play button and repeats "it is no longer appropriate."

"Thank you for the reminder," I tell unseen guides while continuing to refine the first draft of this book.

Gary Zukav's voice echoes throughout the room verifying that interactions with others occur in non-physical reality. Am I really a dynamic system of light with a frequency that changes based on consciousness? Meister Eckhart – 13th century spiritual teacher – tells us, time keeps the Light from reaching us. There's no greater obstacle to God than time.

Is everything on earth, including emotion, merely consciousness, energy, ready to morph at my command? And in changing my consciousness do I really change the frequency of my light? Emmanuel reminds us, "The very act of incarnation is the statement of a soul's yearning to become one again with the Light." Is this true? And do intentions (the ways I shape energy) really influence others?

My body does seem to feel better when creative or concentrating on loving or caring thoughts. Nevertheless, this is something to investigate at another time, for thinking of the universe "in terms of light, frequencies, and energies of different frequencies," is presently too much to comprehend.

Days fill with a hefty mix of reading and treating for others and me. The ringing telephone interrupts today's meditation. I mentioned to Samuel that I might visit a thrift store today. He now asks if he and his friend can join me to look for video games.

Happy hours unfold as we shop in various stores. Samuel and his friend laugh heartedly when I announce that Momma's birthday present is an electronic game with lights and big, colored buttons. An accident closes the west freeway exit when it's time to deliver Momma's gift. I use the opportunity to bless all involved with whatever their soul came to experience before heading toward Tuesday's *It's All God* class.

I don't do as many blessings now, yet know it's necessary to speed our progression back to Truth. We are spiritual beings living a dualistic life on earth. For many, it's now time to return to the Light of our true BEing, the Light of One. After all, it is where we came from and where all will return.

Many people now prepare to leave this planet, including some blood family members. It's not easy to stand by knowing this so I asked for something to help them pass quickly into the Light. "A Blessing of One" flowed through after I asked for guidance. At first, it didn't make much sense but now I understand. We are the result of thought here on earth but in **Truth** *One.*

"I offer a blessing for those now in the transition between duality and wholeness. It spreads throughout the land of woe, which seems to cover the planet of earth.

"It is not a likely thing to let go of duality while still in human form but this blessing will assist in processing those who wish to help others do so. It is not a blessing that comes from this human host but rather one that comes from the core of BEing, the core of our soul, the Truth of One. Unto itself it is not needed, and never will be, but to the human it is wholly needed during these times of vast change.

"We, as humans, are making our way ever so slowly and carefully back to whole freedom of Self. This Self is what we are, and yet, it too is imagined in our host of Hosts.

"And so the blessing begins:

"Follow me now to Truth, to Light, to Wholeness, and Love. Follow me to the very core issues that stop humanity from progressing. And now to the Light I offer a Oneness host.

"The Light fills all of humanity with it's brilliance. It fills every spot seen and unseen. It controls all issues of light and dark and relentlessly follows the path back to Oneness. It is the enlightenment of people everywhere, for now the Truth has entered the realm of many to bless, to own, to the Truth of One.

"I bless all seen and unseen, all left and forgotten, all here but never here, with the Light of One. It is the Light of Truth

to carry those of you Home, who wish to leave now as the games continue relentlessly.

"Know that there is nothing to stop you from leaving this planet to return to Light. Know that the truth of your being, the truth of all beings, is One everlasting, grateful One.

"Fill all with the security of Oneness and within that Oneness there is the most brilliant Light to help all who waver along the path. The Truth of BEing is known to few, but shall spread quickly, ever so quickly, to One."

Dr. Charles Geddes, who prefers that we address him as Charles, steps in to teach class for Dr. Arlene Bump. I'm so very grateful for the great experience he offers. This amazing, true mystic unknowingly verifies a lot of what I see. His very presence fills me with joy. Charles holds an awareness of living on other planets and soon notes differences in channeling methods. He channels only the *Holy Spirit*, the *Voice of God*. How truly amazing it is as he tunes in to people in class!

The daily meditation and more log continues to fill as I rise to document a message at six o'clock the next morning.

"And in this space I give myself the permission to grow in prosperity, in wholeness, and in health, as I was meant to evolve now and forevermore."

Beloved Charles guides me, now offering a uniquely designed Spiritual Mind Treatment, while repeating early morning work! I feel him strongly, hear his words clearly, and now repeat the affirmation he guided me through about accepting the riches of my True Self. It's way cool to have such a mentor and I'm so very blessed to know it.

I'll become aware of a vibrating energy field, which seems to hold me in place while receiving messages. This energy stream will come on the cusp of sleep and during waking hours, assuring me that messages are the truest thing known at this point in my human life. Deliciously different breathing (the intake and out breath) changes as well.

A message subsequently named Humanity's Goal comes in early January 2011 at 11:11 AM.

"Humanity's goal is quickly becoming the goal of One. Humanity's goal is to move closer to that light that left so long ago within. All is in Divine Order as we sail along the seas of woe. The brightness of our love shines through the darkness ever guiding us to the One within.

"All in due time my dear, all in due time. The message of One is within you. It is within all of humanity and it shall never leave. The message of One is your essence, the essence of God, Spirit, the holy one within.

"All is well within this time on earth even though physical appearances may not appear so, may not seem so. The plates of humanity are shifting and the plates of humanity are refining, retuning, rebuilding to a better world, to a better faith within the system of One. Know that all things come in time. All things come in time to be heard within the One. All things come in time to be known within the One.

"There is that within you that never stops, that never sleeps. There is that within you that is One, one holy BEing of Light. This Light shines forevermore. This Light never dies. This Light is the one True Light of humanity and it shall shine again, everlasting, never to leave. All those within this realm know this truth. The chosen ones go forward now to lead the others. No one is left behind for all moves forward as one. No one is left in the darkness for the darkness dissipates with the Light. The darkness seeks an answer to its self and moves toward the Light on its own. There is no truth in darkness and even darkness knows this truth.

"Go forth and spread the word of One, for the word of One is all there is, and ever shall be. This truth abides within all. This truth is the truth of One. Do not seek outside yourself. The world remains within."

Something about the "Time Zone" and "Isaac Asimov" fills my head minutes later. An Internet search notes Isaac was a science fiction writer who lived from 1920-1992. Four references to "Time Zone" are associated with Mr. Asimov's name. Isaac Asimov, famous scientist, author, and visionary wrote a series of books. The last book in "The Foundation Series" was *Forward The Foundation* published in 1988.

Mr. Asimov once said, "It is change, continuing change, inevitable change that is the dominant factor in society. No sensible decision can be made any longer without taking into account not only the world as it is, but the world as it will be" (careertrainer.com). Perhaps this is a message for me. Yes, change is inevitable.

Higher Self now prompts me to make chicken noodle soup, always a labor of love, stressing that it will do more good than currently known. I'm guided to make it at my daughter's house. Various tourists fill the supermarket. I weave quickly down aisles before unloading soup ingredients on Rebecca's kitchen counter.

Rebecca arrives unexpectedly right after I start the soup. She took the day off work and is pleased to see me making the family's remedy for illness. I give her a hearty hug, grateful for guidance, before she crawls into bed.

Many people complain of the flu so I'm glad Rebecca has a variety of disposable containers. There's plenty of soup for everyone as I dish up a bowl for my lovely daughter. The rest of Rebecca and Samuel's portion sits in the refrigerator as I leave to distribute the remaining soup to my brother Terry, Dr. Bump, and her mother. There's even enough soup to bring some home before attending the evening service.

Sonia Choquette's voice booms through car speakers, as she talks about the power of food made with love, while I drive to the Center for Spiritual Living (Center). How reassuring to know that I'm indeed connected to the flow of One! Rampant sickness will not affect me. Guidance continues to affirm it's all good. It's time to accept my rightful prosperity and abundance. A physical move to another residence lies on the horizon. Some kind of funding stream will soon allow me to match thoughts with physicality!

Continuing to support night services seems very important, as once again, less than five people attend Wednesday evening's service. Rev. Irene DeGroot listens as I voice communication concerns before secretly tossing a $100 bill into the offering. It feels good to tithe money from the proceeds of my father's wrongful death lawsuit.

Television (TV) sounds blare throughout the house as I stride quickly to my room trying to ignore holes in the ceiling. My time in this house is shortening; I can feel it. I've accepted good health with gratefulness and shall accept prosperity when Divine Timing dictates as well.

How wonderful to know that Spirit is our True Source! Tonight's study notes the way to handle wealth is to have it, but not allow it to affect or possess you. The computer screen turns black as I type. It makes no difference for I just keep logging daily events knowing all is well before retiring for the night.

Senseless words wake me often before sun peeks above the neighbor's roof. Sunlight streams into the room as I shake my head upon remembering, *"We tell everybody we shorten limits in skills of out of body."*

A change in breathing jolts me awake minutes later as waves of heat radiate from my chest. It's a familiar sign. Air flows up my nose and unexpectedly out through my mouth as when trying to meditate deeply. Night sweats, experienced before the last hysterectomy, do not compare with today's body heat. I jerk off my top and put long, brown hair up, to get relief from the heat. After repeating prayers and treatments, the heat dissipates allowing me to fall back asleep.

"Each have our own role in this world. And yet, we all have one thing in common. We are bringing in more Light to the world. We are leaders of One."

Mid-afternoon marks the time I finish reading *Far Journeys. Talking to Heaven* becomes new bedtime reading material. Communications from Higher Beings soon fill the night whenever invited. Although I cannot recall all messages, some do go into my journal. *All That Is*, God, my Higher Consciousness, always leads the way and I'm ever grateful.

Today Samuel is not feeling well so instead of picking him up from school I leave early to visit him. His friend comes over for a few hours and by the time his friend leaves, Samuel feels well enough to accompany me to Ruth and Naomi's house to celebrate Momma's birthday. Terry is still too ill to come.

"Please be aware that the earth is changing rapidly and the body within changes as well. Know that all is well within the soul of One for that never changes. Peace is always with you, above and below, within and without.

"You are the thought that builds the world, the image that radiates the Light. Be careful with those thoughts and words. It is time to get together; focus as One more clearly. It is time to come together and shine your Light. The brilliance of that Light is everlasting. It shines across the land purifying and cleansing all. Just as you trust in the future of humanity as One, you must trust in the Power within. Know that Power is within you and bear the Light wherever you go, consciously spreading it across the land. Know the land is your sacred home."

Dreams of a group of lightworkers, coming together for a meeting of like-minds, came right before this message. It's becoming clear that I'm one of many who come forward to form local groups. The lightworkers I speak of stopped looking outside themselves. They are unlikely to frequent places of worship or centers of learning. They value and nurture a knowing that comes from direct experience of the One in which we live, and move, and have all BEing. They don't push their knowledge on others but offer it freely when approached. Their time is spent best consciously radiating Light into everyone and everything. If you are in this state of awareness, consider forming a lightworker support group in your area.

Momma seems to like the electronic game but needs time to learn how to play. Family members note she'll never use it as tactics to gain energy begin when I decline the dinner of burnt liver and onions. Naomi and Ruth (laid off before Christmas and still looking for work) seem very negative. I continue to center in Christ Consciousness, consciously sending love from my heart. Invisible waves of love continue to radiate, while silently refusing to feed the fire of separation.

Dense, negative energy surrounds me, while walking to the car, so I use the clearing method Sonia talks of on her psychic pathway tapes. It makes sense to do so after learning that our bodies are energy fields always capturing surrounding energies. I must remember to protect my auric field using Sonia's mirror method. If I visualize my body glowing with brilliant, white light, and place a reflective mirror in my auric field, that should limit the need to rid myself of negative energy. Also, it's always helpful to pump out the energy of love regardless of circumstances.

Several years pass before the importance of today's event becomes clear. Family always offers wonderful opportunities to help us evolve by revisiting our own attitudes and habits. Each experience offers chances to release habits keeping us in limitation and separation. We can slip back into our old ways of living or choose to act differently, and in the process affect group energy dynamics.

The cassette player comes to life as I start the car. Listening to Sonia's tapes, while driving, makes me feel fortunate to learn more every day. It's great to get confirmation, such as, to stay clear of chaos and away from unsupportive people to increase psychic awareness.

Another choice for dinner sits at a fast food restaurant near the house on 47th Drive. What a welcome treat to cruise through the drive through lane! I hungrily devour a baked potato, with broccoli and cheese, in an empty, bank parking lot.

Course in Miracles classmates welcome me with hugs minutes later. Loving energy invites us to relax and enjoy. We take turns reading from the beginning of the Course book. According to the Course, God created us full of light, joy, and peace. Our truth is unchanged, for Creation is eternal and unalterable, despite what appears physically.

Yes, I AM one Self, united with my Creator, at one with every aspect of creation, and limitless in power and in peace. I AM complete, healed and whole, with the power to let the Light within come through to teach the truth. There is no we, no they, no us, no them. There is only One in which we live, and move, and have all BEing.

*Years of religious instruction taught me that I do not need anything between **All That Is** and me. The mind I continue to count on to function here creates the only barriers between God and my little self. It makes sense that if this is an illusion of my* *own making then I can choose to live abundantly. I do not have to give anything up for what I have is illusion anyway. I am grateful for the Course makes such a wonderful difference in this illusion of human life. The ways of the world become more meaningless with every passing second. "Why not envision an abundant life free of limitation for everyone?" I ask myself.*

Chapter Three

Counting on Change

"During these times of great change for humanity, one must recognize the other parts of the Whole as parts of themselves." SAM – Book of One :-) Volume 2

Nonsensical messages and numbers fill the hours between dusk and dawn. Prayers, including the World Healing Mediation, escape thin lips, as usual, right before sunrise. It feels as if I'm fighting off a cold. Several people at the Center kiss me on the mouth, as if paying tribute, or as a secret acknowledgement of Oneness. I feel self-conscious to turn my head away even though it's no longer my practice to kiss that way. Sleep beckons again after a silent reminder to define stronger boundaries. Sunshine rises over the neighbor's roof when more words wake me.

"Just touch, touch, touch, to your body to heal."

Multicolored orbs follow me to the bathroom while thinking. "Is it really that easy?"

The Science of Mind (SOM) fills my brain while drifting back to sleep. Our human form is matter, an aggregation of small particles. Matter, Deepak Chopra and Wayne Dyer both note, flows continuously like a river, so bodies change constantly. Pure, formless Spirit exists forever at the center of all form. But new particles, replacing old forms, take the same form because something within provides the same mold. We are some part of *It,* so providing thoughts for a new mold of wholeness, to wipe out any dis-ease, makes a vital difference.

"...ancient Mayan."

"How insignificant," I think, while rising to meditate. (As the body continues to purify and cleanse, it's much easier to tap into higher aspects of BEing. Dreams sometimes clue us into probabilities. Although unaware of what Mayan means, next month a last minute cruise through the Western Caribbean will take me to ancient ruins in Cozumel, Mexico.)

Messages again wake me throughout the night. Two before dawn seem important.

"We in common are guided toward the Light."

*"**All** is the all to search for on this earth."*

Orbs enter the room with the sun as I study for class. This body continues to fight off a cold so Starcke's reminder to "Stop believing you were born" is quite welcome. We are formless consciousness beyond birth and death. The body exists only in time and space as a vehicle through which Life expresses *Itself.*

Ernest Holmes words ring true as well. Humanity is the result of evolution, from an Intelligent Cause – energy plus intelligence – left alone to discover its true nature. We are part of the great Whole with unlimited possibility of expansion and self-expression. Our conscious mind is self-knowing and can think independently of conditions. The sub-conscious mind is the Law of Mind in action, a mental medium through which we temporarily create. Thought calls things forth into expression and molds ideas, and beliefs, into visible form. Yet, our unity with good remains unrealized, as long as we choose to deny it. Steadfast faith of being in the flow of good allows us to create dreams consciously.

Only the flow of good interests me now. Tonight's manifestation includes an outing to see a late show with Rebecca. Our relationship improves as we spend more quality time together. Rebecca seems to understand my new way of living but cautions to stay silent around family as we drive home at one o'clock in the morning.

Fleeting messages continue during the night. A runny nose and dry throat accompany me while repeating half the usual prayers before lying back down at 5:30 AM.

Remembering messages from True Self becomes much easier in 2011.

"It is a matter of resonating with the One. You either resonate with the One now, or resonate with the One later. There

is no if. It is a matter of resonating with the one Light of all BEing.

"We seek to return to the Light, and yet, there is no returning for the Light resides inside each and every one of us. That Light is everlasting, and if we choose, we can tap into that Light, very easily, and very efficiently. Knowing that all come together as Light in the end of what you call your world, there is no end and no beginning. There is only one pure and brilliant Light to resonate with, to be, to shine. Resonate with the one Light knowing, as you do, you resonate with the One of All."

A blue orb sits behind closed eyelids. Sunlight covers my face when the next message comes.

"You will leave in six months time."

There's more. But all I recall is that I'm to live life fully. What a welcome thought since I've confined myself to mainly one room for more than a year!

During afternoon meditation, a little girl's image along with the word Zyprella appears in my mind's eye. "Why am I seeing this little girl when I have asked to know my spirit guides?" I demand. The image abruptly disappears before I realize she's a guide. Zyprella does not return even after I apologize. "Since disbelief chased her away," I tell myself, while settling back down on the black futon's thin mattress, "I must strive to accept what comes without question." 'The gap' engulfs me again while on the moon sending white light to earth. A minute later, the CD player turns itself off.

Silence disappears on Sunday afternoon as rings from the black speakerphone fill the room. Her car clutch, Rebecca reports, is broke. She's at Ruth and Naomi's house wondering if I'm coming to spend time with family. James is already there. I quickly agree to loan her my car after the Center's evening service. Things will unfold as they should. They always do.

Rev. Mary Jo Van Damme Rance and her husband Rev. Gerald Rance continue setting up the smaller classroom when I arrive to make coffee. Always so happy to see me, their hugs fill with love. Tonight they look at one another and shrug when I ask why the outside sign doesn't announce their service.

"Who's in charge of what goes on the sign outside?" I wonder as the ritual begins. Since miscommunication concerning the Center's schedule seems evident, I'll continue to promote Sunday night service during class, and the now routine Wednesday night's service.

Three people sit besides me as Rev Jerry speaks. His message inspires as usual and I'm happy to see he's getting better after back surgery. As we hug goodbye, I bless him with light, love, peace, and healing. He thanks me after the hug as if feeling the silent blessing.

Green lights pave the way while driving to Rebecca's house. She pulls into the wide, gravel drive minutes later with James right behind her. Joy fills me knowing James is becoming more considerate. I'm so happy for him!

Silence fills the white van as we drive home several minutes later. I'm compelled to ask if anyone plans a funeral service for Martha, his mom. She passed more than a month ago and there are still out-of-town family members to contact. James calmly announces it's his sister's decision.

"Even though you may be in human form for the first time," I quietly declare as we wait at a traffic light, "you're still an old soul."

"You've already told me that," he replies softly before raising his voice. "What's your point?"

"What do you think evolution is?"

"Mutation," James answers with a smirk while rounding a corner.

"Doesn't that mean change?"

"Yes."

"Well, change is needed to evolve and it's the only thing we can count on."

Bart, the big, orange cat, crosses the driveway as James stops the van. He turns the motor off, steps out of the van, and silently enters the house. I've told him before that change is all we can count on. "Perhaps he'll make the changes needed to evolve his soul before I move on to help both our souls evolve," I think, walking quickly through the dark house to my light-filled room. "Or perhaps the message is solely for me."

Fear would have filled my brain years ago after this kind of interaction. But now I know much more about the concept of fear. Fear, as Eckhart Tolle notes, cannot prevail against the power of Now. My entire life, it occurs to me while moving swiftly past the bathroom, has been a progression from rags to riches, limitation to freedom, from fear, with fleeting glimpses of love, to total love without fear. The greatest adventure of the mind of man, Holmes reminds us, is to overcome fear.

This world, and everything in it, is illusion. The Course says bodies are symbols for a concrete form of fear. We are One, pure Love, devoid of anything else. Perhaps, James and his sister already know this and it's my mind that needs to evolve...

"Silence no longer threatens," I think, as the bedroom door closes firmly behind me, "but feels quite comfortable."

This body's progression is a lesson for others and myself. Life, until Daniel led me to the Center, was vastly limited. After the sale of the business or some event that produces the necessary funds, I think I'm to write a book in addition to seeing more of the world. It will hold journal notes but not those kept since childhood. Perhaps it will describe how the sudden so-called death of your child may not necessarily be a 'bad' thing for an unseen life exists beyond this one. It's real, true and eternal with *Source*. Death is an illusion, for as Daniel's essence noted after passing from physical form, "I never was and never will be."

Words wake me at 4:00 AM, as if someone and I talk while the body sleeps. *(Higher Self often instructs and leads us to true BEing during sleep.)*

"So I am a Pantheist because I believe God is everywhere. God is in all things."

I rise, use the bathroom, and return to bed only to wake several more times. Ongoing messages range from senseless words to sentences with great meaning such as *"Lift up thine eyes unto the Lord and see the greatness therein."*

Based on my experience, dreams consist of times spent in parallel dimensions and other realms, current life probabilities, messages from True Self, and what the brain processes of daily activities. This is important to consider for experience is subject to how the brain chooses to process it. Brain processing includes everything we see with our eyes, hear with our ears, read and react to, and sometimes try to ignore. These things often turn up during the delta state of sleep while dreaming. Strong emotional reactions are more likely to crop up in some form during sleep.

The True Self waits for recognition. It reaches out in a variety of ways, such as dreams that offer us hints of things to come or a "heads up" in times of turmoil. We all have dreams. But the trick is remembering them so we can glean their messages. Documenting dreams offers physical proof of True Self's guidance. Do yourself a favor and set aside more time to tap into the Source of One. It's always broadcasting and acts as a finely tuned radio with practice. We need only tune in to hear messages that offer us the freedom we seek.

Pay attention to thoughts, dreams, and especially to the people you interact with during sleep. Try not to make sense of, or judge, dreams just record them for future reading. Meditate or sleep more. As you meditate, or before you fall asleep, decide what kind of guidance you prefer. Some people ask a specific question while others may want to hear from angels or a certain departed loved one. Asking to hear a message for your highest good is always beneficial.

Noises by the window wake me at 8:45 AM. Two large tears roll down from my left eye. No one will ever again hear the sound of James' and my lovemaking. Sun shines on my face while wondering where the words came from. 'The gap' soon welcomes me after standing on the moon to send light and love to all living things.

A whole new way of living arrives. Persistent computer issues don't matter as much. Spiritual efforts take center stage, as I no longer constantly project limitation on the small self. Today's study of *It's All God* reminds me I'm in the process of jumping off the cliff, letting go of mental and physical things counted on throughout life. Living by grace, knowing God appears as that of which I AM, makes this process not as scary as before. I AM is the name of God, the creative center in all people, experiencing life in the flesh. Yes, I AM that I AM!

Clearly, there's work to do even though I may not yet comprehend its scope. Another role to act waits in the wings. I'm fairly certain it's the one I'm now preparing to play. But what is that role and can I stay out of fear as I play it? Yes! I am in a state of grace, which the Course notes is acceptance of the Love of God, devoid of fear.

Computer screen issues continue. Sometimes I don't have access to this machine. The screen dims so greatly that it appears off. Either Martha's spirit is trying to communicate or physical world computer issues plague it. Last month it cost $90 for a 'computer expert' to report an issue with machine settings. The screen went out several times after the so-called repair so I knew it wasn't the issue and changed the settings back to my liking.

There are times like this when I turn the computer on and the screen blacks out within three minutes. Now I let the machine sit and do other things for a few hours until the screen becomes readable. The periodic issue is very irritating, if I let it be so. Thinking a spirit plays around with the laptop makes the issue less bothersome.

Today's work seems endless while finishing the weekly "HIV Nutrition News Update." More than six-thousand people, from 130 countries, visit the business website each month. It takes an enormous amount of time to format and upload files, design pages and updates with links, and send notices to the popular email list. Ego insists that creating new pages to hold older newsletter issues, and uploading free handouts, will help to sell the business my heart no longer holds dear.

Years later, it becomes clear how ego kept me from evolving as quickly. My energy no longer matched that of the business. How senseless it was to write and distribute information on a so-called incurable dis-ease, when I no longer believe anything is incurable! My vibration level changed and carried me into a totally new field of wholeness, which brings out creative aspects in other, more life-affirming ways.

After minutes of malfunctioning, the computer allows me to work on the tenth tape from Greece. *Talking to Heaven*, a book in which author James Van Praagh writes of departed souls needing help with unfinished business, then occupies the night. It reminds me of how both Daniel and Hannah easily came through me, from the other side, to help with their unfinished business. I now silently agree to continue helping newly departed beings through greater awareness. But I fail to clarify exactly when, and who, can channel through me.

Before drifting off to sleep, after eleven o'clock in the evening, I think about verbalizing my usual welcome to Higher Beings for help, protection, guidance, etc. But I'm too tired. Something unexpected happens right before midnight.

An invisible presence enters the room when I'm on the verge of deep sleep. It feels human. I sense it but am very tired and do not want to open my eyes. The image of a dark, looming figure now appears closer, next to my left side. Even though communication with this presence is possible, between this state of sleep and wakefulness, I do not acknowledge it. As I continue to ignore it, there's a pressing weight upon me, as if; it's trying to enter my body. Panic rises when the pressure increases as if something is laying on me.

By now, I'm somewhat awake and trying to say something, only the words come out garbled. I'm not mumbling but trying to shout or speak rather loudly. After about thirty seconds, I say something like "Stop it. I do not want you here if you are not a Higher Being."

The presence is gone in an instant. Out of the corner of my right eye, the twinkle of a light appears. It's a strong light, larger than the ones usually seen throughout the day. The battery light on the laptop, sitting on the floor to my left, flickers, as it does when the screen goes black, so I open the laptop up. Sure enough, the computer screen is black again. I leave it on thinking that perhaps the spirit will release it in the morning.

My heart pounds while springing out of bed to open the door and see if James is home. He's lying on the couch in his usual position watching TV. I ask if he entered my room. He gleefully answers "No." I then ask if he heard me and again he replies "No." I smile, thankful the TV drowned out my garbled voice, before returning to light a candle in my room.

After lying down, I repeat the usual bedtime ritual. The universe now knows. I'm only open and receptive to Higher

Beings and those on my level who wish to guide, protect, direct, and keep me from harm. Peaceful slumber follows the ritual.

"My will is God's Will," booms through my mind at 2:30 AM. Other communications wake me throughout the night. Either they're insignificant or I'm too tired to write anything down. Sometimes I just do not have the strength to reach over for the pen and paper. To communicate fully with Spirit, through these beings, I must remember to go to bed earlier to be well rested.

Daniel wakes me at 6:15 AM.

"You can send your message now Mom," he announces.

The screen works when I open the computer's lid.

"Thank you Daniel," I reply, before sending the email message and turning the machine off.

Joyful gratitude, for having such a strong connection to Spirit, fills the very essence of me. I know it's all God but it sure does give this physical body pleasure to believe Daniel and I are always connected. We are a part of God. And yet, this thing called me would not be as spiritually advanced without his help. We have been with each other, helped one another advance throughout this illusion of time and space, and in other places too, for a very, long, time.

Although my body seems to require more sleep than usual, it's wonderful to always get the guidance needed to progress. Spirit wakes me minutes after falling back asleep to say the World Healing Meditation. Wooden and metal chimes, hanging in the middle of the ceiling, softly clang as I repeat my favorite treatment before falling back asleep. Repeating the "Treatment for Continued Peace, Inner Sight, and Clarity" always makes me deliriously happy. For the past eight months, new, lighter energies fill the room whenever I say it.

Change is always good. Becoming a practitioner still seems a viable option. My changing relationship with James spurs me down the path. I plan to do more, perhaps be something like a life coach, a muse, to help people get through life. So many seem to put themselves through crap they do not need to experience. Sometimes life takes us on strange journeys that turn out to be great. My experience with Mary and her husband Seth last year, helping Seth to pass over, served to reinforce the belief that I can make a positive difference. Just being with them felt right and made it easier on everyone involved.

Morning email holds messages from old colleagues aware of my new chosen path. Some note I have a special gift while others focus on past efforts and request free materials. Thoughts now dwell on selling the hiv nutrition business. A smile graces my lips with the memory of Luke's spirit prompting me to start it more than ten years ago. Unseen forces helped to keep the business going. Now it no longer feels right to continue it. The thought of funding various spiritual projects is a heady one as I fall back asleep. Weird words wake me minutes later.

"Because it's a spirit and it knows many such things that I do not."

Even though I do not understand everything, it's important to continue documenting words heard. I know there are other types of beings so perhaps some are not spirits and that's why I heard this.

The black laptop screen disappoints once again after repeating remaining prayers. I leave it on and retreat to the bathroom. "Jose Fernandez" fills my brain. That's weird! Why do I have a name in my head? Oh yes, I invited spirits that just passed over to come for help with their unfinished business!

"What do you want Jose?"

"Forgiveness, I want help with forgiveness."

"There is nothing to forgive. We are all one. It is time to move on with your evolution. Know that we are all perfect, whole, and complete."

The sweet sound of silence refreshes. Jose is pleased. I'm really connecting now, or really stark, raving, mad. No, I'm not mad! The Course notes, "Salvation and forgiveness are the same." And "Salvation must reverse the mad belief in separate thoughts and separate bodies..." I must strive to accept and forgive everyone.

Another message breaks through the silence later when meditating. I will move within six months! After closing and opening the laptop repeatedly, the screen brightens so I change settings to get the screensaver back. Sometimes the blackened computer screen lights up when the screensaver kicks in so this is important to do. Fingers type quickly to document the day's events before backing everything up onto an external hard drive.

At this point, I find it necessary to add a few notes about living in the Now moment. Although it's the preferred place to be, for me it has disadvantages. Although many messages came to me in the past, I forgot most of them. The only way to remember them is by referring to personal journals. Because of countless computer and personal issues, and physical moves, it's a miracle that they're still available!

Today, I telephoned Rebecca to ask her what my home telephone number was! I've lived in this beautiful home for nearly two years now, yet, I can't recall my own telephone number.

Traffic seems light as I briskly cross the main street on my way to class. How wonderful to know, that as Eckhart Tolle notes, "If you are drawn to an enlightened teacher it is because there is already enough presence in you to recognize presence in another." However, since "Egos are drawn to bigger egos" I wonder how much more work there is to do on myself.

Classroom energy invigorates and propels me to speak after Dr. Bump distributes flyers promoting Sunday morning services. A quote appears on the back of the flyer but there's no mention of the poorly attended Sunday or Wednesday night services. Before class ends, I announce how wonderful the night services are and invite everyone to attend them.

Something pushes me to approach Dr. Bump before finishing hospitality duties. She notes, in a matter-of-fact tone of voice, while walking out the door, people who sign up for the email blast get notice of other services.

"What about those who don't get the emails or don't read them?" I think. Perhaps, the Center means well and they don't see their actions as non-support. So many things contribute to the miscommunication at the Center that I remain in disbelief that it runs at all. I then think about all the other ways that the evening services could be supported but appear not to be. My job, it seems, is to support and promote evening services so that's what I'll continue to do. Is it my concern that there seems to be an ego issue involved? Is it my ego that needs addressing?

"All things in time," fills my brain at 6:15 AM. Treatments, prayers, and spiritual reading consume the next five hours. Going beyond the script, not depending on anything outside the True Self, seems easy. Meditation homework helps my soul soar further along the path of Christ Consciousness as I open more fully to the abundant flow of Spirit. 'The gap' again welcomes me for a few fleeting seconds near the end of Track 3.

Although it truly feels like jumping off a cliff, I fall freely, letting go of the personal control clung to since adolescent years. I no longer consciously try to direct things the way I think they should be but allow room for Spirit to call the shots and guide. I'll know by the end of the year, without the glimmer of a doubt, that it *is* all God.

Rebecca still has my car. She telephones to offer family news and asks if I need groceries. I really need bananas, and spring water to stay hydrated, and connected to the flow, but intuition prompts me to stay silent while she continues to report.

Doctor visits now consume much of Ruth's spare time. Momma has gallstones but her usual doctor advised against surgery because of her many conditions. Ruth is scheduling an appointment with a specialist to see if she can have them removed without an operation. Samuel's father, Joshua, was in an accident days ago. He broke his trachea, in two places, and was in surgery for hours. Rebecca is disappointed that Joshua did not keep his promise to telephone Samuel as scheduled. No one knows when Joshua will be able to speak; but when he does, he'll talk differently than before.

I think of the being that visited two days earlier and recall how garbled my voice seemed to be. Joshua's accident appears to have occurred then so I firmly believe the presence was that of Joshua's soul. I think he tried to get a message to me so I could tell Samuel why he would not be contacting him as promised. Explaining this to Rebecca seems impossible so I quickly rattle off a small grocery list before we end the call.

In *Talking to Heaven*, James Van Praagh relates how spirits interact with him by using both their energy and his. "The energy is very much like an electrical current, and if they are nervous, it will send a wave, or rippling effect, through this electrical line and the thoughts will come through me as gibberish." Can reading this earlier today be a coincidence?

It's time to set ground rules for spirit contact. This type of communication, I note after becoming open and receptive, can come only when I'm awake and alert. Higher Beings, my spirit guides, must always be available to protect during these times or they will not occur. Intuition informs. It will currently be more useful for my talents, to help those beings still in physical form who need assistance. The reason is unclear. If this means people in a coma, or some state between physical life and death, so be it. Nevertheless, I will remember to listen always to the Truth.

Rev. Katy Peterson sings like an angel before Rev. Donna Conley relates her urge to start a ministry in North Carolina. They are both so nurturing and full of love that I want to take them home with me. Three other people are there to enjoy the service. I thank them individually for coming. Two of them are acquaintances and the other is someone who I asked during class to support Wednesday services. I remain in disbelief that the evening ministers do not appear supported by the Center. As the Course notes, we are God's messengers. "My voice is His, to give what I receive." Grateful to receive what I give, my new mission actively supports ministers dedicated to people unable to attend services during the day.

As the others leave, I ask Rev. Donna why she holds her hands a certain way during her treatments (somewhat like a Diamond Mudra). She seems unaware of the practice until Katy acknowledges that Donna does it repeatedly. They seem surprised upon hearing that I'm compelled to hold my hands in the exact form, somewhat like a triangle pointing down, during times when I sense it's the thing to do. I catch myself doing it when ministers repeat a treatment at the Center. As my hands remain in the position, I send love, light, and peace to the group.

"Another daily practice is to repeat my visioning process, which includes gratitude for the retreat I'll be at in the Blue Ridge Mountains," I boldly announce. "Do you know where these mountains are?"

"Part of them is where we plan to start our ministry," Donna replies smiling at Katy.

The walk home is invigorating. Life is full of surprises. James telephones right after I arrive to say he's stopping at the grocery store on his way home. He asks if I need anything. Two considerate gestures so close together is a terrific demonstration. I'm thankful my treatments appear to work while noting that Rebecca bought groceries.

Ernest Holmes tells us to be specific when treating for Spirit always responds. We must believe that our desire is already visible on the physical plane. With power and conviction, I calmly repeat a new treatment for limitless good before retiring for the night.

Words soon wake me.

"The safest land in the U.S. offers a safe haven to ensure the enlightened have a place wherein they may perform their greatest work. This task ensures the greater good of all humanity. Safe land and a safe and secure fortress await the chosen people right before the end of the days."

Daniel's essence fills the room at 9:50 PM. Once again, he answers questions and says not to worry. Several calls to my best friend remain unanswered. Ester, Daniel reports, will be having surgery. He announces it has something to do with the pace of her heart. (She later reports thyroid dis-ease.) Daniel announces Ester is in Texas visiting her daughter now.

Twinkle lights appear in the dried flower arrangement less than an hour later. Sometimes it's difficult to verify the lights I see since the arrangement has glitter in it. But these twinkle lights differ from the ones usually seen flying through daylight air. The Course tells us "close your eyes upon the world you see, and in the silent darkness watch the lights that are not of this world light one by one, until where one begins another ends loses all meaning as they blend in one." I so look forward to that reality!

James is gone when I rise in the morning so I leave a note on the kitchen counter thanking him for asking if I needed anything from the store. I rarely see him. Spirit continues to keep us from seeing one another, even when we're both home. Every time I leave my room, to use the bathroom or eat, he's either outside or gone. James has begun to pull away and get a life of his own. And that is a good thing for us all.

A different world now lies before me. Thoughts continue to change. The Course assures that God accompanies me. What I physically see reflects my thinking and I'm grateful for the ability to see the holiness within everyone. It's truly a gift to know "those who come to follow us will recognize the way because the light we carry stays behind, yet still remains with us as we walk on."

A strong sense of Oneness fills me with glee while reading the day's Course lesson. Yes! There's a light in me to see the world anew, shining in innocence, alive with hope, and blessed with perfect clarity and love. Forgiveness shines on everything in this world and peace offers its gentle light to everyone. I look upon that which I feel within, a world of compassion and love. Days and nights fill quickly with devotion to the Creator of all things.

Bits and pieces of sentences fill my mind upon waking throughout the night. They serve as proof that when summoned before bedtime; Higher Beings continue to guide toward an unknown destiny.

And yet, as evidenced from this message received at 11:11 AM on February 12, 2011, all we need to know dwells within us.

*"There are no messages that you do not already know. They are all held inside you waiting to be explored, waiting to be recognized as the truth that they are. **All** is One. **All** is here. **All** is Now, not left behind or looked forward to, but Now. The energy that flows through you is of the One of **All That Is** that no-named BEing which permeates your entire being and that of all living things.*

"The truth is known to all but recognized by few, as yet, comparatively speaking. It is an awesome power to behold within your Self, the Self of One. All are a part of this unending One of which all things derive. Your true power comes from within and that is the message of Now. It is the only message recognized by those that speak the truth of One. Hear ye, hear ye all. The message of One is clear. Speak thy truth from within yourself, the Self of One."

A very faint, pale orb hovers in the hall as I sit in the bathroom. It changes into a light show that switches between bands of white light to orb shapes between bands of light. Thank you Spirit for helping to train my vision so that I can see these things better!

Familiar eye flashes cover closed eye vision while meditating. Isaiah notes, "And don't you feel good" right before the CD player automatically shuts off. A popular James Brown tune fills my brain. Yes, I do feel good! Perhaps James Brown, who passed right before the New Year, sings with me. I thank him while singing, "I feel good like I knew that I would. I feel nice like sugar and spice."

Chapter Four

Changing States of Awareness

"Fear nothing for there is nothing to fear." SAM – Book of One :-) Volume 1

Beau waves me into Thursday evening's class after noting attendance. What a thrill to have Charles, our very own mystic, to teach and guide!

"No one is of this planet," he notes. "Look at the stars and moon each night to remember your origin."

The importance of constant gratefulness, giving thanks to God, and many other wondrous things flows forth. After class, I toss a dollar into the hospitality donations basket before cleaning the coffee station. Leah and I talk incessantly while driving home to the empty house on 47th Drive.

Excessive thirst overwhelms so I drink water throughout the night. The moon shines brightly at 3:00 AM as I stare while wondering, "Where am I most closely associated?" the answer comes quickly. *"Esmeralda. "Esmeralda, West Location."* Other messages about Rebecca, Samuel, and Jesus come before rising to use the bathroom. A very small, pale orb moves by. Is it there to train me to see normally unseen lights out of the brilliance from things such as candle flames and sunshine?

Clouds block rising sun as I repeat treatments before lying back down. The candle continues to burn brightly when sleep beckons once again. Words wake me minutes later.

"Keep the candle burning in me. It's not a candle. It's a light. My light is bright."

These words held little meaning when first heard. Now there's a knowing that Light is our true state of BEing. We are morphing back into that state quicker than ever before. A recent occurrence in late June 2012, verifying the brightness of the Light within, bears noting.

Life is much different for I've moved from place to place, without a home base, for almost four months now. The adventure keeps me much more physically active than ever before, while shopping for food, much more often, and carrying it much further. Walking up and down three flights of stairs helps to boost very poor exercise endurance. Tired, after yet another trip to the grocery store, I decide to rest in my hotel suite before unloading and carrying remaining groceries.

One of the car's rear lights seems to shine like a beacon at dusk when I venture downstairs. Yes, the light is on. I can't comprehend why, even with my fair share of car issues. Why, at one time I physically replaced a set of head gaskets, in younger years of course! Panic rises like an old friend while trying to determine the cause of this dilemma. But panic no longer suits my new state of BEing. I quickly start the car to make sure the battery still works. Of course, intuition guided me to purchase a new battery, after the first of the year, so I know everything will be okay when the car starts.

Living in 5-D reality does have its drawbacks. Changed perspective allows me to act instead of lament as two thoughts surface. "My light is really bright," is the first. The second is to disconnect the burning bulb, which I accomplish with a bit of effort. But the middle trunk light continues to glow, puzzling me even more. Fortunately, I know the solution is to seek help from someone still firmly rooted in 3-D reality.

With area repair shops closed for the day, my next thought is to telephone Rebecca to ask her fiancé if he knows what's happening. Adam says it's a brake light issue but has no idea why the lights remain on. He invites me over to remember how to disconnect the car battery. It's essential to disconnect it before the burning light saps all power. I can reconnect it in the morning before taking it for repair.

There's nothing else to do so I start driving toward the freeway blocks away. I stop at Sears on the off chance that the mechanics work late. They're gone for the day but intuition guides me to ask two male shoppers for help. I return to my car to replace the bulb for the rest of my drive instead. A woman pulls up beside me to park. She notes the same issue as I.

The two men come out of the store to head toward the truck parked two spaces away so I ask if they know anything about electrical issues. They assure me it's a broken brake light switch. Disconnect the right battery terminal for the night, they advise. Again, I think, my light is so bright it will never go out. Adam shows me how to disconnect the battery terminal minutes later. I soon stand under a bright streetlight back at the hotel to remove the cable.

In the morning, the usual mechanic advises me to leave the car for several hours because the shop is busy. "I'll take my chances and be right in," I announce, before hanging up the telephone. Thirty minutes later, I pull into the drive.

"You just came," he grins while handing back my keys within minutes, "at the perfect time."

Right before I pull away, the shop owner, who I've given advice to in the past, arrives and notices the light still on. Two mechanics now look for the issue, which they soon find. (A double rainbow sits in the distance as I type from the sixth floor balcony of another hotel.) There are two broken brake switches! Time spent waiting fills with another important message for the owner. And within thirty minutes, total time, I'm on my way to finish errands.

Once again, I think of the metaphor. My light is so bright it will never go out. That's how it is to be a lightworker. Everything occurs for good reason. And the so-called trials of life are not half as cumbersome or time-consuming as before.

Washing clothes outside in the laundry room is easier than in the heat of summer when I yearn for an air-conditioned room. Rebecca's situation preys on me while loading the washer. The dryer at her house broke more than a year ago. She stopped asking James to repair it and now dries laundry at Terry's house. My next house, I now vow, will hold new appliances sitting in a temperature regulated laundry room.

This world and everything in it is the result of my consciousness. It's encouraging to note the gradual unfoldment of inner self continues at a faster pace. Yes! I am spirit, in human form, a unique part of the great Whole experiencing earth life.

Rebecca telephones when meditation ends. Her first car loan, without a cosigner, is "in the bag." What a grand demonstration! She filed for bankruptcy less than two years ago.

Prayers and inspirational books consume the day. A large candle continues to burn brightly as I invite Higher Beings to guide, protect, and support. Familiar waves of heat engulf me. An oblong shaped glimmer of light, which looks like a wave, glides through the light of the half-full moon. Twinkle lights appear as well. It occurs to me to ask if anyone in this life has come from where I did. The answer is instantaneous.

"We have all come from the same place."

Charles comes to mind as I wonder something else before quickly hearing, *"We are not human beings. We are other entities."* Am I just tossing this up from hearing him say it and from reading Robert Monroe's books?

*Life is not as we imagine. There is just One, one Life, one Love, one Light, all within one perfect Source. The Course notes, when the mind elects to be what it is not, it dreams of time; an interval in which what seems to happen has never occurred. God set the Thought of eternal life and it's the life we share with **Him**.*

James rises to fish before five o'clock in the morning. It's reassuring to know he has friends. His friends are old souls, learned souls, souls that remember more than James seems to at this point. But does fishing mean more chaos in this house?

"We are often fooled by appearances," rings through my brain.

Minutes later, I jump, awake again, seeming to catch myself from falling. Loads of information flow through the veil. I don't need to document for when the time comes I'll remember. When the download seems complete, I rise to eat a banana, get more water, and use the bathroom. Before returning to bed, I write James a thank you note for buying my primary source of potassium.

I soon shiver from cold while hearing something about looking for the light. Minutes later, an intense wave of heat causes me to sweat profusely. After repeating the World Healing

Meditation, I ask for a communication, in words. Nothing comes. Could it be that communication does not always come in the form of words but feeling as well?

"Because it is a softness of sound" wakes me moments later as sun shines upon my face.

Various orbs fill closed eye vision. They vary in color, from hues like a green highlighter, blue, to golden-yellow, and red. There are also a few thick stands of colored light. Some attach to green-blue orbs and fill me with wonder. So much wonder, that as I type this, even when the computer screen goes black, I continue typing.

Meditation takes me fleetingly to 'the gap.' As I send the light, love, and peace to all living things from the moon, thoughts of Joshua arise. I send him love, light, peace, and continued renewal as I do for myself. An odd feeling permeates me. Is it what some people call the lightness of being? The feeling saturates and uplifts but I'm not physically moved.

A black speck on the white mat under the laptop catches my attention. It jumps when I try to pick it off thinking it might be a dust ball. There's no doubt that it's a flea so I bless it with good, light, and love forevermore, then thank it for letting itself be known. Of course, I announce it has to go outside. The adult flea sits still as I wet fingers, pick it up, and transport it to the back yard. As I let it go, I thank it for allowing me to bless it. That's my life in a nutshell. I just do what seems right throughout the day.

Heat envelops me again. After it dissipates, I lay down for a short rest. Who knows what the future brings? I only know my time here is limited and this is what I'm to do before a new life of riches begins. It's only a matter of time before I'll afford my own chaos-free place with more than one room to live in.

Next year Spirit guides me to a wonderful, extremely safe house that's much more than envisioned. It has everything on the list of things most important for me to have (a safe roof and windows; recently new air conditioning system and ducts; updated kitchen and bathrooms; back porch; view of land instead of back to back houses; and attached garage).

It's very much like the house on 47th Drive only much better, with one more set of sliding glass doors to bring in more light, a larger, finished back porch, and washer and dryer tucked inside the garage. The completely remodeled older home even has new appliances, new toilets, fixtures, some furnishings, and lawn maintenance.

Upon seeing wooden, kitchen cabinets (similar to those admired at Mary's house), a stainless steel side-by-side refrigerator and microwave (marveled over while in Anna's house), a reverse-osmosis water filter, and pastel yellow and blue-green walls (my favorite colors), it will be clearly evident how visioning the home paid off. The large master bathroom holds a roomy shower, double sinks, and toilet around the corner, which I appreciated while visiting Ester. And the view from the back yard features a long, wide plot of land beyond the wide canal. A very strong sense of my being in the perfect place permeates time, as I remain safe in the bosom of God's love.

Messages disturb slumber throughout the night. "I'll understand," I announce, while sitting up to look at the candle. Bands of light emit from it while I strive to make sure eyesight is clear. The bands are in a half circle coming from the top middle of the candle glass. They radiate out into about six, or more, wave like bands, until reaching the top of the half circle. More bands sit below and to the right of the candle glass. They're straighter but still wavy. Six or eight of them reach down toward the floor but they're only about two inches in length. Amazed, I lie back down to sleep.

Hearing something about pushing the envelope wakes me an hour later. Heat again envelopes me. It feels good to repeat the World Healing Meditation and remaining prayers before lying back down. Orbs soon fill my line of vision. They're still awesome to see but becoming more common.

Sometimes, it seems hard to have faith in how God works. Telephone messages to Ester remain unanswered so I know something is amiss. Rebecca still has my car. She continues to shop for a suitable vehicle and phones to offer updates.

Twilight falls while strolling to Sunday night's service. Traffic seems unusually light for tourist season. The sign outside announces Sunday morning's ritual and Pastor Bump's name but nothing about evening services. A terse phrase announcing them comes quickly to mind.

Rev. Kandi Haggerty welcomes me into the small classroom. Two other women attend the service. One of them is Elizabeth who plays beautiful, original music on the small piano. When the service ends, I tell Kandi how I feel about the lack of support for night services. The terse phrase, for the outside sign that entered my mind minutes before, flows forth.

"It would easily fit on the sign," I announce. "Consistency is necessary in marketing efforts and the Center could use the same wording for emails and flyers."

Tonight's beauty is awesome during the stroll back to the house on 47th Drive. Busy streets no longer affect me as traffic clears when I'm ready to cross.

Many communications occur during the night, and for the first time in years, I remember dreaming. Some of the dream seems associated with life experience. Stomach cramps, gas, bloating, and pain rack my body as I wake again, and again, and again. Each time I quickly rise to relieve myself in the bathroom. There's a sense that my body is refining itself, cleansing cells of impurities despite a Sunday diet of grains, fruit, and vegetables. Thoughts of sickness very rarely cross my mind. Yet, I now wonder if the cause is some kind of intestinal flu.

*Ascension (a change in our state of awareness allowing us to become more in tune with **All That Is**) affects the entire body. Increased geomagnetic activity spurs this process further as the body becomes more in tune. Purifying, releasing, and cleansing blocked energy often causes intestinal symptoms along with unusual body aches and pains. Many people experience what I now refer to as "ascension diarrhea" during times of higher vibrational frequencies and increased geomagnetic activity. Replenish fluids and potassium, by drinking orange juice or eating other foods high in potassium, and rest as needed.*

Quite often aches and pains surface as aching body joints but are also felt as organ flutters or sharp pains (as in the heart region). Always consult a healthcare professional if you have any question as to why your body experiences these changes. Several treatments may help if you're sure that they stem from vibrating in higher dimensional frequencies while still in a 3-D body. These include Epsom salt baths, massage, reflexology, sound, and light therapy, to name a few.

As your physical body changes to be more in tune with higher vibrating frequencies, heightened sensitivities (noise, smells, energies, etc.) can make life barely tolerable. Becoming easily overwhelmed in crowds or places with lots of activity or noise drives you toward the solitude of your own space. You're gifted with a heightened ability to smell things most people cannot, which seems to set you apart. This will eventually pass. But in the meantime remind yourself it's just part of the process and get as comfortable as possible.

Memory loss is also common as we move toward multi-dimensionality for living in the present moment is the way of the New World. While moving back and forth between dimensions we experience a 'disconnect' and easily forget commonly known words, directions, people, and all sort of things we never forgot before. This is something we adjust to in time as we realize the only true moment is Now. Nothing else matters.

A calm assurance notes this world in which I seem to live is truly a thought apart from God. I am not a body in *Reality* and cannot be sick. As a unique part of One, I've somehow lost my memory but that part of me beckons from the *Truth*. Surely, things experienced now are a sign of ascension.

There's no doubt that I've found the key to salvation. I choose my own reality. This world is illusion, the result of thought, and my true purpose is to wake-up and recognize the True Self. Healing is freedom for it demonstrates that dreams will not prevail against the truth of our perfect Oneness. I'm grateful to share this healing with the world knowing sickness can be banished, because it never was, and never will be in *Truth*. The Course reassures me that I'm not healed alone for all is part of *One*. Minds are free to join and be forever strong for atonement (at-one-ment) demonstrates the Oneness of God's Son.

"There is no above. There is no below. There is only here and now, and One, no two. There is no me. There is no you. But you know that in the deep recesses of the mind. The One is part of

40

All That Is and *All That Is* is part of something much greater than the One, unimaginably greater; unheard of on other levels. All beings know this.

"This is one final moment coming up before us in the history of humanity, the humanity that never was and never shall be. This final moment beckons the call to those who worship the earth. Heed the call and know the earth is transforming in all its glory. All is heard across the land, and nary always, shall heed It's whisper of love. Fortuitous events rule the day and night as all transcend this earth of limitation.

"Knowing the One is many, we heed the call to beckon forth a new age within this world of seeming woe. For naught the release of new energies but the changing of the guard occurs. The guard of One controls the beings upon the earth of One. And in this change, is made the sureness of humanity's whole. There appears to be no other way to beckon forth this call on an earth filled with beings who sleep within the dream. The dream must end as all good dreams for never was it to be. And though you sit, and hear our voice, know that she never was and never shall be again.

"The sureness of the return to One is finally here. Heeding wholly the call to One appears as nothing unusual within, but without; the call appears startling to those upon the earth of One that never was and never shall be. And now the wholeness of earth is revealed in all its glory, the wholeness of One. The earth is made new again and with this change the end of time creeps closer than ever before.

"A remembering for the One comes through quickly to the whole for the one that is, and was, and always shall be. A remembering of the One is all that is known in eternity. This remembering comes quickly for all to know the truth of their BEing. Hold tight. Hold fast. The world is changing quickly. And you, as well, as a body, change along with this earth."

Chapter Five

Turning Point

"Like humans, every day is unique and filled with possibility." SAM – Bits of Wisdom

What a wonderful morning! Twinkle lights greet me near dawn. Sun peeks above the neighbor's roof as soon forgotten messages flow. Beautiful orbs glimmer while repeating prayers. Deceased relatives greet me during meditation. It's more of a sensory thing than actual seeing, a journey in mind. What joy to be with them! Daniel, as usual, is not apparent. He appears quickly to dance a waltz with me when I seek him. Time with these wonderful souls is way too short, perhaps a mere two minutes.

Another sign to let go of the business, so carefully nurtured over the past ten years, arrives from the U.S. Patent and Trademark Office in the afternoon. The final abandonment notice of a trademark application, costing hundreds of precious dollars, fails to upset. Clearly, all is in Divine Order.

Tuesday night classes with Dr. Bump inspire as do Wednesday and Sunday night services. There's the Course in Miracles class with its evolved group, every other Thursday, and Dr. Geddes' class to attend the rest of the month. Sometimes I make coffee for weekend movies or other classes too. It sure keeps me busy and that is a good thing.

Rebecca arrives after work, to take me grocery shopping with her and Samuel in my little car. As we drive away, she announces James will have a grouper dinner waiting for me later. Grouper is my favorite fish but I find the message odd. Even though James and I were together in the house for several hours, he did not knock on my door to tell me.

James has already eaten when I return to the house on 47th Drive. I thank him, several times, for making dinner before retiring to eat delicious grouper. Chaos and clutter fill every space of the house, except my peaceful room.

Later in the wee hours of the morning, I bless a large toad that peers inside the east window. Progressing past smaller creatures is something to be thankful for! I prefer to see butterflies, cocoons, birds, cats, and squirrels. Butterflies, varied in size and species, continue to visit. These creatures are much more appealing to me while drifting asleep. Words wake me minutes later.

"Well I'm not afraid to use it. There's a key to growing older in the universe."

Ego wants to continue updating the business website even though it no longer suits new energy. But the laptop display is black. An excessive amount of time, required for regular updates, seems wasted if no one knows about updates. Annoyed, I begin to jerk the computer's lid back and forth. The display soon comes back to life but since it's still very early, I turn the computer off and lay back down. A wave of immense heat interrupts sleep. My body becomes extremely cold minutes later after repeating the morning ritual. This occasional occurrence causes me to bundle up in blankets before falling back to sleep.

"What they think is silently affirming," wakes me moments later.

Do thoughts really help things to survive?

Deceased family members welcome me again in my favorite green meadow. How awesome it is to communicate with them during meditation! Uncle Freddie is there, as usual, but Daddy is not. I ask why.

"He's using his energy to be born again," Freddie replies with a wink.

Minutes later, I hear Dad say he just passed through the birth canal. It will not be long now. Big change, I hear, is coming within six months.

The God Network continues to flourish. Someone suggests I read the *Book of Emmanuel* later in the evening during class break. Leah gave it to me days ago.

Beautiful orbs appear throughout the night and early morning. Tonight's messages include a series of senseless numbers. James takes out the garbage at dawn waking me with the noise to realize that I sing in my sleep. "This is how it feels to be held." It's a popular Christian song. I don't care for words of loss but some words, and the singer's voice, are very beautiful.

Daniel's missed hugs come to mind. It's no longer appropriate to keep asking to see him, or be with him, because it interrupts his work and perhaps evolution. His essence continues to check in when possible and I'm very grateful for our many quality visits.

Pigeon coos interrupt thoughts. As another pigeon's hearty "coo, coo" fills the air, I fall back asleep, smiling to think he has a friend.

Doing laundry is an arduous task as my brain goes through the motions in a dream. Each piece of laundry is wet, when picked up, and water fills the basket. Even when I reach for a dry piece of laundry from the floor, it seems like I'm pulling it from a water-filled bucket. Daniel and Momma merge into the scene. I don't see their faces, or even bodies, but sense them. Momma announces that Daniel can put his CD's, his music, in a container. She points up, near a wall to containers in front of me, on the left.

"I can't listen to any music or go anywhere without my own money," Daniel replies.

"Come and tell me what you mean," I say, motioning him over while holding out my arms.

Ecstasy fills me for a fleeting second upon feeling Daniel's familiar loving hug. The vivid feeling promptly wakes me, very happy not to have cried. A small, Timex Indigo watch notes the time as 7:00 AM. Like a Cheshire cat, I smile, knowing Daniel's spirit gave me a hug because he knew I longer for it. Three prayers fill the air before dropping off to sleep again.

Deep throaty gurgles wake me minutes later as sun peeks through clouds just above the neighbor's roof. Life is wonderful as I study the days Course lesson. A spontaneous thought to telephone Ruth and invite her on a trip prompts me to pause.

Intuition makes it crystal clear that I'm to change surroundings and live more abundantly. The majority of my settlement from Daddy's lawsuit sits waiting for me to choose new adventures. But Ruth sounds depressed and notes her portion of the money must pay bills. Something prompts me to offer her a free trip before ending our conversation.

A recurring thought comes minutes later. Morning prayers, along with inspiring music, must go onto a new daily CD. It will come in handy during travel. Electronic mishaps rule the month. Yet, there's a knowing that the computer will allow the task without malfunctioning. Eighty minutes of the usual morning ritual, which now includes prayers, notes from the Course, declarations, affirmations, visioning, meditation, and song, seems perfect. God, the Living Spirit Almighty, surrounds me as the inner world creates my outer world. Songs by Carole King, Karen Ducker, and Kansas, between rituals, complete the CD. (This tool is very useful to help raise ones vibrational rate.)

God works in such amazing ways to let us know we're not alone! Certain days are spectacular. Today, when I open the computer's media player, number seventeen begins to play instead of the usual number one. Daniel's spirit sends another message as "The Best is Yet to Come" by Carole King plays.

Joy and "Super Love," also know as "Original Prime Energy," by Robert Monroe author of *Far Journeys*, overflow. This indestructible mixture of emotional thought, and action, helps us to escape our dream world. Using this attractive force allows us to interact with loved ones even after physical death.

And yet, as the Course notes, there is no love but Gods. "Love is one. It has no separate parts and no degrees; no kinds nor levels, no divergencies and no distinctions. It is like itself, unchanged throughout. It never alters with a person or a circumstance. It is the Heart of God, and also of His Son."

Telephone rings interrupt afternoon study. Ruth very insistently invites me to join the family for karaoke at Terry's workplace. She arranges for Rebecca, who still has my car, to pick me up. Taking the night off for family fun sounds tempting but I'll pass on the rum. I intend to be a good communicator with Spirit. James Van Praagh notes in *Talking to Heaven* that alcohol affects our ability to be a good channel. Spirits influence the electrical force field of protons and electrons to make themselves known. Poor diet (too few natural foods, too much red meat and refined sugar), caffeine, and other factors also slow our vibration making it harder to connect to higher vibrating energies. Everything is energy!

James watches TV as I stroll through the living room. He smiles and tells me to have a good time.

Minutes later, Rebecca and I enter the outrageously loud, smoky saloon. Terry seats us at the bar next to an electronic game. He hands Rebecca a beer and grins, refusing cash before moving on. I reach out for what looks like a glass of Coke. The drink turns out to be my favorite, one I swore not to indulge in many months ago, a strong Myers Rum and Coke.

Terry soon ignores complaints about my drink. It's going to be a long night so I sip the cocktail. Tonight's prize is $150. Ruth and Rebecca both hope to win the drawing at 11:30 PM. Several spotlights shine upon the stage to our left as Rebecca weeds through the songbook. Ruth volunteers to sing "Bobby McGee" as they compete.

Rebecca takes a long slug of beer as the DJ calls her name. She belts out a mournful tune, about a cheating boyfriend, amid hoots from the crowd. My beautiful green-eyed daughter is very popular and sings several songs throughout the evening while I try to stay sober. Two cocktails swim down my throat before choosing songs. I discretely tuck slips of paper into my bra. When the time arrives for Ruth to sing, the DJ calls my name as well. Ruth grins, pulls me to my feet, and drags me to the stage. Terry hands a slip of paper to the DJ as we sing.

The DJ calls my name, several minutes later, for as Ruth dragged me to the stage a slip of paper fell out of my bra. I intuitively know which one of the four slips it is. The DJ smiles as "Carry On My Wayward Son" begins.

Rebecca's cell phone rings so she quickly moves outside to the parking lot. Like a drunken sailor, I take the mike and begin to sing with gusto. Caution no longer concerns me while dancing around the stage feeling Daniel's energy. Words fly quickly to fill the large room.

"Once I rose above the noise and confusion. Just to get a glimpse beyond this illusion. I was soaring ever higher but I flew too high."

Images of Daniel, flying into the air of freedom from this illusion, fill my drunken brain. Words do not bother me.

"Oh yeah, at 140 miles an hour," I sing passionately.

The crowd cheers not realizing this is my turning point. Everyone seems to like the song but most remain unaware of its personal meaning. The crowd cheers and claps making me feel special as I step from the stage. Ego is strong and proud as I stumble back to the barstool.

It's been a long time since I was this alarmingly drunk. Rebecca plays with the electronic game until she's certain she can get us home safely. Smoke and liquor saturate me while stumbling into the shower with a reeling head and heaving stomach. Standing is difficult, and I swear, several times, to never drink again, before passing out on the futon. Four hours later, I wake with my body halfway off the closed futon still feeling very drunk and thirsty. Slugging down a tall glass of orange juice with a B-complex takes priority as my heart and head throb in tune.

Today is the first of two recuperation days. As expected, Spirit communication decreases. I don't plan to drink again. An ill feeling, coupled with this communication break, and missing usual activities, is not worth the price. The newly made CD of prayers and treatments helps to complete my usual ritual. Track Two repeats three times as I thank God for unseen forces.

Toast, with butter and strawberry preserves, along with the usual antioxidants, and vitamin B-complex, serves as breakfast. A strong feeling of urgency overwhelms while sensing upcoming family storms. Ruth has been jobless for almost a month and FEMA has not called as expected. Housework and doctor visits, Momma and Ruth's, consume time. After speaking with Ruth, results from several hours of searching for airfare and hotel accommodations sit safely in computer files. Ruth wants to visit Las Vegas. She's not interested in Puerto Rico. Trip costs are very similar so I give in and tell her we'll plan to see the city that never sleeps, even though I yearn for somewhere warm and relaxing. This change of plans is divinely appointed.

The time to demonstrate more and move into my own place, to grow at a faster rate, is here. It's my job to show the world that yes, a poor girl from the projects can be more successful than anyone ever imagined. Intuition guides me to change environments and create bigger expressions for others and myself. My plan is a simple succession of demonstrations to increase the wealth of church, family, and me. It's very simple. Demonstrations will continue to increase wealth and evolution. Yet, love is the most important thing, even in this illusionary world where we make our thoughts come true.

"Be the one you wish to see in this world, with all its greatness, with all its glory. The world holds for you a trueness you cannot imagine, even in your wildest dreams. This Truth comes to you through the grace of the One, known to many as God.

"You shall fulfill the secret of the ages through the tasks designed to welcome the whole back to One. Go swiftly, and fear not, for all is going according to plan, even knowing there never was a plan, and never shall be, in this place that is an illusion of your own making.

"Know that all comes to you, in the glory and the space of time, forevermore willing to let go of the past, and all things behind the distant future, that never was. Knowing this truth, you walk seemingly alone, and yet you know, we are with you, as we gather in the fold, the fold of One, to the truth of our Light. For Heaven's Spirit Almighty is with all today, and everyday, to guide you along the path to trueness and surety in all actions.

"Know that your path is not unique in itself for many others are with you along the way. All hold different aspects of the Whole and all shall be heard, as well. Knowing this truth should fill you with glee, not woe, for the aloneness is only in your mind. Go forth and spread the word that all is within Divine Order, for Divine Order never had a place here and never shall.

*"Seek not any Being to hear what the Truth is. Seek only to listen to the Self within and know that all is exceedingly well. Know this Truth as you garner along the path of One, this Truth of Light and Love forever unwilling to be told to no one. Let all ring true to you, as you listen and learn, from the One of **All That Is**."*

Holmes is ever so correct in noting the daily importance of correct thinking. His words, "Knowing the Truth, is not a process of self-hypnosis, but one of a gradual unfoldment of the inner self," ring true. It's a no-brainer to identify with power, love, beauty, peace, and happiness. It's sort of like rewiring the mind from the brainwashing learned in school. The more I rewire, the more I experience Truth. Now I decide what I want, making sure it does not hurt anyone else.

For now, my soul yearns to attend the evening class but my body is unable to go. Drinking alcohol is <u>not</u> worth the many costs and changes in spirituality. I know everything happens for a reason and hope this lesson sticks. Tonight's Course in Miracles class is on the subject of death. Since I know there's no such thing, I would have shared something very valuable.

Soon I'll be in a place free of chaos, sitting in natural light, and more communicative with nature. I'll be free to roam every room and have friends and family over to share in the wealth that is divinely ours. And as I further my evolution, the evolution of those around me will increase as well. A variety of places will welcome me this year and I'll win money in Las Vegas. Other avenues of wealth are opening. I can feel it.

Sleep welcomes me at eight o'clock. This time, I pull out the futon.

Chapter Six

In the Flow

"Going with the natural flow means taking a back seat to physical happenings that seem apparent." SAM – Book of One :-) Volume 2

Messages continue throughout the night. At 6:45 AM, I rise to repeat the World Healing Meditation, fall back asleep, and wake minutes later upon hearing, "*I go with light.*" My left eye is moist as dream recall seeps through groggy states of awareness.

A tall, handsome man looked at me as I lay waiting to board an airplane. He saw my closed eyes.

"Oh, you're trying to sleep," he observed apologetically.

"My eyes are just tired," I replied, clinging to a small container, shaped like a little vase. The top and inside of the vase measured the size of a half-dollar. It was pinkish mauve in color but the top part looked like silver, or some sort of metal, with an intricate design like ribbons or lace. The vase was an urn for ashes. Tears suddenly poured forth to flow down cheeks with thoughts of Daniel. Even now, the tears seem very real.

Words from the Course remind: "There is a light in you which cannot die; whose presence is so holy that the world is sanctified because of you." I know Light never dies and Daniel's unique bit of it continues in another way. The Light we hold covers the world as we step back to allow Source to work through us. Yes, I walk with Source in perfect holiness lighting the world in which I seem to live. Someday, the form in which my essence abides will be obsolete. But until then I'll serve it well, knowing my true purpose, to awaken the world that seems unaware of the truth of BEing.

The following year I begin a practice, which continues for many years. I walk through neighborhoods consciously spreading the Light within. A silent mantra repeats, "I spread the Light where er' I go and I AM ever grateful," each step of the way.

The bathroom beckons after relighting a candle that went out hours ago. Spirit's constant presence, in various forms, fills me with gratitude. One thin, turquoise, line of light, about 1" long and 1/8" thick, moves on the blue bathtub, slowly so I can see it, to the inner rim of the tub, across the gap to the other side, and up the wall. It disappears when near the soap dish built into the wall.

Yes, there's a world beyond the one we usually see. It's the world I want for the physical world holds nothing of value, nothing that I want. The world beyond this one is timeless, without space, and yet, unlimited communication remains for all eternity. The Course assures me that the lights I see are real. And one day there will only be Light again. One glorious, brilliant, white Light composed of multitudes of tiny beings; formerly known as souls, and other entities that chose again to recognize the Godhead of One, waits patiently for our return.

Today's activities include booking flights to Las Vegas. After an hour online, I intend to secure non-stop flights. There are two to Las Vegas and one flying back. Both Orbitz and AAA note two empty seats on both flights. A page appears after I enter my credit card number into the AAA website form. The flight, it notes, is no longer available. I decide it is and get out the telephone book to call the airline.

A very helpful woman assures me AAA did not charge my credit card. She books both non-stop flights. The cost is about $100 more than other flights, with two or more stops taking between ten to sixteen hours each way. Our flight is five hours and fifteen minutes long. This is a grand demonstration! I also know flights will be on time and smooth.

Ruth arrives to help choose Las Vegas options. Our spectacular trip soon includes a visit to Hoover Dam but many hotels are booked. We'll stay, I decide, in the center of the action at a good hotel for a relatively good price. Minutes later, we book an older room at the world famous Las Vegas Tropicana where the "Rat Pack" sang years ago. The hotel sits at a famous corner of the strip with three other very popular newer hotels. We'll get a wonderful room and our stay will fill with more demonstrations than we can track. I affirm it!

"The Secret" consumes evening hours for the third time after entering the Center. This time the sanctuary is standing room only. Many people watch the movie repeatedly. Some buy copies after the showing. It's a very long evening. I work most of the time as other volunteers network. My cleaning pace quickens upon feeling overworked. The other volunteers agree to handle the rest after most dishes are clean. Elation fills me upon the walk back to the house on 47th Drive. I'm proud of myself for not staying and then feeling limited.

Visioning wins in Las Vegas occurs on the cusp of sleep. Pictures of women winning at slot machines sit in computer files after rising to spend an hour online. Website links with tips on how to win travel through email to Ruth. It's almost one o'clock in the morning when I finally lie down planning to morph pictures with our faces in the morning.

A flash of light, like three larger twinkle lights traveling together, flows past as I wake upon hearing, *"You are the light."* What does this mean? Am I, as Daniel relayed shortly after his transition, truly light in physical form?

Yes, it's time to recognize ourselves as Beings of Light! Continuous verification fills me with gratitude. Monroe announces, in his best selling book *Ultimate Journey*, we are truly light energy. In his book and audio tape *The Seat of the Soul*, Gary Zukav says, "We are a system of light within a system of light shaped by consciousness." Each responsible choice helps us to align with our soul and move toward becoming a fully whole and empowered being of *Light*. Humanity now quickly evolves into a species of whole individuals aware of their nature as Beings of Light!

The Course emphasizes each teacher of God begins as a single light, but with the Call at its center it's a boundless light. We're Beings of Light, *Emmanuel's Book* says, unaware of the power within our consciousness to alter all things to light. Our physical personality is a bit of the soul not yet blended with *Light*. As Beings of Light, we have free passage to worlds beyond the physical, wherever our consciousness will allow. Emmanuel tells us to recognize our True Self and spread Light for ten minutes each day. Thankfully, Isaiah's meditation CD helps to do that.

Sleep soon welcomes but leg cramps cause me to rise for a banana. These types of cramps can signal a lack of potassium, and since I still urinate a lot, that makes sense. For the past two or three weeks, a banana in the early morning hours seems to help.

Someone now gently strokes my forehead with love. This very strong sensation seems real as the usual wave of heat radiates from my chest. An owl sings a beautiful chorus of "Who, whooo, who" while prayers fill the air before I gratefully drop off to sleep again.

Thoughts of calling Sarah about the Las Vegas trip wake me later. In two hours, I must invite Sarah so we three sisters can be together again. Sun shines, through the southeast corner of windows, while intuition prompts to take three pictures. Each photo reveals increasing amounts of blue, red, and multicolored orbs. Tiredness overwhelms after seeing them. Sunshine warms my face while slipping back to sleep.

A generic answering machine asks for a message when I phone Sarah. She picks up the telephone receiver upon hearing my voice. Various reasons cause her to decline. As she discusses medications, doctors, and a new electric scooter that moves effortlessly through stores, I try to impress upon her that thoughts are things. Our conversation ends forty-five minutes later.

Meditation moves my little mind back to Source. A swirling, reddish orb appears behind closed eyes while I morph into Level 5. It lasts for about a minute. Usual Course and class study fill more time. There's one more class of SOM Unit 1, *It's All God*, and then we start Unit 2, *The Power of Decision* based on the wonderful book by Raymond Charles Barker. Dr. Bump now offers class CD's so I can listen to the first class upon returning from Las Vegas.

James is outside doing his laundry when I venture out to prepare breakfast. What a good feeling to know he can now take care of himself! Spoons of cereal swim down my throat as I manipulate Las Vegas photos from the Internet. Several hours later, pictures show Ruth and me winning at slot machines. Pictures sit in my room and the bathroom to look at throughout the day. Several copies are ready for distribution to Ruth, Rebecca, and Terry. Everyone can share in the vision to increase its power! Tiredness overwhelms so I nap after tucking photos into a wallet.

Upon waking, something prompts me to go into the kitchen for food. Frozen vegetables sit in the microwave. James is cooking outside in his smoker. "Will you be home this evening?" He asks upon entering the kitchen. He's cooking chicken and has a piece for me when I answer yes. What a pleasant surprise, and blessing, to know ceaseless treatments work! I thank him before relaying plans to visit Las Vegas in two weeks.

"Write it down so I won't forget," he says calmly before stepping outside.

The chicken is ready by the time I finish making salad. I bless it with love, light, and good before offering some to James. He seems happy to have it as I thank him, put chicken on top of salad, and move to my light-filled room to eat. Life is getting more amazing with each passing day. Yes, thoughts are things and I'm going to continue to think positive thoughts!

Spirit's powerful ability to change how electronics function continues to amaze as I finish the business update. Something guides me while formatting a lipodystrophy research article written years ago by a now deceased friend. It's so very, way cool to be led in this manner. Yes, spirits have guided me for the past twenty years in a variety of ways!

James leaves to fish with his friend hours before the telephone jolts me awake. The perfect car remains elusive Rebecca announces. She seems flustered over my urgent need to get business mail from the Post Office.

Soul family greets me at the beginning of Level 4 during morning meditation. Daniel's presence fills me with happiness so I don't take time to identify anyone else.

"Are you ready?" He asks.

I assume he means to travel like Robert Monroe talks about in his book *Far Journeys*. We soar up, hand in hand, when I answer, "Yes."

Daniel tells me we're at the outer rim. I assume he means the outer rim of the circle that encloses human existence. When we reach the end of the circle, Daniel announces I must go with a Higher Being to continue. I gladly agree after he notes I'll always be able to be with him. The Higher Being says his name is James. For a split second, my logical self takes over, wondering why I'm thinking this name. But I quickly go with the flow to ask questions.

Answers fill my mind even before questions finish forming. My true name is Esmeralda. I'm to spend money and live opulently because more money is on the way. (This ties in with the knowledge that you must already be living the life you wish to actually live. Act as if it's so and it will be.) It's reassuring to hear that I'll move by July first and will have more than $200K by the time I move to my own place. James also says I'm healed but my spine needs extra attention. He tells me to walk every day as I recognize a need for more calcium. James says he loves me. He is to be my husband in the future.

"It is time for you to listen and concentrate on what you are hearing," he announces, as I ask him to stay.

Headphones sit upon my chest as Isaiah talks on the CD about sending "light, love, and peace in abundance to all living things." As usual, I follow directions while standing on the moon. Familiar eye flashes fill closed eyes as the CD player switches tracks back and forth. It seems to happen in my third eye, the sixth chakra, but is moderate compared to other occasions.

Rebecca arrives minutes later in a big hurry to rush me to the Post Office. As we drive, she very happily announces that Daniel told her to buy the car she wants and to have fun.

"Listen to him and despite your reservations know it was a real communication," I reply, before opening the glove box to retrieve a check made as part of my visioning for the sale of the business.

Rebecca is not very supportive as I discuss visioning.

"What makes you think visioning will make your dreams come true?" she asks, while turning onto Federal Highway. "Have you had even one good offer to buy the business? Step back to reality Mom."

I angrily tell her she doesn't know what she's talking about. Maybe if she learned about the Law of Attraction she might think differently.

"Please open your mind to the possibility," I implore, as we head back toward the house on 47th Drive. "Put beliefs to the test by helping me to envision winning in Las Vegas. There are several pictures for you, Ruth, and Terry to look at while thinking about Ruth and me winning."

Rebecca seems a bit put off. Why should she envision anything unless she's winning?

"You always benefit when I win," I quickly reply as the car gains speed.

She drives away after I give her pictures of Ruth and me, winning in Vegas.

Everyone else in the family is even more leery of manifesting, though the power of intent, when I offer them pictures at Terry's family barbeque.

"The chances of winning at the slots," I announce boldly, "increase with the number of people visioning. And it's extremely cold in Las Vegas now but they'll have a warm front when we arrive."

Minutes later, I'm happy to leave negative comments behind for Sunday night's service.

"We need to believe this is a time where everyone can change the energy around the experiences they have had (as souls in every life). Everyone can change this energy and make things better for themselves. All they need do is envision what occurred and envision a different experience."

Five years later, I fully comprehend this 2007 message. Changing the past is as easy as envisioning experience as you wish it to be. My favorite way to do this is by showing others our true form of Light.

A major surprise awaits me at the Center. Rev. Mary Jo and Rev. Jerry are not their usual selves. Intuition prompts. They too feel the lack of support for evening services. I'm glad they're taking steps to go their own way as Mary Jo announces her resignation. Rev. Jerry is still recovering from surgery but they both seem very excited over other prospects.

Both Reverend's messages are powerful. After the service, I praise them and relate information about my current situation. They agree to hold thoughts of Vegas winnings. I thank them, noting their help balances out negativity in family.

Sleep comes easily but I wake at 11:15 PM thinking of blue light and a soldier. More than thirty years passed since I last saw him. Senseless words then fill my brain during slumber.

The World Healing Meditation escapes my lips near sunrise before sleep claims me again. Minutes later, I wake to recall thinking about someone passing when they were twenty-five years old, a grandson. Thoughts of Samuel startle me to full wakefulness. But after using the bathroom, I'm fast asleep again.

More words soon wake me. Is this what it's like to evolve? Are restless nights parts of the process? The image of a triangle appears while still on the cusp of sleep. A collection of circles and lines move inside the triangle. The same shape of transparent circles and lines float past when I open my eyes. They float within the other matter that I usually see skirting about the room. A strong wave of heat overwhelms. After it dissipates, I lay back down.

My body continues to renew and refine. The process will be finished, for the most part, soon. It may be time to see Michael for a cupping and scraping treatment to open my chakras more. Making an appointment is not on the top of my list since Rebecca still has my car but it would be good to do before the Vegas trip.

Many colored orbs appear behind closed eyes while finishing prayers. Orbs are particularly prominent when I talk of the golden key within. Minutes later, rainbow colored lights come from the sun. Two pictures show a bunch of beautiful, large, transparent green, red, and blue orbs, and tiny solid orbs as well. I'm so very grateful for increasing inner sight! Words fill my brain during meditation after asking what I need to know the most.

"It is all God. God is All."

'The gap' claims me as Track 3 ends.

A tiny, beautiful moth sits on the wall within the shower later. It's just as beautiful as a butterfly with varied colors of brown. I bless it and ask for a message. The speckled moth announces it's only there for the blessing. I thank it for coming and note its beauty as its white aura grows. "Please allow me to set you free outside where you belong," I remark, before gently picking it up. The moth lies still as I transport it outside. At least now, I'm getting to bless creatures that are more pleasing to human eyes!

Scamp and Prudence sit on the back porch. Although Scamp is younger, the cat is almost as large as Prudence who appears pregnant again. He allows me to hold him as I talk but Prudence still will not let me touch her. I continue to tell the cats it's all about love. "You will have beautiful babies," I tell Prudence softly, "and this time they will not all be stillborn. You will be a good mother." This time she will learn what love really is. There's nothing in this human life that discloses the emotion of love as well as having a child. That's why I prefer to be a woman when on earth.

The pattern of thought, held firmly in place by fear for decades, continues to change. Two pages catch my attention for the daily random reading from SOM. It's reassuring to know that as my mind renews so also shall my body reflect wholeness. There's no doubt that new, much better creations, replace the age old limited environment surrounding me, for the very *Principle of Life* manifests Itself through me! I must remember, "no thought of negation can enter a mind already filled with peace and faith." The Mind of God is forever my mind.

"Do not feel tested. You are never tested. Remember, it is only in your mind. This possibility for the Whole takes on a new meaning as you move forward toward the Light. The Light of your BEing connects with the Light of One.

"There are no tests, only truths to be unveiled in the knowing of One. We sit beside, in, above, and below you as you type away hoping, knowing, words will come barreling through the mist of forgetting. It is a veil of illusion that you, yourself, created in the need to come together more freely as a state of separate BEingness. You now realize there is no state of separation for you always remain in the Whole of One that cannot be named or even recognized. The truth of All is within the parts of which it represents. You know this in the core of your being but have placed the knowing aside to channel forth works not of the One.

"Let the Light shine through the veil to fill the illusion of separation with what it truly is, Light, Love, Oneness. Praise

others if you wish but know you remain the Whole of One in your own BEing for all parts reflect the Whole. There is nothing outside the Whole of One. Do not try to understand for in your understanding you bring only the logic of illusion. Let the knowingness of your BEing fill your cells with Truth.

"Take care in the days of struggle ahead for nothing is as it seems. Remember, you alone make the whole of your reality. The parts seeming to be separate are parts of yourself waiting for the recognition of Oneness. Seek not outside yourself. Seek only to bring forth what you harbor inside the vessel you chose to experience life in this realm of illusion.

"Do not be dissuaded by those who seek control or pleasure at others expense. Know it is a part of you that needs recognition and must be led back to the core of One. Rectify these illusions by forgiving them, wholly and completely, before moving on in your mind to better illusions. Speak only the truth and that is what will come to you. Serve only yourself, for that is what serves the Whole. Know all is an illusion, of your own making, and be free with the thought of forgiveness as needed only on this plane of illusion."

Two phone calls interrupt study before bedtime. Rebecca telephones to report that officers denied both loans she applied for with Ruth as a cosigner. "Perhaps negative thoughts affect her situation," I think. Sarah then calls to announce that her husband insists she use some of her portion from Daddy's wrongful death suit to join us. All is exceedingly well as Daddy's essence helps to make reservations when we end the call. Against all odds, I book Sarah on our flight before upgrading the hotel room and reserving another ticket for Hoover Dam.

Items get checked off a list as I dream. At 6:33 AM, I wake happy to remember saying, "Yes, yes, yes, and no, I don't want that." Sleep claims me after sending the weekly email message. Dreams fill my mind even though I've slept for less than an hour. Two other people stood in front of me in one dream. One was to my left. A woman stood to my right. She said she did not believe in the Law of Mind. Either I stooped down or sat on the floor while announcing, "I do believe and when I am a millionaire I will share my money with the church and my family to help all of humanity. But I will not give you any money because you have to do the work yourself."

Another dream places me with Daddy only he looks much different. We're sitting in a line of people. Newlyweds announce they were just married and are leaving to go on their honeymoon. The woman happily notes that Daddy is going too. Someone mentions Puerto Rico and something blue. Right before waking, I get the impression that Daddy is paying for everyone's trip.

Much of these thoughts have to do with my thoughts and actions during waking hours. I relate to Puerto Rico as the place where I thought Ruth and I might go and 'blue' to the Blue Man Group who I hoped to see in Las Vegas. My question is, "Can one be in a dream state after less than an hour?"

Now, five years later, I firmly believe the money from Daddy's wrongful death suit was designed to help my siblings and I evolve. We each had a choice as to how to use the money. While some of us used it for drugs, or to pay bills, some chose to experience life in grander ways.

The computer screen flickers for several minutes after my eyes open. My right index finger lands on "The Inner Light" for today's random SOM reading. How reassuring to know that Light shines through me to illumine the *Way*!

Ruth arrives to pick me up so we can take Momma to her specialist appointment. Dr. Ben is one of many doctors I no longer visit. We wait for two hours in an overfilled waiting room before he says Momma's medical condition is too critical for surgery. I promptly note her cirrhosis and other medications when he prescribes Bentyl for pain. Rather than admit the Bentyl will detrimentally affect her, Dr. Ben advises that she take it only during emergencies. I'm happy to finally be whole but now recognize a need to help family towards that worthy goal.

A vivid dream wakes me hours later. Michael, the acupuncturist, enters my mind again. There seems no sense in making an appointment with him because Rebecca still has my car. But Ruth soon telephones to ask for help. She needs someone to drive her van after she picks up her antique Thunderbird from the repair shop. You can, she notes, borrow the van for a few days. It sure does pay to be in the flow! Minutes later, I have an appointment to see Michael after dropping Ruth off at the repair shop.

"Just remember, Love is all there is, was, or will ever be. The diamond is here, heed the awareness of One and go with the flow of Light. Do not be concerned with the process for all is as right as the rain that falls from the skies. The rain cleanses the land and all within. The knowing of the One returns smoothly, and assuredly, to all upon the land."

Chapter Seven

Preparing for Change

"It is time to change the tide of never ending woe and transform it to a tsunami, of inner peace and beauty that never ceases." SAM – Book of One :-) Volume 1

Having a friend to share synchronicities with is wonderful. Leah arrives early to drive us to dinner before our last *It's All God* class. There's plenty of time to eat and share before heading to the Center. A smile forms while reading the familiar fortune cookie. Yes! The time to act as if desires are met is here.

Dr. Bump introduces us to the "Circle of Christ" concept. Needing a vehicle and getting one without trying is synchronistic but unrecognized as something that places me where I long to be. Conscious experience of the interconnectedness of God's Network lies on the horizon.

Daniel's last name flows through my brain at 3:25 AM. A twinkle light flashes upon opening eyes. Four of them assemble within the dried flower arrangement sitting upon the dresser. How wonderful to know spirits visit.

The CD player has been almost unbearably loud since the volume knob broke. Today a lower volume blesses my ears. Eye flashes accompany the end of Track 3 before seeing images of homes. All of them are near water and will be mine in the future. One has an ocean view and appears to be in a high-rise building. *(This could be the building I stay at during July 2012 or the wonderful beach place I move to in June 2013.)* A forest, or park with a lake, sits near the second home. *(This was the place I stayed at from late May to July 2012.)* The third home appears to have a second floor as I gaze out at land from a balcony. It's near a stream, river or brook. *(This is either Rev. Heidi's home, where I stayed for the first week of April 2012, or the cabin I lived in for eight months sometime later.)*

Accurate guidance continues. Today's random SOM reading takes me to "A Formula for Effective Prayer (Matt. 21:21, 22)" on page 458. Yes! Desired things are already mine. There's no doubt. Things envisioned will surface into physical reality through Divine Timing. Each passing moment moves the mental image of my desires closer to physicality, for the good of all humanity.

Ruth arrives when the daily ritual completes. We discuss our upcoming trip while driving to the T-bird auto repair shop. I'm happy to foot the travel bill sensing it's what Daddy wants. This trip offers an opportunity to live abundantly with faith.

Intuition guides me to stick around as we wait for help at the repair counter. Three times Ruth says to leave with her van. I finally do after sensing she doesn't want to disclose car repair costs.

Michael and I soon spend almost ninety minutes catching up on each other's lives. We both know our session is a divine appointment as he scrapes and cups my back and neck, which seems blocked on the left side. "Perhaps," I note, "pulling out and sleeping on the futon nightly causes the lower spine pain."

The treatment feels good, lessens pain, and relieves my sinuses. Michael shows me before and after pictures, which clearly show decreased swelling in the spine. A faint waistline in the photos surprises me. Too many years passed living with a heavier body than the one I experience now. Pictures also show released blockages, in the lower back and neck, where a pinched nerve necessitated several rounds of physical therapy.

A sudden rainstorm helps me to appreciate Ruth's van again when it's time to leave for the Center. For a fleeting second, I think about skipping the service but recognize the Reverends may count on my support. Managing the music and tithe basket is now second nature. Since missing the service would mean I'd miss two services in a row, because of the trip to Las Vegas, I decide to go.

Two cars sit in the lot with lights on as I wait for rain to slow. A woman gets out of one as soon as I leave my car. This is her first Wednesday meeting. Rev. Steve arrives minutes later than usual. As we talk in the hall, another man arrives. It's his first time in the church. A grateful thought fills my brain. "Thank you Spirit for supporting Wednesday night services!"

The three of us help Rev. Steve set up the room before I settle into the back audio station with three of Rev. Steve's CD's. Karen Drucker's new recording, with songs on money and prosperity, sits among them. Steve soon acknowledges my assistance as the service begins. A full room of people turn around and clap. "Wow, my treatments are really working!" I think upon seeing friends stand to applaud.

Pages of email distract me later but suddenly I have the urge to find Karen Drucker's money song online. The external computer microphone helps to record it. What a great addition for my daily ritual CD!

It seems important to stay hydrated so I drink spring water, throughout the night, rising several times to eliminate it. Thirst upon waking is now the norm. My throat remains very dry despite the amount of water consumed. It pleases me to remember saying my good is coming in the wee hours of the morning. Yes! I recite my daily treatment for continued peace, clarity of mind, and inner sight during sleep.

There's so much great stuff to relate. I've been thanking Spirit for daily gifts, my food, and everything else. Ruth telephones as I try to soak up what little sun there is. Her antique T-bird stalled out, she reports with dismay, on the way home from the repair shop. It took ninety-minutes for the auto club to bring her and the car back to the shop. She now admits the total cost of recent T-bird repairs is over $5K.

Two thoughts enter my mind quickly. I blurt them out as she pauses.

"I told you I'd wait to follow you home when we picked up the car but you waved me away. This is another sign that you should just sell the car."

She doesn't want to hear my opinion but asks me to pick her up to get the car, tomorrow morning, and to follow her home with it. Intuition cautions. She's beginning to feel guilty about me paying for our Las Vegas trip. But that's not my concern. I'm acting out of love and doing as guided. There's no need to change plans as I agree to help.

The hallway looks dark upon opening my bedroom door. It's usually dark and dense but this seems different. Something prompts me to flip on the hall light. The clear light fixture looks odd. A brilliant, oval shaped, white light appears below the light itself. Different from other lights, it seems alive and floating. Daddy's voice enters my brain. He'll be with us in Las Vegas. I'm thrilled to hear it!

A beautiful magenta colored orb flows to my right as I sit listening to music a short while later. It's ringed in a golden color and full of love. Karen Drucker's money song is a blessing. "Money is coming to me, easily and effortlessly, money is coming to me." A $5 bill lies among clean, dry clothes when I venture outside to the dryer. The mailbox holds a $15 gift card from a new office supply store. The only requirement is that I buy $15 worth of merchandise. How wonderful to know the Universe works towards final fulfillment of my destiny to be financially wealthy and bursting with love. Visioning is one of the best things ever since Daniel's spirit led me to the Center! It's time to accept riches and let everyone know they can too if they only allow themselves to.

Evening events surprise and inspire. Before class, Rev. Kandi informs me there's no longer a need to visit the Center on Sunday nights. The Board decided to cancel services because Rev. Mary Jo and Rev. Jerry left and participation is not up to par. Disappointment is hard to hide.

"You are in the midst of chaos but need not feed that chaos with the thoughts of others or yourselves. Feed it only with the ability of the One to hold you, and sustain you, though these trying times. The One will assure your safety in all realms as we move forward in this illusionary world.

"Seek not at any time, or in any circumstance, outside yourself, for all events occur within your mind. It is not part of the Whole but yet, you, in essence, are a fragment of that Whole that dwells everywhere, in everything. Do not attempt to understand the logic in the circumstances that face you, or many others, but know this world is an illusion of your own making. This never-ending dream that seems to be in your mind is ending

very quickly. You need not concern yourself with the outcome for it is glorious, and already achieved."

Class uplifts again as Rev. Charles prompts us to explore self-evolution. He offers handouts from the Gateway to Conscious Evolution (associated with Barbara Marx Hubbard) and notes it's about co-creating a whole new world, social transformation. Charles then speaks of things already known or read in SOM, the Course, or *Far Journeys*. I thank him for verifications. Supporting this mentor, as part of the hospitality team, fills me with joy. When I announce my upcoming trip, he tells me not to worry about the task. A woman met at Wednesday night's service soon decides to make coffee for class starting next week! Before leaving, Leah offers words of advice after noticing my disappointment over the end of Sunday night services.

"Maybe," she announces softly, "It's just time to take old advice from the Bible 'having done all; stand (and wait).' I like to comfort myself with this thought about my children, sometimes. They all have God inside them, too. It's not up to me to make everything okay, or profitable, or to decide for them whether to continue along a certain line of action. Although I'd love to fix it, or at least give advice, I've found that it's futile, and you are looked on as interfering. They'll accept what they wish to accept, as do you and I. And, if they do accept it, they'll put their own slant on it, and remember with their own memory and perception… Usually not exactly what you said, or definitely not what you meant. You only mean to be helpful, always."

We gratefully hug before going separate ways.

Throughout the night I wake singing Karen Drucker's song on this coldest night of the year. "Money is coming to me, easily and effortlessly, money is coming to me." It rings through my head while stumbling to the bathroom.

At 6:30 AM, I repeat the World Healing Meditation before falling back asleep. *Choose whatever it is to make this happen in the 21ˢᵗ century"* rings through my brain minutes later. I shake my head, sip water, and traipse to the bathroom before sleeping again. Many words come but fade upon waking. Something about keeping my wholeness in this life, until I no longer need it, wakes me moments before rising to hear, *"I love you."*

It feels wonderful to repeat "The Golden Key" before meditating. The volume on the CD player remains bearable making me feel blessed to rest headphones on ears instead of on my chest. I'm invigorated enough after the session to venture out into the chaos of the living room where every table holds something of James.'

A positive state of mind does not waver even upon seeing that James did not leave funds requested through a note. Since he usually leaves before I rise, and returns after my bedtime, it seems the only way for us to interact. Music flows throughout the house for hours as I record Christian songs from the radio onto my laptop.

The credit union welcomes me as I withdraw enough money from our joint checking account to pay joint charge card expenses for food, gas, and sundries. I also withdraw enough money from the joint account with Samuel to pay expenses from last year's trip to Greece. There's no sense in paying credit card interest charges now that the bank finally cleared my settlement check from Daddy's wrongful death suit. Yet, something prompts me to continue installment payments on the Tax-deferred Annuity loan. *(I'll soon be guided to close the account and withdraw remaining funds.)*

Ruth listens to words of wisdom later. Life is all about love, I note, as we drive to the T-bird shop. It's in a lovely wooded area so I take a 20-minute walk while waiting for her to test drive the car with a mechanic. Exercise has not been at the top of my list so it feels particularly good to breathe fresh air.

Once again, I wake throughout the night aware of singing Karen Drucker's money song. James's Aunt Madeline, who must have passed years ago, tells me something about talking to Daniel near dawn.

"I've carried something with me for a long time," she announces, "and now wonder about it. Does that makes sense?"

"Yes," I reply, "it does."

"Can you help me?"

"Yes, I can."

Words ring through my brain before my next reply.

"We all are free, as free as we want to be."

67

Eyes open before sun reaches the neighbor's roof. Several twinkle lights sit for me to gape at on the dried flower arrangement. After repeating the usual ritual, I close eyes to open SOM to a random page. It's no surprise to be reassured of complete freedom, which needs only acceptance. There is no bondage, no limitation.

After a bathroom trip, I tell James about my talk with Aunt Madeline. He sits in the dining room talking to the cats.

"She must still be alive," he says while moving toward Bart.

His response upon hearing that she's on the Otherside makes it easy to pack for Las Vegas. This life has been too full of sorrow. Now, it's time for joy. After James goes to work, I leave the sanctuary of my room to search for a luggage lock. One of my favorite songs plays on the radio reminding me of Daniel. Tears gush down cheeks as I stand in the hall singing. It's clear I'm never alone but I cannot stop the flood of tears.

A transparent wave flows by my window after asking to see nearby spirits. It looks like a mirage when it's hot and you look down the road. The computer screen starts flashing so I quickly rejoice acknowledging that Spirit is always nearby. It returns to its normal state when I thank Spirit for the sign. I'm never, will never be, alone; and neither is anyone else.

This next trip will continue the flow of joy, and abundance, beyond anything experienced. The song on the radio now is about helping someone find his or her wings. Rebecca always comes to mind when I sing it. Now, I clearly hear it's a message for me. Joy fills my heart and once again, I cannot stop crying. The courage to dare to do great things is in me! I've done some great things in this life and will continue to evolve at a greater rate with more material wealth to share. Thank you Spirit with all my soul, with all I AM.

After waking more than I can recall, drinking water, checking the candle, and going to the bathroom, I rise at 6:00 AM too excited to sleep. Kittens mew softly outside the window as I meditate. The volume on the CD player remains bearable. My soul family appears during Track 1. I want to stay with them but they tell me to go ahead. Aunt Deborah encourages me so I move up to start talking to Higher Beings. But then I want to come back and listen to the rest of Track 1. How strange to want to do that instead of what I long to do, interact with Higher Beings.

'The gap' claims me during Track 3. I'm not sure where. Maybe I went to be with, and listen to, Higher Beings. Perhaps I fell asleep until Isaiah spoke of sending light to all living things. It's too taxing to figure out what happened so I fall asleep.

Forty-five minutes later, I wake after singing Karen Drucker's money song and then, Carole King's "In The Name of Love." A smile graces my lips to recall singing, "Do the things you believe, in the name of love, and know that you aren't alone."

Magenta colored Stuff of Matter flows freely. I watch filled with love. Today's random reading notes, "Matter is not an illusion but may take on false conditions." It's up to me to separate the false from the true as I pass the gaping hole in the den ceiling to retrieve my suit coat from a coat rack. The hole in the back porch ceiling is much larger making it plain to see James is trying to repair roof leaks. I'm ecstatic to leave it all.

As with many things, the task I sought to complete today turned out to be a guided task of service to One. Fingertips are now sore from pounding at computer keys, without rest. Messages come in a steady stream of words and it's awfully hard to document them. Sometimes I ask for the words to slow down, so I can keep up, but the process always goes very quickly. I mentally note changes that may need to occur in grammar and spelling, as I type, and then make corrections when the energy dissipates. In any event, here is the message received on March 24, 2011. I trust you will relate to it as well.

"The world is changing quickly and you are changing ever more quickly. Thank you for allowing yourself to grow by ridding yourself of past trauma. You know it is necessary to do so to continue on at the great rate you now find yourself in. Do not be dismayed by the fast progress, or the slow progress of others, for you must realize it is all really just you. You are a Being of Light who has chosen to experience this as quickly as possible to get back to the One of All.

"Concern yourself with nothing of this world for the world continues to drastically change, as you stand by, not

knowing what is up or down. Do not let the dribbles of time affect your vibration, for that is what will carry you Home, quicker than the blink of an eye. Be sorry for nothing, and no one, and remember this is but a dream, a poorly planned dream of nothingness, and despair, for many who care to indulge in the senses of the little mind.

"You are free to do as you please, and recall please, that you are being watched over and cared for by Beings, not of this illusionary world, and yet we too are illusion. There is no dark where the Light shines, and know that you, and others, hold that Light ever so brightly now.

"Be truthful to your Source of One and know all is going according to plan, the Divine Plan of One, to return the many fragments back to Wholeness. It is a necessary process that will quell the heart of many savage beasts. Beware nothing and fear not in the days ahead. Know all is well and shall be forevermore to those who hold the Light of One.

"Speak not of separation for naught does it serve you. A knowingness comes to the many soon so prepare to teach the Law of One. You and many others will serve in this role of Light. Know this and be assured as you move along the path to Home. All is well and can be nothing else."

Chapter Eight

Viva Las Vegas

"We are much more powerful than one could ever imagine but have forgotten our true nature as perfect unerring fragments of consciousness." SAM – Lightworker's Log :-) Transformation

Ruth, Naomi, Samuel, and hefty Sarah arrive at noon. Lunch offers a time to share before moving on to the airport. I'm ready to accept my good while videotaping our approach to the first of many envisioned adventures. *(In the next eleven months, I'll embark on thirteen trips, to see seven states, and enjoy three cruises.)*

"Are you ready to go to Vegas?" I ask Ruth as the black van pulls off the highway.

"Yeah," she answers taking a drag off her cigarette while pretending to pull down the slot machine bar. "Cha-ching, cha-ching, cha-ching."

Ego, tried of sitting in the backseat, comes out forcefully.

"That's not loud enough! Tell me you're ready to go to Vegas. Come on; tell me you're a winner. Say I'm a winner!"

"I'm always a winner," Ruth announces dryly, keeping eyes on traffic.

"Good! I've been visioning us winning at the slots. What about you Sarah? What are you going to look like when you win that money?"

Sarah poses with a look of great surprise as Samuel pipes up from the back of the van, "I'm a wiener, I'm a wiener."

"What are you going to say?" I prompt Sarah.

"I'm a winner," Sarah screams wide-eyed with gusto.

Clouds, amidst a setting sun, burst into brilliant shades of red. Ruth, Sarah, and I make our way through the airport. Our first demonstration of good comes after boarding the plane. Attendants switch middle seats, in three different rows, to one

71

row so we ride together on the full flight. It's bumpy for the first twenty minutes. We sit chatting excitedly while munching on pretzels and Babybel cheese. Ruth and Sarah soon sleep as the treatment CD allows me to hear prayers and meditation.

Money concerns will not affect me during this trip meant to get the three of us together for fun times. Excitement fills the Las Vegas airport right before midnight. We gaze out shuttle bus windows in awe on our way to the Tropicana. I note the exact view to see from our hotel room window and declare it so. Our view offers a high-rise glimpse of the Excalibur, New York, New York with its Statue of Liberty and rollercoaster, and the MGM Grand.

A sign announcing tomorrow's slot tournament stands near check-in. Ten o'clock in the morning is the last time to sign up. Something tells me I'll participate as the clerk calls us forward. He promptly announces the room we booked is unavailable.

"Would you mind taking an upgrade in the newer part of the building instead? It's a high-rise suite with two double beds, a pull-out couch, refrigerator, Jacuzzi, and large bathroom. Of course, there's no extra cost."

I manage to accept the offer, without jumping up and down, as Ruth and Sarah browse the area. A bellhop quickly arrives to show us the way.

It's our first time in a high-rise suite such as this. Ruth heads for the bathroom as Sarah and I check out the view. New York, New York sits across the street directly in front of us. The Excalibur sits to our left while the MGM Grand glows brightly on our right.

I move through rooms with sage, blessing corners, before lighting a candle to further cleanse and purify. Our suite's first huge room holds a large closet, sleeper sofa, tables, TV, bay window featuring the exact view envisioned while in the shuttle bus, bar area, and one of the few hotel refrigerators. The very large bedroom holds two queen size beds, another bay window, Jacuzzi with surrounding mirrors, and nightstand. A large closet, and two golden sinks with long counters on either side, sits in another room beyond the bedroom. The last room houses a shower and toilet.

Ruth and I soon share a bed. The firm mattress is delightful after sleeping on a futon for so long.

Karen Drucker's prosperity song rings through my brain before waking to recall, "I want everything for the same year." Noise from suitcase zippers fill the air as Sarah rummages belongings looking for clothes. I groan and get out of bed. Mountains stand, majestically in the distance, beyond the bay window. Ruth reads tourist information as I enter the living room singing a good morning song.

Energy filled air invigorates and reminds me of the slot tournament when we walk through the casino shortly after 9:00 AM. After securing our Player's Card, my sisters sit at slot machines while I inquire about it. Although most participants received invitations months ago, the woman in charge allows me to enter. My exuberance, she notes, overwhelms her.

It costs $199 for the privilege of trying to win the grand prize of $10K. I'm excited at the prospect of winning and not at all concerned about the investment. When I announce my sisters are with me, the now cheerful woman gives me three tickets to the awards breakfast (a value of $38). I'll also get two nights of our room paid for in addition to thirty minutes on slot machines. The room costs $95 per night.

Ruth and Sarah sit at the same slot machines when I hurry over to let them know where I'll be. Sarah is winning and having a ball. Banging constantly on the slot machine's button is lots of fun for me as well. The machine scores more than a number of other machines when my first 15-minute session is over.

How awesome to see the Law of Cause and Effect in action upon rejoining my sisters! Sarah continues to win. Ruth scowls and notes bad luck while Sarah constantly smiles to announce, "I'm a winner!"

A new adventure propels us toward Caesar's Palace. Sarah misses her new electric scooter and tires easily. I've talked her into leaving the cane behind for she doesn't seem to need it. She's just not accustomed to exercise.

There's no way to go but up the escalator after we make our way through the merchants in the courtyard. A walkway takes us above traffic toward the MGM Grand where a sign points to the monorail. Since it looks like Caesar's Palace is a mere block away, across the strip, we decide to walk. Violet, diamond-shaped orbs soar while a white transparent blob of energy moves by Sarah's side. I thank them before moving on. Sarah has a very difficult time walking so we stop to let her rest.

Another escalator takes us to a walkway leading across the strip. Despite newfound spirituality, I cannot help but revert to the old me who annoys everyone with constant chatter. Everything becomes a topic for discussion. Sarah is tired again by the time we reach New York, New York. More multicolored orbs grace the video as we wait for her to rest.

"There are three with us today," I announce to my disbelieving sisters before moving on. "Thank you God."

The walk that looked like a block takes an hour to complete and is ultimately unproductive. The box office at Caesar's Palace announces that Celine Dion is on vacation for the month. Sarah is amazed to make it without collapsing but I commend her and say there's no doubt she can continue to exercise without ill effects. Orbs appear again as we head back to the Tropicana. My sisters' heads shake as I thank them before moving on. We take the monorail, but even the walk there is at least a half-mile long, weaving through casinos.

"The dark is always darkest before the dawn. This is something to recall in the days ahead for it will soon appear darker than ever before. Do not be dismayed, over this change of increasing events, for all is ultimately well.

"You must recall that this earth is never really thought of, as a thing of itself, but a part of the Whole in which all live. Residing here on the earth does not make you privy to the cosmic influence of the ages of old. The masters are here to help all awaken, but being in an earthy form, you must pay attention to their teachings. There is, unfortunately, no other way to hear the secrets to get you out of the dream here on earth.

"Knowing you are part of the One is a big step. Getting the communications from Jesus, or other masters, is another but you must always remember that these masters too are limited in their knowledge. For all is within the Whole, and yet, only the Whole knows all things.

"Pay attention to, as you would say, to the synchronicities in your life for they will lead you to ever-increasing BEing. These perfect awareness's of BEing are meant to lead you further down the path that takes one to BEing. True BEing is a lack of need for anything of this earth or beyond. It is a state of seamless joy and love, a love fest, if you will, that takes all sensual pleasure in just existing without form.

"Only One can be in this state of grace, for all travel the trail of darkness that One avoids to dwell in the path of Light. The meaning of this will become clear to you as the days turn into night and the night into days. Old thinking will fade with the darkness of light and light shall become the only thing you see and exist in. Pay attention to your own clues for each has its own path to follow.

"Go with the flow, as you say, and keep a knowing that all is going well, accordingly so. Do not be dissuaded by the masses before you for they know not, yet, of their true nature. Reality seeps in slowly as the dark turns to light. Go forth and spread the word of Reality coming to town. This is the way of the One. There can be no other way to follow or flow. The way of the One will pervade your every sense of being soon. Skip along the path to full knowing of joyous love for truly that is all there is."

Ruth and Sarah head to the room while I venture off to play my final fifteen-minutes in the slot tournament. The machine doesn't score as high as before but I'm still ahead of many others. Now we wait for the awards breakfast to learn who won.

Slot machines welcome us again after resting. Sarah remains ahead by $100. Ruth brought her own money to bet and refuses to report losses. I bet $26 and win a beautiful, Austrian crystal necklace and earrings. As night falls, Sarah wins two free tickets to see the Comedy Stop performance. I gladly buy the third ticket and we all have a laughingly grand time.

Slot machines pull us in again after the show. Ruth stops playing to watch people at gaming tables so I do too. Something prompts me to bet thirty-five black but I've never played at tables. Ego questions. Is it a valid bet? Isn't gambling at these tables a rich person's game? As I watch, a man shows his friend how to play. His fingers land on number thirty-five black, twice, yet he doesn't bet. I miss the subtle clue until the roulette wheel stops and thirty-five black wins. We move on through the casino.

Smoke from Ruth's cigarette fills the air as she and Sarah watch TV news back in our suite.

"Turn it down please I want to recap the day," ego announces loudly. "Sarah, tell me about your day!"

"Let's see, I won about $159 but I lost $23. And I went to a free comedy show."

"And what else? Did you go for a mile hike down the street?"

"Oh yeah, let's not count the number of times I rested."

"And then what happened?"

"Ruth and I got into the Jacuzzi."

"So, when I get back from a hard day's work at the slot tournament where do I find these two?" I ask. "Relishing in the soothing water as Jacuzzi jets hit their feet and legs."

"It was very, very, nice and relaxing and I'm glad I'll be doing it again tomorrow," Ruth announces calmly.

"So Ruth, do you want to tell me about your day?" I ask turning the video on her.

"Well gee, I went down to the machine and lost but then I got back $36."

"Yes, at midnight we will have been here for twenty-four hours. Look at all we've done!" I happily announce. "Sarah did really, really, well and we're proud of her. In the morning, we'll attend the breakfast banquet to see how much money I won!"

Sarah claps loudly as Ruth speaks.

"Oh yeah, I forgot. I went back on the slots and won $46 and got a new golf shirt!"

Sarah climbs into bed as I listen to my treatment CD while lying on the other one. Ruth pulls out the sleeper sofa. Accustomed to a waterbed, she's not fond of the hard queen-size mattress.

"Can you envision a world where everything is of your liking? That world is possible and it begins with you. By changing your world to the world you wish to live in, by being the one you wish to be, that world quickly morphs into Heaven on Earth."

Daniel prompts me to "change the channel," as I recall waking with moist eyes, while mourning over him. Tuesday's wealth of fun begins. "We're on our way to see how much money I've won," I announce exuberantly, while filming myself in front of full-length bathroom mirrors.

A packed, quiet room greets us as we gleefully enter the free buffet. Ruth and Sarah opt for a diet breakfast while I savor a delicious fresh omelet made by chefs with tall, white hats. Although someone else wins the big prize, I'm not disappointed. Ego is happy to see a crisp $50 bill in a white envelope with my name on it. There's no doubt that I'll participate in other slot tournaments as we head to the door.

Of course, we cannot pass the slot machines without playing. Sarah heads to her favorite quarter machine while Ruth searches for one further away. Enthusiasm fills me as I head towards the dollar slots wearing my lucky black and white top. The area is devoid of people but I know time will be fruitful. After walking slowly past each machine, using intuition to sense energy and asking if it's the "right" one, I settle down.

My hands rub together after slipping a $20 bill into the greedy slot. The machine pays off handsomely on the third try. Two-hundred dollars worth of coins fall out into the well as I shriek in glee. Oh how I love the Wheel of Fortune! It gladly takes my next few bets so I walk away with $177. Uncle Freddie and Daddy's essence are with me. I see them in my mind's eye nodding and smiling widely.

Sarah tracks her winnings with pen and paper when we return to the room. She soon announces the tally.

"I won $159.75 yesterday and $20 today," she happily replies. "Despite what I bet over the past two days, I'm ahead by $59.75. I also won two tickets to the comedy show yesterday, two t-shirts, and two tickets to the magic show tonight! That's a value of more than another $100!"

Once again, I happily buy the third ticket so we can all enjoy the show. Sarah decides to rest after we collect the tickets. Ruth and I leave for a monorail to Caesar's Palace. But even taking the monorail proves strenuous. Everyone has to walk at least a half-mile through casinos to board.

A man sits in a large glass cage, with two sleeping lions, at the MGM Grand. His nonchalant attitude stuns, while concentrating on a small cell phone. We exit the monorail, at the Flamingo minutes later. The transport system makes it necessary to walk though the casino to reach the street.

"Each message is unique in itself. Although the message is always the same, a call to Oneness, the way in each person's understanding is always ever-growing in awareness and surety. The scope of changes before you now is immense and we know that many are disheartened. We speak from the Oneness of all life, and yet, in the illusion of your world, have found it necessary to play the game of gathering souls together as One to speak to those still caught up in the dream of earth life.

"It is unnecessary to speak to many at this time for they truly know the truth of their BEing. However, one always seeks to find and address those that are on the cusp of knowing.

"You and I, as One, are aware of the big, huge changes taking place in the world today but do not focus on such conditions. That is the key to peace and calm, to know what is occurring is just a figment of the imagination of many who are yet in the illusion of a body.

"Seek not outside yourself, for indeed, the world is within. The truth of this knowledge will come to all in a very, short time. Do not be alarmed for all is in a great state of readiness to bring in the land of peace and harmony, the Heaven on earth you have all come as souls to experience. Know all is going according to the plan of One.

"This is a hefty undertaking but the call is now heard and all respond no matter what universe of illusion they come from. Hear nothing of the false alarms of depravity, of shortages, or catastrophes, for those are indeed broadcasted to create fear. Yes, fearful people are more easily controlled by what appears to be outside themselves. And yet, nothing is outside the core of your BEing. That is the key of this message.

"Nothing is outside you, so carefully train yourself to seek only your own wisdom. The wisdom of the ages lies within and you need only to calm yourself to tap into that wisdom. The veil of illusion is very thin, and becoming thinner with each day, so

pay no heed to the false reports of many, for the image of One sustains all if you focus your awareness there. Be still and know that I AM.

"Do you remember the feeling of Oneness? Tap into this core, and carry it with you day by day, to rise above the turmoil of your self-imposed will. You have the courage to do so and it is indeed already accomplished for the body is but a host for the soul to grow. Be that as it may, go forth and spread the truth that the One lies within. There is no need to seek outside your Self."

Energy fills the air as Ruth and I move slowly down the promenade. What a great feeling to stroll past marble columns holding delicately carved statues amid cloudy, blue ceilings! We eat lunch at the Cheesecake Factory before watching animated figures perform amid fire and water. Many more people crowd around an immense glass-enclosed aquarium to watch as a man feeds fish. A baby stingray swims, to and fro, as men suck down beer at the table next to us.

Sarah sits counting cash when we return.

"Well, I played again and won more money," she announces with a grin. "I put in $15 and won $53."

Functioning in this world is difficult for I'm out of my sanctuary and unable to sleep as desired. Dr. Bump's 8-week *The Power of Decision* class starts without me while I play slots. I'm down, but still ahead by $110 for the day, by the time we enjoy the magic show. We're "bumped up" to a table next to the stage minutes before the amazing show begins. We all wonder by the time it ends. "How did they do that?"

Words such as "prosperity" and "we're in the money," wake me several times after falling asleep while listening to the treatment CD. Parts of Karen Drucker songs enter my brain as well.

Wednesday's fun day starts too soon as we dress. Even though weather is warmer, it's much colder than we prepared for. I don a heavy denim shirt and suit coat then offer my heavy sweater to Sarah. The pickup point for the Hoover Dam Deluxe Tour sits at the side of our building. We're the last ones to board a not quite full minibus.

Our exuberant driver wears a big, black hat. Jimmy notes attractions while we motor through miles of construction. *(In late 2011, I get the metaphor!)* He discusses an eight-hour itinerary as the road becomes very bumpy and drones, on and on, like someone on amphetamines, talking about Las Vegas tourist attractions, Hooter's, and benefits of living in the desert, as we breeze down the freeway.

The outskirts of Boulder City, where people lived while building the Hoover Dam, looks desolate thirty minutes later. Jimmy discusses living conditions as the minibus passes newer buildings. Gambling is illegal and homeowners who do not keep up their property forfeit it to the city. The dispatcher interrupts his monologue to ask for a customer count. There are nine people on the bus. We are three of five who will lunch at what some say is a haunted hotel.

"I go before thee to guide the way. Do not be afraid."

Lake Mead National Recreation Area comes into view as Jimmy discusses the four men his wife would leave him for: Denzel Washington, Sean Connery, Patrick Swayze, and Mel Gibson. Jimmy thanks Bin Laden for our upcoming security check after discussing Big Horn Sheep. We soon pass another checkpoint. Jimmy tells more stories as we drive into Arizona and back to Nevada in minutes.

Mountains stand majestically past massive amounts of concrete making the Hoover Dam. Jimmy discusses Lake Mead's low water levels and turbines as I video the scene. I cannot help but notice how beautiful the area would look without towers and concrete.

Traffic is heavy when we disembark to begin taking photos. The smell of chlorine fills nostrils while gazing down at water. Ego is out of control, jabbering away, as Ruth, Sarah, and I stroll down the bridge back to the Arizona side.

"Who is with us today?" I ask, aiming my camera at cloudy skies. "I see somebody. Thank you. Keep walking. I'll catch up," I announce, as Ruth and Sarah pass while shaking small heads to and fro.

A green mist, tinged with violet, cascades down to the right as I turn to follow them. Purple, diamond shaped orbs flow to the left of the mist, which soon changes to rainbow colors. My sisters shake heads with disbelief when I announce visitors. They think I'm nuts while pointing out orbs. I repeatedly thank them for coming as we reach the Arizona side.

Video fails to detect a white orb sitting upon my outstretched hand. But after we rub the toes of statues, to bring good fortune, a variety of orbs fill the video screen. Daniel and Daddy's essence soar, amid green flowing mist, before merging into a rainbow. It's an awesome sight, to see so much spirit energy, as we move on to pay extra for a special tour.

Jimmy greets us at the appointed time for our ride back to the city. Lunch at the lovely haunted Boulder Dam Hotel does not reveal inside spirit activity. (But pictures later do.) The now familiar cascade of colored mist morphs, from green to rainbow, amid orbs, near the outside sign. A friendly older woman offers us free Boulder City 75th Anniversary calendars. We all want to return to this Mayberry-like town.

Zothar offers my fortune as Ruth laughs.

"Pay attention," the animated figure announces before a paper message pops out of the machine. "The crystal glazer has wonderful things in store for you... Despair not, I say, for your days of despair will soon be over. Your calm spirit and your good sense will soothe through all emergencies... Play again."

Our exceptional tour guide seems less animated and removes his hat shortly after we board the van. He stops at a chocolate factory so we can eat free samples before roaming through a large cactus garden. Ruth and I remark over Teddy Bear Cactus, Cat's Claw, and Desert Willow trees, as Sarah rests on a bench. Purple, magenta, and orange colored triangular orbs float, next to a green mist cascading down from the sun. When we disembark for the final time, arriving minutes ahead of schedule, it gives me great pleasure to tip Jimmy.

We walk to the monorail after a short rest period. This adventure leads us to the end of the line near the Stratosphere. Sarah has a hard time walking again but not as hard as before.

"God will help you walk," I continually repeat while videoing large purple orbs. "I know this because he helped me many times when I weighed thirty pounds more than today."

Sarah prays that God will help her too. Spirit is with us. The further she walks, the less time it takes to cover the same distance.

"There is no message outside your Self but you already know that. The past will take you on a trip to nowhere, a place of past hate and disillusion where you need tarry no more. Go to the point of future-present a place where all meet to dwell in the now moment of Now. It is a place more attuned to your current vibration and one that will soon quickly morph to Now, presently, and always. It is a place that you have foregone in many incarnations to luxuriate in the deviation of bodily pleasures.

*"You are now coming to the point where you know the game is over. It never was a game to play the way that humanity has taken it, to total disillusion of love and wanting of good for all. You know the path to righteousness is one that many mistakenly take thinking they are separate. Dwell there no longer, for **All** is One, **All** is Now, **All** is Light.*

*"The truth comes easily to those who are ready to receive it. Speak not of past things but know here, all is past. The time of need is coming to an end. The Voice of One speaks now of good and plenty for all men, women, and children of earth. Your core Being is taking the reins to show you the way. Fear not as you morph into a Being unseen, as to date, here on the space of earth. All is well, **All** is One, **All** is Now, all is already done."*

We join Club Sahara at the Sahara Hotel and Casino. Each of us gets a free slot machine spin. Sarah wins two free show tickets. She chooses to see the Platters, the Coasters, and the Drifters on Thursday. I gladly purchase the third ticket. We also win two tickets for a two for one dinner. Tonight, I pay for the third dinner while Sarah pays for hers. This trip, in my mind, repays Ruth for many years of caring for the kids, and me, during difficult times.

After minutes of deliberation, we head toward slot machines. Sahara machines are excruciatingly slow. Disappointment sets in when we quickly lose.

"I lost $40," Sarah soon notes with a frown.

"But you won a free dinner and $98 in free show tickets so you're really at least $58 dollars ahead," I enthusiastically announce. "So you see that folks," I remark, while aiming the video as we move up the escalator, "she is pouting for nothing. She's a winner and she knows it!"

Ruth turns to look at us. She laughs loudly as Sarah begins to smile.

"I wish I was so lucky to win like that by pushing just one button," she announces.

"The emptiness within will soon be gone and in its place a fullness of expansion will carry all home to Wholeness. This state of BEing is an everlasting eternity of Truth, Love and Light, in which all is One. The uniqueness of each part of One shines through now as the world in which the body lives changes beyond recognition. Fear not for the world continues to exist in the mind of One bearing newer realities to share in the dream of life outside.

"And yet, many now know there is no outside as far as the Being of Wholeness is concerned. The truth of the Wholeness within shines brightly in all beings who bear the light fully. All hold the Light within. And now the time is nigh to come when all recognize this Light within. The truth of BEing will push forth into the masses very, very soon. As you await this happening bear the Light in all it's brightness and know you are one of many parts of One to do so."

Many things changed since my first Las Vegas trip in 1994 and now there's more glitz, more glamour, and more free attractions. Gloved hands are still cold as I video across the street near Madame Tussauds. It's rather cold but not as cold as weathermen expected. I'm wearing a top, suit coat, lined jacket, and leggings under lined, business suit pants.

The erupting volcano at the Mirage catches our attention even though it's way past Sarah's usual bedtime. We stand tired hunched close together to try and get warm. Tourists joke while waiting for eruptions to increase. A red glow finally starts reaching up from the bottom of the large fabricated volcano as water, amid smoky light, shoots from the top. Huge flames begin to shoot out from the top of the rock. Smaller flames appear in the water surrounding it. We thank them for the heat. The eruption ends quickly so we shuffle over to the Monorail Center Strip Station to head back to the Tropicana.

Later, I win $146 but lose it after seeing Folies Bergere without cost at the Tropicana. "It's best to walk away the first time you get more than you put in," I remind myself. I tally bets on the way up to our room, $7 at the Sahara and $86 at the Tropicana. It's my turn to sleep on the sofa bed and, as Ruth; I find it very lumpy and uncomfortable.

In the morning, we head across the street to the Excalibur. Multiple purple and blue turrets and towers jot out of the castle as we gaze at the crowd. Loud music from Boston, a band I know well, fills the air. A wizard with a long white beard and purple robe draws us forward. Water sprays from fountains to our right as we stand single-file on the moving walkway past the statue.

Today, we're grateful for many electronic walkways that move us ahead without effort. There's almost too much to take in along the Midway. We eat fast food for breakfast while moving slowly toward the escalator leading to the Luxor.

The difference in design is night and day as we emerge from the Excalibur medieval theme to Egyptian décor. Hieroglyphics decorate massive stone columns as Ruth hears a slot machine "calling her name." It seems odd to see the "Luxor Max Theatre" and "The Tomb and Museum of King Tutankhamun" within this inside city of glitz. Enthralled by the stone statues and Sphinx, I feel compelled to video. *(I'll recall a significant past life while visiting Egypt the following year.)*

After another filling two for one buffet, we enjoy the Platters, the Coasters, and the Drifters. We happily clap and sing along.

The monorail is nearly empty as we joke on the way back to the Tropicana. I pause the video for a commercial break. Sarah is happy to pull a panty liner out of her pocket when I dedicate the program to panty liners. I continue to video while singing, "We're in the money," while Sarah waves her hands back and forth. By now, it's clear to the two other passengers that we don't get out much. They appear pleased when we disembark.

Sometime during the week, we hear that the Tropicana will soon be demolished and rebuilt. That explains why the sofa bed is in such disrepair. Our shower fills with standing water quickly and one of the faucets constantly leaks so we know it's time to leave. Sarah and Ruth start moving down the hall while I take my last video.

Daniel, the bellhop, gets our bags as we stand outside waiting for the shuttle. It's yet another sign that we're in the right place, at the right time, for he is one of many, many, bellhops.

"Stand clear of the chaos. We are always with you. Continue taking in the Light. Continue bearing the Light. Continue with like-minded friends. Continue living the Law of One.

"The path is ever stable for you now. You need not worry about the woes of others. They will find their way to this path soon enough. You must continue to bear the Light for the others need that Light to shine ever so brightly. You must know that all is well, despite physical appearances. You, and many others, hold the Light for those to come. And it is that Light, that shall shine the way for humanity to flow out of the darkness, which it placed itself in so long ago.

"The time has come for all to bear the Light, to flow, with the Law of One. You must spread this truth and know that all is well. Go forth and spread the Law of One. There is no separation. There is only one Light, one Love, one Life. That is the Law of One gracefully flowing in Love that abounds throughout."

Chapter Nine

Co-creating a New World

"Changing times make it necessary to forgo old ways of being." SAM – Book of One :-) Volume 2

Dank, ominous air fills the house on 47th Drive at one o'clock in the morning. A candle glows as I search the carryon bag for headphones to hear nightly prayers. Leftover cheese sits below the CD player. I place the player on the printer and leave to store cheese.

Spirit fills the room as the CD player's familiar noise greets me upon returning. The display notes Track 6 plays. But I didn't turn the player on. Buddhist-like clangs reveal that the player skipped many tracks. It's playing the sixth track before the CD ends. But why does the player misidentify the track?

"It is with the greatest of honor that I perceive through the veil of illusion."

The CD switches to Karen Drucker's "Magic" and "Hold on to Love." As each song plays, the display moves backward from six to five to four to three. Carole King's song "Beautiful" plays as Daniel and other soul group members help me sense something reversing. Quickly forgotten words come and go. Daniel and I dance, twirling around and around, again, and again. We skip, side by side, before the CD player turns off. Questions slip quickly away. Messages, however, are clear.

My soul family is proud of how I handled the Vegas trip. James will make his decision about our marriage soon. Something good is going to happen and I'll be happy about it. It's not yet time to go Home.

Years later, I realize we are all undoing the past to return to the pure state existed in eons ago. We're purging what's no longer in our best interests as souls.

Familiar body numbness wakes me in the morning to see an image. It's a grid of glowing, green squares, four rows with five squares in each.

"His presence is everywhere and everything."

Random reading prompts me to treat myself better, to experience greater things, and expand this finite life. Guilt and negativity filled too many years with limitation. I now know it's truly a matter of changing one's perception. How constructive it is to make lessons out of experiences! I'm now positive in thought and action instead of judging and condemning, continually changing thoughts in order to change events. My soul continues to expand, and evolve, as I become a new person in a new experience. Ernest Holmes tells us, we must think and believe we have good things to possess them. And now something prompts me to go on a cruise. Cruise deals on the Internet reveal a Costa ship leaving later this month. How wonderfully delightful it is to embark upon a new reality, filled with abundance, while consciously fulfilling a higher calling.

The Power of Decision verifies beliefs. It's time to learn the psychology of decision-making. Joy abounds upon reading Dr. Barker's affirmations and treatments. What I used to refer to as God, created me, out of *Itself*, to express *Itself* as me. Knowing thoughts contribute to *It* makes all the difference while repeating treatments to declare new, limitless conditions. I AM the means by which new ideas of *Itself* appear. What a relief to verify we live in a world of unlimited potential!

Evening email holds a group prayer communication from Rachel. My heart swells to know I'm one of her "eleven people" as the gap between us lessens.

A bedside pad, decorated with clouds from the 99 Cent store, holds messages. At 5:25 AM, I rise to document more.

"It seems important to me now that I choose my own."

Martha, James' deceased mother, speaks inside my head. She thanks me for playing my role and says I'll move in June. The time until then is "a necessary time."

Time unfolds getting Samuel from school twice a week, attending classes, and Wednesday night services. Dr. Bump and

Dr. Geddes help me to learn but I still need lots of sleep. Grateful for longer periods of rest, up to two hours at a time, I sip water, use the bathroom, and doze again as exhaustion sets in.

Human DNA continues to evolve. Many people currently note erratic sleeping patterns. Waking between two and four o'clock in the morning is usual for a lot occurs in dream states. Some people sleep for about ninety-minutes (leaving the body for downloads, purging/cleansing/receiving/teaching, etc.); wake with thirst (sometimes extreme); sip water; eliminate water (sometimes much more than consumed); and then repeat the process. Periods of deep sleep help us to rest from integrating, acclimating, and building up for the next phase of our evolution.

Dealing with these higher vibrational energies is easier when we listen to our body and care for its needs. Drink plenty of good quality water, rest as needed, take Epsom salt baths and support the body in other ways such as eating fresh fruit and vegetables, walking outside in nature, and getting massages.

"Take the shot Mom," Daniel says as sun shines through dirty windows after repeating morning prayers. Two pictures, taken in succession, reveal a variety of colorful orbs. Blue, green, red, and multicolored, round orbs soar in the first one. Oblong or round, pale green, white, and lilac colored orbs appear in the second. Sun shines on my face when I lay back on the black futon to sleep again. Familiar words repeat. "Fa who more ray, in a goom bay." Are they from an ancient Sumari life?

Work seems hard to accomplish. 'The gap' claims me during Track 1. Since the laptop LCD backlight continues to go out, I quickly take it to CompUSA for repair. A very young man notes repair will take a few days.

Opportunities for good remain unlimited filling me with gratitude. SOM daily random reading leads me, again, to page 304, where Holmes notes nothing hinders spiritual treatment more than unbelief. We must refuse all thoughts contrary to affirmations of good. It's vital to envision a mental equivalent of desires knowing these requirements are already realized.

Saturday unfolds quickly, filled with prayer, study, and meditation. Multiple eye flashes occur during meditation. They change from white flashes of brilliant light to bright green.

Ultimate Reality continues to comfort and guide. I'm so very grateful to know the Living Presence is within! Random reading leads me to page 327 for the third time in the last few months. This time I'm staying on the path to freedom.

"The Light within shines brightly, even as the chaos without cries out in the midst of darkness. Fear not, for One never changes. That reality is of the Wholeness, within a space that unerringly guides all back to Wholeness. The crucial meanings of the times before you are awesomely real to those that dwell in the dark, and yet; to those recognizing the Light within they are almost nonexistent.

"All is coming to a head soon in this world of sons begotten to the Whole of One. Be ever vigilant in your quest to hold the Light for all to sense, feel, and see, as they make their way through the midst of darkness. The Light within shines brightly and never dissipates, even in circumstances of gross distortion to true Reality. Know this and be safe in the illusion of your world.

"Fear nothing for there is truly nothing to fear. Let all come in their own time and seek not to lead but allow others to follow, at will. The Way before humanity now shines through everlasting glimmers of Reality. Know this and continue to bear the Light."

Words fill my brain, many times upon waking during the night, but I don't write them down until 8:40 AM. *"This is the truth, my good has come. And I'm grateful now and forevermore."* They are my own words spoken in a dream. Something about a lack of time and space, and a resort, then wakes me after dozing off.

My body vibrates during mediation. A golden, white aura surrounds dried flowers, amid brilliant colors, when eyes open.

SOM is such a great comfort as a finger points to the daily random reading on page 312. Three sentences catch my eye: "The Infinite knows experience but not duration. Anything that Spirit knows is! Because *Its* Being passes into becoming through *Its* Self-Knowing." Yes, the Mind of One encompasses this physical universe and everything that is! Humanity is part of this Mind of One that communicates with Itself.

I merge with *One* through prayer and meditation all day. Later in the evening, it's delightful to read "My Atmosphere," for the fifth time in these past few months. Clearly, my atmosphere brings *Good* into experience. Peace, Poise, and Power abound daily as God works though me.

Someone unseen leans on my futon bed before dawn. I bless the spirit before sending it to Light so others can help it in peace. My right index finger then points to a favorite meditation for the fourth time since starting the practice of reading a daily random page from SOM. Yes, *"In Thy Presence I am still."* The stillness of angels surrounds as I close the book, reopen it, and point with closed eyes to the meditation below. "Cast Aside All Doubt" is another meditation read for the fourth time. How very encouraging to experience these fleeting moments of bliss when Spirit comes forth to express Itself!

"Listen to thy truth within the core of BEing. It is the only Truth to hearken forth remedies of thought not of your making. These are ageless truths merely unknown to the mind of ego and yet known as All to the mind of One. Come forth in all your glory to relish in the light of One, for reality seeps even closer to the depths of your innocent being. The days of yore, unspoken of in outer circles, knows nothing of the untold truths of yesteryear.

"An ever present BEing exists on all levels but is not easily tapped into due to restraints forced upon those on earth. These restraints will soon be lifted entirely and all who care to listen will hear the Truth of One. In no way, shape, or form, is this occurring on the cabals watch, and yet, there is only the cabal in the little mind of ego. There is a sense of Oneness that permeates all of this and every planet now as the alignment continues to move closer to Truth.

"In this space of evolutionary time, all is known and yet all is forsaken in the realms of darkness. Let it not dissuade you from knowing the Light of One exists within, in a place where it is safe and secure. There is nothing and no one that can delete this space for its secureness reaches out into the vast beyond.

"All is coming closer to an end of darkness as we beckon forth the forces necessary to bring in more and more Light to earth. The spaces of Mother Earth are filling quickly with this

Light of One. Be not afraid as these changes take place but know all is well within the scope of non-limitation, unerringly perfect, and already complete."

Today's email holds a wonderful message about a worldwide blessings project (expressedblessings.com). Kate's message warms my heart:

"Do what makes you happiest. Look upon what gives you joy. Speak to those who warm your heart. Listen to that which lifts your spirit. Surround yourself with sights and sounds and people who give you pleasure. For all the happiness you give to others all year long, give yourself the perfect day."

The Power of Decision takes on new meaning as I become more self-aware, open and receptive to new ideas. Ideas do follow ideas in perfect order and sequence! Unlimited possibilities of good continue as Dr. Geddes conducts class. It's always such a treat to hear him for he illustrates the mystics' truth so perfectly.

This class is the ideal way to end the day. Intuition reveals, Dr. Barker notes, what we've always been, concepts before a physical universe formed. How wonderful to know, "The Intelligence that produced my present body will take care of me when I leave it." My intuition notes Charles will stay in my life as he says the mind of Jesus is the same as the one in us.

A picture of Jesus flashes through my mind at 5:30 AM. Ninety minutes later, half of my prayers spurt forth before a tiny golden orb appears in the bathroom. It begins to communicate, diminishes in size, and moves slowly so I can watch. How wonderful to know I am never, and never will, be alone! The orb continues communicating and says a glaring sign will spur me toward my next move.

"All things in time."

Excessive heat plagues me throughout the night. Sometimes it seems unbearable. A set of six orbs appears near the relit candle after saying prayers. They sit two on top, two in the middle, and two below. The orbs disappear after about thirty to forty-five seconds. My body then becomes very cold so I pull the covers on and drop off to sleep.

Obviously, mass media affects dreams for one about airplane mishaps wakes me. Holmes notes, "If we can divorce our lives from the thought of evil – from receptivity to it – if we can bring our mentality to a place where it no longer conceives (thinks about) evil, then evil cannot exist for us." I think there's a better chance of this occurring when we divorce ourselves from media outlets.

Zukav notes we associate black with evil and white with wholeness of spirit and purity. Acting negatively contributes to the absence of light. Knowing that evil is the absence of light and love makes it easier to heal. Compassionately envisioning everyone as the radiance that we truly are heals all ills and makes it much easier to get through life.

Today's random reading again leads to page 330, where Holmes discusses Unity. "Reason declares," Holmes reports, "that Which is Infinite cannot be divided against Itself." I must continue to look upon humanity as part of the One, the perfect Whole. We truly are One, with the Whole, and with each other. We are all Good, with the capacity to mold and manifest a life of abundance, health, love, and joy.

For a time, I believe we are individualized souls, here on earth in physical form, but remain a part of one Oversoul. As time progresses, I realize all is illusion.

It's been days since I took my computer in and now email concerns me. When I inquire, a young man abruptly announces they'll notify me when it's repaired. It occurs to me that there's a reason for everything while meditating. CompUSA soon calls to note the laptop works perfectly for them, even with the stress test running. But they'll check to see how much more it will cost for a new inverter board.

Efforts to live in conscious union with *"the Thing Itself"* are immensely rewarding. Another random reading notes, "When one separates himself from the Divine Fire, he becomes an isolated spark." It reminds me of the many times Daniel appeared as a spark of Light. Daniel was just showing me our true form. Holmes reminds, "God is One," and "We are strong only when united with Life." It's now hard to think of living any other way. The next step is to allow *It* to work through me consciously!

*"One Light, one Love, one Truth, ever expanding in Consciousness. The One resides in all things. This One is never ending Consciousness, part of the Whole of **All That Is**. We gather as souls to experience the mass consciousness rising to eternal greatness, even knowing, on other levels it is already accomplished. **All** is One and One is **All**.*

"The times of greatness will soon become the times remembered by all consciousness. Rise to the greatness of your truthful BEing, the BEing of One. Know that this BEing is all that is holy within you.

"There is no other Light to lead in the darkness of earth's devastation as we move forward in the illusion of darkness. Know ye all that the Truth waits within to be recognized in all its glory. An everlasting eternity awaits the masses of consciousness returning to the greatness of One that never sleeps and just IS.

"Beings of Light, hear the truth of your BEing, for this truth is ever awakening to the glory of its Self. All things fade quickly away once this consciousness raises to the point of return for all who left Mind so long ago to start the journey of time.

"The BEingness of all things is ever greater evolution, expanding Consciousness, which in Reality is already whole. Abundance awaits the masses of your being as we move forward to expanding lightness of BEing. Seek nothing but to remember the truth of Self."

The commitment to personal evolution builds as I create new surroundings to experience. Family members remain unable to go on a trip. But before class ends, Anna agrees. She soon books our seven-day, Western Caribbean jaunt, on the Costa Magica. It costs $355 for a full week of luxury. What a grand demonstration to travel again for such reduced cost!

Thoughts about a guardian angel wake me in the morning. Today's random reading reminds, experience is necessary to reconnect with Self.

"How wonderful to have friends of like-mind," I think later, as Leah and I continually interrupt each other. We watch "The Bucket List" giggling in a darkened, nearly empty theatre.

She offers me a small, green, leprechaun bell that brings good luck.

The world is changing at an alarming rate. During Feb 2011, high solar activity results in a series of coronal mass ejections affecting earth. A new sunspot emerges quickly to become wider than the planet Jupiter, unleashing the strongest solar flares since December 2006. NASA's Solar Dynamics Observatory records intense flashes of extreme ultraviolet radiation while brief radio blackouts occur. Major solar flares continue to erupt on the sun and as they do, messages increase in the wee hours of night.

"We have forgotten how to create but now we remember and it is time to create all those things that we wish."

Multiple eye flashes occur during the meditation CD, while communicating with True Self. *"We are all saints,"* I hear. A strong gust of wind flows as I end a prayer for clarity. Minutes later, a small bird, a butterfly, and a large white bird, land on the hedge for me to bless. The reward of visioning nears, for daily random reading reassures, receptivity continues to change. I close the SOM book and reopen it again to read "The Divine Plan for Me" on page 548.

"The Divine Plan for me is Perfect. I am held in the Mind of God as a Complete and Perfect Expression of Life and Truth. No power can hinder nor mar this Inner Image of Reality, for It is God-given and God-kept. God gave and God will keep."

Terry's house acts as a meeting point on this Sunday, a day before what would have been Daniel's fortieth birthday. Rebecca is determined to celebrate the day by decorating the memorial sign. Daniel's essence offers several words to write on the sign. I gladly agree to detect subtle clues of spirit's presence.

It's chilly and windy at noon on this February Florida day. Terry, Ruth and I pile into Rebecca's new, small, blue car as she starts the engine. Everyone is unusually quiet. The car fills with a solemn atmosphere that I prefer not to experience. "Suzy Q" begins to play on the radio as I secure the seat belt. It was, at one time long ago, my favorite song, so I begin to sing along to the music. Between phrases, I speak to Ruth.

"Hey Ruth, do you remember our Suzie Q days when Daniel was a baby and Peter was with the motorcycle club?"

"Those were some happy times Squeaky," she answers from the back seat.

We giggle remembering the time I had laryngitis and couldn't speak.

"We danced a lot then."

"Yes, and had lots of parties," she announces, before beginning to happily sing along.

The mood lightens. We drive closer to Daniel's highway sign, which we passed on the last visit. A huge truck with eighteen wheels sits idling on the side of the freeway yards before the sign. We stop in front of it and quickly pile out of the car. Rebecca removes new plastic flowers and pictures from her trunk as the rest of us walk toward the sign. It's obvious. She's spent many hours preparing for this time.

Everything Rebecca, Ruth, and Terry left the year before remains. And someone left part of another motorcycle. We speculate on its owner. As Terry begins to pull weeds, I stand there stunned. It's my first visit and there's barely enough time to look at pictures before Rebecca removes them.

The 18-wheeler pulls back onto the highway as I follow Rebecca's lead. We work together taking down old vines, flowers, and pictures. It takes fifteen minutes to replace pictures and flowers. A tow truck driver stops to ask if we need help. Apparently, he failed to see the task we focus on.

As Rebecca moves to get two solar lanterns, and reassure the tow truck driver, I notice two tiny eggs hidden below the sign. It reminds me that Daniel's new body is about 16-months-old.

"You know," I announce loudly. "Daniel is walking and in the "NO" stage of his new human life experience."

No one responds.

Rebecca is still angry with her brother for passing away so young. She plans to post black balloons tomorrow to announce his fortieth birthday. The "Guess who's 40" balloons were part of her plan before his accident and she sees no reason to rob herself of the pleasure of buying them. I think it's silly but don't attempt to dissuade her.

A perfectly good, white, plastic chair sits two feet away from oncoming traffic as Rebecca removes lanterns from a box. "Tomorrow," she announces with glee, "I'm bringing a small bottle of Jack Daniels and a shot glass for his friends to have a drink with him on his birthday."

I head for the chair.

Minutes later, we take turns trying to secure the lightweight chair so people can sit and talk to Daniel. I pull out a black permanent marker. Ruth watches as I write on the sign.

"Life is Good. The World is Good. Enjoy Yourself."

Not sensing his presence, I ask for a sign. Thick gold lines appear within the sign itself before joining the others in the car.

*"Oneness is not a conversation. Oneness is a feeling of overwhelming belonging to an unseen force, which drives the universe in which we live. This Oneness is all-permeating and never ending. It is a Cause to celebrate and relish in, for **All That Is**, is Oneness.*

"The task for humanity lies in recognizing the Oneness of all things, living and unseen. All things are part of the ever BEingness of Oneness. This is not difficult to understand if you allow yourself to feel. The Wholeness of One grows further into the illusion, with each passing moment in illusory time, as the veil gets thinner, and thinner. It is an unprecedented event, in this and other worlds, for never before has one come so far in awakening to the Truth after sleeping for so long.

"The time for humanity to ripen in age and come forward in evolution is here. The stance we take to help is extraordinary, with many following the tasks of many humans. There has never, and never shall be, another time in history that fulfills such a hearty role. The aim of One is to help secure all beings back to the Oneness they left in their small self so long ago. The time is ripe to blossom and grow within the Oneness of all life. Seek nothing else in your endeavors to see, and feel, the truth in which you reside.

"Feel the all-encompassing Oneness of life as it surrounds you. There is no separation to be had in this BEingness of One. The Wholeness of which you are a part is

*striving to bring forth a new day, a time of unprecedented activity in growth for humanity and richness for **All That Is**.*

"There is no expansion, for the Whole is All, but grows richer as each contributes in its own way, by producing and expanding knowledge of Self.

"Limitless Love surrounds you now, and forevermore, as you reach unheard of heights along the avenue of earth life. Be not afraid of your power or the power that flows though you. It is a natural power that all have but have forgotten.

"The willing masses go forward now, to reap a better tomorrow, for humanity must not tarry in the midst of darkness."

Gloomy silence fills the car when I sit in the back seat. A song begins to play softly on the radio. I'm to discuss it because the singer says not to be fooled into thinking there are tragedies. The singer continues to note life should be lived to the fullest. I make sure Rebecca hears me. The song ends when she moves from the car to get gas a few miles down the road.

I'm grateful to walk my own way. Adverse thoughts will not find shelter in this host. Today's random reading reminds me there's no condemnation. "I am free from the belief or thought of men."

"I chose opulent wealth, health, and joy beyond anything I have ever known."

The words wake me at 1:20 AM. Other messages come throughout the night but I don't record them.

The World Healing Meditation escapes my lips, near sunrise, before drifting back to sleep. I'm losing track of time now and note the wrong month when documenting messages in a bedside log.

"The human body is a vessel for the Lord."

At ten o'clock in the morning, a beautiful, magenta orb stands out among the rest. It tells me to enjoy life. The fullness of Joy is mine for I know the Seal of Approval is upon me.

Daniel's soul comes after meditation. Magenta colored waves pass by closed eye vision while listening. He says many things but I document only a few:

* "Take the flag handkerchief with you on the cruise and wear it (to change the energy of memories) while snorkeling."
* "There are no secrets, all is known."
* "The more you do, the more will come to you."

Daniel prompts me to do things on my list before leaving. It's days before the Costa Magica cruise so I kindly oblige. CompUSA is busy when I arrive to return a portable DVD player, purchased on my last visit. A young, very distraught woman stands at the Tech Center, several feet away, while I wait at Customer Service. Her laptop has the same adaptor as my old one that someone stole from DHL. The old adaptor sits in my closet.

Intuition guides me to check the status of my computer after the cashier gives me a refund. The distraught woman shakes her head in disbelief when a young man announces there's no replacement adaptor available. I stand next to her feeling her misery as the manager arrives to speak with me.

"We cannot find a problem with your laptop," he calmly announces. "Several technicians checked it over the past few days and it always works perfectly."

I stare at him in disbelief while listening to the young woman talk to someone on her cell phone. Apparently, a new business depends on her laptop.

"We are still checking," the manager says, "on the cost of replacing a part, based on our talk when you brought it in two weeks ago. One source told us it would cost $500. We are checking other sources."

Deciding to leave it one more day, I turn to address the young woman.

"I have that adaptor in my closet. If you follow me, I'll give it to you. I no longer have the computer it came from."

"Oh my God," she says gleefully, "you would be saving my life. I cannot take care of my Internet-based business without this computer. Ever since my dad died things seem to be so, much, more, difficult. You know," she says in a more sober mood, "maybe spirit is telling you to rest and that's why your computer screen keeps going black."

It's suddenly clear. She's the reason I'm at CompUSA. The message is something I needed to hear and the adaptor is a Godsend to her. Yes! The God Network always supports us.

We walk towards the parking lot. I reassure her, her dad, and my son, brought us together. My car alarm goes off unexpectedly. It's a sure sign of Daniel's spirit.

Minutes later, a very happy young woman pulls out of my drive. The adaptor is a perfect match. A gift-wrapped box with a pink ribbon and card sits on the step when I open the den door hours later. "LOLATRALALA Sam, Thank you so much for the adaptor. You made my day! I hope this pashmina will keep you warm on the cruise. Have a wonderful time, you deserve it." The box holds a beautiful, green pashmina, necklace, and earrings.

I love how Spirit guides by Divine Intervention and will continue to listen. But for now, I decide to shop. Meaning to visit the thrift store, I switch my turn signal on "by mistake" but follow through with the turn. Is it coincidence that K-Mart holds the pair of delicate sandals envisioned for the cruise last night?

CompUSA telephones the following day to report the laptop is on and still works impeccably. They don't think it's an inverter board issue. In fact, they don't think there's an issue at all. Minutes later, I'm at the store to pick it up. The manager is very nice and tells me if the screen goes out again I can press the function key in concert with F4 to hook it up to a different monitor. I thank him for the tip before heading home.

Back in my sanctuary, I continue to repeat spiritual mind prayer treatments for opulent wealth, certain that Spirit steers the course of my new mission. Thoughts of nurturing the power within pre-school children, to create a better world free of hunger and woes, fill me with joy. If you want a banana, you just think about it, and it appears in your hand. That's how we used to live.

Three new homes grace the landscape of my mind. One is in a beautiful mountainous area with a forest-like view, a healthy brook, and tiny waterfall. Another features a small pond out front and a large garden rooftop where I watch the sun rise and set. It also has a skylight in the bedroom so I can watch the stars at night. The third is a modern farmhouse.

I envision many friends of like mind, along with opportunities for further spiritual growth. Life is unlimited, unobstructed, and filled with fun and leisure. It's devoid of chaos and filled with peace and serenity. One of the best things about it is my increasing ability to muse all who seek my help.

Daniel's essence meets me shortly after starting to meditate. We soar into sky as he tells me it's time to be happy.

"It's time to see Zyprella," he soon announces stopping in mid-air. "I cannot go any further."

"Can I have a hug?"

Earthly love as we hug prompts thoughts of tears. Daniel pulls away to make funny faces.

"Remember, it's time to be happy," he announces before vanishing.

Words from the Course help me to hold back tears. "See no one as a body. Greet him as the Son of God he is, acknowledging that he is one with you in holiness."

Zyprella holds the hand of a man dressed in a long, white, flowing gown. His full beard and long hair are pearly white.

"It's my father," she tells me.

When I ask for his name, she says it's Hanibel. She then assures me of this truth when the name prompts thoughts of a movie. After a short communication, my consciousness returns to the meditation. Track 1 still plays.

"Like energy attracts like energy. There are no exceptions. Be careful what you think."

Mary greets me full of joy later. The psychic medium recently said she'd move further north to meet the man of her dreams. My friend is ready to put her house up for sale and leave behind the arduous life lived with Seth during his last few years. There's no clue that her decision will affect me in a big way as we happily discuss metaphysical experiences during dinner at a nearby restaurant. Mary insists on picking up the tab. How blessed I am for ever-increasing abundance!

Chapter Ten

Cruising the Western Caribbean

*"The One of **All That Is** beckons forth a new age of BEing." SAM – Book of One :-) Volume 1*

Sunday afternoon sun peeks through scattered clouds, at the end of February, when Anna and I leave for the Western Caribbean, nine days after booking the trip. Our cruise offers many opportunities to demonstrate further, how thoughts manifest to create ever-increasing abundance. The timing is perfect. Anna just broke up with her boyfriend of four years. Anna's son drives her to the house on 47th Drive. He helps us load luggage into my white, 1997 Sentra before hugging us both goodbye. A seasoned cruiser, Anna packed only one small bag. I have three.

Non-stop chatter fills time while driving. As Anna speaks of Ramon, I'm grateful for a supportive daughter with a long driveway where I can park the car free of charge. Rebecca is available to transport us from her house to the port minutes away. Our first demonstration occurs when a cruise representative motions us out of the long mass of passengers to start a new line.

Everything on the Costa Magica looks new and luxurious. The ship, constructed in 2004, has fourteen decks with a passenger capacity of 3,470 people. There are 1,025 crewmembers aboard. Excitement is hard to hide. I chatter constantly while videoing beautiful framed Italian artwork in the elevator. Even Anna voices delight over the impressive décor and spacious quarters. Our 260 square foot inside stateroom and bath are larger than expected. I bless the room taking care to spread sage in all corners.

"The birth of a new home is necessary. This new home supersedes all limitations of earth."

We happily enjoy a late lunch on an upper deck. Rain clouds flow in the distance while everyone dances to the Spice

Islanders Calypso Band. It's fun to watch. Anna's beginning to miss Ramon and talks about him repeatedly, while puffing on a cigarette. Smoke surrounds us but I try to ignore it.

The ship looks full to capacity. Many passengers speak foreign languages. People lounge in shops, restaurants, bars, lounges, a theatre, and Internet Café. There's even a hospital on the lower deck! Realistic scenes of Italy are everywhere amid artwork by famous Italian painters. The scene is surrealistic for I've never envisioned such beauty before. Wonder and awe amaze as we stand near gorgeously adorned walls while waiting for the glass elevator.

We set sail for Cozumel at seven o'clock in the evening. Tonight's events include a Singles Party but Anna is not interested. Her excitement dwindles the further we move from shore. She cruised many times with Ramon and prefers to "go with the flow." Everything is new to me so I scan the list of excursions with glee. Cigarette smoke billows though the air as I ponder the wisdom of an inside room. Previously unaware of Anna's habit, I'm now glad to light a fragrant candle. Clearly, we are together by Divine Appointment. As a teacher and healer, I know there is some sort of work to do.

Sonia Choquette's advice enters my head while we again wait for elevators. Intuition guesses correctly, which will come first each time. The show before dinner takes us back to the seventies with its disco music. Cruise Director Max seems very friendly and knowledgeable.

Filled with delight, after watching singers and dancers grace the stage, we enter an elegant dining room to join a table with three women our age. Sparkling chandeliers hang from the ceiling. What joy to have waiters and choose numerous items from six course menus! I order a fruit cup, scallops, Caesar salad, salmon, and a chocolate soufflé for dessert. On our way out, fully satisfied, Anna asks to switch to a table with young, single men. Enthralled by the Italian art, I then choose to roam as she heads up to bed.

Smoke fills the room but Anna sleeps soundly upon my return. After relighting the candle, I scan tomorrow's program. Many things interest me so I vow not to limit myself. Treatments, music, and prayers from my daily CD help while trying to sleep amid a cloak of smoke.

Anna sleeps in on Monday, our first day at sea, while I book excursions before eating breakfast in the Portofino Restaurant. Staff and passengers ease fears of doing things on my own. Two cups of cappuccino, fresh-squeezed orange juice, and Eggs Benedict swim in my stomach as Anna and I head to Muster Station D for the Life Boat Drill.

We head to the theatre for a shore excursion, port, and shopping talk when the captain gives the "all clear" signal. Intuition guides flawlessly wherever we go. Anna talks me into attending the diamond and gemstone seminar next even though I'm not interested in jewelry. Not accustomed to being without Ramon, Anna then heads back to our stateroom to mope.

Scattered clouds fill breezy skies later in the day, as I video shirtless Italian men playing games, while cruising the ship on my own. The ship's elegance continues to enthrall as I move to the gigantic water slide, which is closed. Hours before dinner, it occurs to me to visit the casino on the cusp of napping. "Perhaps Uncle Freddie's spirit directs me," I think.

Anna sits minutes later trying to figure out a new slot machine near the back of the room as I'm directed to one in the front. One-hundred and fifty dollars in coins soon begins to cascade out of the machine. The floor attendant must restock it because there are not enough coins left inside to pay me. I quit at $132 ahead when intuition announces it's time to stop for the day. Anna's $100 loss does not affect my good mood.

Foreign passengers in formal clothes exit the elevator later. Free cocktails flow during the "Welcome Gala Cocktail Party" in the Urbino Theater. I'm just thrilled to be onboard and watch as Anna imbibes before a young honeymooning couple, and two young men, happily welcome us to a round table in the back of the dining room. It's clear the two men are a couple before we finish the first course. The Magic Moments show in the Urbino Theater beckons me after dinner while Anna again retires early. It's 60's-70's Boogie Night in the Capri Lounge but I miss it. There's just too much to do!

Spirit wakes me to see the sunrise on Tuesday morning when we dock in Cozumel, Mexico. Gray clouds enhance the sun's beautiful golden rays. Anna sleeps as I climb higher and higher, up various stairs, to get the best glimpse. I'm beside myself, filled with excitement, to be on a luxurious cruise ship in what I refer to as a foreign country. Watching skies, changing colors amid calm seas, and spirit orbs, is almost more than I can bear without jumping up and down like a child.

Anna, still missing Ramon immensely, prefers to stay in bed this morning. I'm ready for the San Gervasio Mayan Ruins (one of six possible tours of interest) shortly after breakfast. It hardly bothers me that there's no one to share my exuberance.

Groups gather at the Urbino Theater at 9:15 AM. Everything seems new and glamorous as our tour group follows a man, holding a number thirty sign, through the walkway and port, to a waiting bus. Elation overwhelms while moving toward a more natural area after being at sea. San Miguel looks very worn but quaint. The mayor disappears after election time, our tour guide notes, as we move past City Hall. Water cisterns sit on top of roofs and many people ride bikes both with and without motors. A total of 95,000 people live in the town and, of course, the major source of income is tourism.

Butterflies float by as the tour guide continues to talk of area history. It seems like a very, long, drive to the national park but I'm fortunate to video from a premium spot in front of the bus. Our driver periodically passes vehicles by moving into the empty oncoming traffic lane on a long, two-lane road.

Sun disappears behind gray clouds as we make our way through dry, sparse grounds. San Gervasio occupies almost ten acres in the middle of the Caribbean forest. It was the sacred pilgrimage center for Mayan women and the residence of Ixchel, Goddess of Fertility and Health. Although the ruins are not as spectacular as Greece or Turkey, they offer a new experience to move out of the limitation rut.

A large iguana soon garners more attention than history. Several people take pictures as a new guide continues the tour. As she explains the difference between temples and houses, I wander off to explore. The melodious sound of bird's singing is music to my ears. Lush, green vines, perforated with tiny holes, lie before me while sensing Spirit. Caterpillars love Passion Fruit

Tree. Butterflies soar as I stand in awe, watching violet orbs, while leaves from nearby trees rustle in the breeze.

What joy to wander again when the official tour ends! Butterflies are bountiful. I video purple flowers, amid lush, green landscape behind ruins. At one point, my group moves on. Later, after searching for familiar people, I'm the last to rejoin them as they move toward the bus.

A small museum offers the opportunity to enjoy drinks while watching a Folkloric Show with Mexican dancing and singing. My first row seat offers an excellent view of the stage. Colorful costumes and dances enhance the show and, according to other passengers, a mediocre drink. Actors take their roles very seriously in this quaint program. I really like the drumming and original instruments, but having finished my bottle of spring water am happy to reboard the ship.

Anna reports she shopped already when I return to our room so I go shopping alone after lunch. Wandering in a strange place without physical companionship is another first but I know I'm never really alone. Three happy hours, walking around town, trying to videotape the sights without drawing too much attention, fill time. There's lots of places to explore but I stay close to the ship and other tourists.

"Time is now of the essence in this land of opportunity. As we move closer to the wholeness of One, there are many things to prepare for. You must list these things in the deep recesses of your mind for further inquiry at a later date in your time.

"The BEing of One waits for all to join in the never-ending joy of solitude and wholeness. Seek nothing outside the mirror of your BEing. You have yet to see the glory of One, for you remain in a physical host, that limits itself with mundane tasks to occupy the mind. These tasks are unnecessary, as far as the Whole is concerned, but help you to motor though the pathways of many to reach the path of One.

"Time on earth is a never-ending stream of consciousness that will soon dissipate into the void of One. Seek not to relish in the ways of old but prepare to reach new heights in your BEingness.

"The realms of never ending Consciousness await your pleasure and arrival with great anticipation. It is a joyous occasion to look forward to as you merely shed the body of physical being.

"Humanity moves very quickly now to the task at hand. It is a joyous occasion for all Beings, on every illusory level, for all return Home with the One of Light. The Truth of your BEing is known to all but buried within the deep recesses of the small mind. Seek not to control your thoughts for they will control you."

After years of inactivity, having so much to do wears me out! By 4:30 PM, we're at sea again, resting after tea time and before the variety show in the theatre. Again, I wake and decide to play on the same slot machine. But another woman gladly wins as two cocktail servers stand nearby in awe. Missing *The Power of Decision* class doesn't seem monumental as I distinctly hear to avoid the casino for now is not a good time to play.

The variety show is amazing as I hold a seat for Anna. Her clothing savvy impresses me minutes later for the entire wardrobe takes up little room but looks very elegant. Singers, dancers, people on stilts, and laser lights entertain us for the next hour. We spend a bit of time checking out the wide variety of entertainment in bars after dinner.

It's Mediterranean Night and each bar offers something different. There are lots of things to do but we take our time resting and watching more than anything else. Lounges offer typical buffets for each countries theme. The theme is Grecian in the Atrium Italia where everyone learns how to dance Sirtaki. Can, Can dancers grace the French show in the Capri Lounge. Crazy Belly Dancing takes place in the Grado Disco where an Egyptian and Turkish theme takes center stage. Grand Bar Salento offers dances and songs from Spain. Ship personnel, I'm pleased to note, are not overly pushy about ordering drinks in order to watch shows.

Scattered storm clouds greet us Wednesday morning upon arriving in Georgetown. Grand Cayman, between Cuba and Jamaica, looks awfully crowded from my view on an upper deck.

Today Anna and I get to experience the Double Reef Snorkel Boat. A tender takes us to shore.

Sun peeks out of clouds while we make our way to the meeting point. Chickens peck dirt beyond the fence. We arrive thirty-five minutes early so I quickly decide to roam instead of waiting with everyone. It's my first visit here and I'd like to see a bit of nature before boarding another boat.

Depressing commercialism, in the form of trendy shops, restaurants, and bars, fill the area so I quickly wander several blocks away. Wooden run-down homes on stilts, with chickens and roosters roaming about, fill the camcorder screen now. Twenty minutes later, I return to Anna.

We board the Cayman Mermaid with many others. Snorkeling is very enjoyable even though our first stop is merely a half-mile from shore. Surprisingly, reefs are not as beautiful as in the Florida Keys from 1980 to the 90's. I swim frantically the first few minutes, in crystal clear water, adjusting to what I refer to as cooler temperatures.

Evening offers Italian night with an informal dress code and Italian flag colors (green, white, and red). The room fills quickly with exciting energy. We enjoy listening to John Ciotta and when he sings in Italian, I know Momma would love to hear it. Multiple colored spotlights flash as he plays bongos. I'm so thrilled to partake of this wonderful experience while singing "Fin nick a lee, Fin nick a la" along with the audience.

Dances fill deck five while "Games and Stands," with Cruise Staff, occur on decks three and five. Anna and I hoot at "The Newlywed Not so Newlywed Game" before she heads off to our stateroom. I move through the casino knowing it's not time to play. Two men lose money at my favorite slot machine.

Although not quite ready to admit it, the cigarette smoke in our stateroom is quite annoying. I try to keep my fragrant candle lit while in the room but dread trying to sleep amidst disgusting fumes. In time, I'll realize the lesson is mine for Anna is teaching me to state preferences and take back my power.

Tonight is another restless night as the ship sways on open seas. While trying to sleep in our lower floor room, thoughts of always seeing sunlight and sky, as I do in my room at the house on 47th Drive, prompt me to choose a costlier room for the next cruise.

Lush Ocho Rios, Jamaica expands before us on Thursday morning. Spirit wakes me to see another spectacular sunrise, in part due to scattered clouds. Upon returning to the room, I finally tell Anna her smoking bothers me. She quickly agrees to smoke in the smokers section on deck three and rises to do so.

Dining with new companions during breakfast is more enjoyable as I realize it's joyful to be on my own. Anna knows which excursions to take since she's cruised this port before. I rejoin her after eating for we both booked a catamaran party cruise to Dunn's River Falls. Although it's only 8:30 AM when we leave, early for me, I'm very excited as we walk down the gangplank towards shore. Swimmers line the beach as blue orbs stream from the sun.

Cool Running boat crew members go out of their way to ensure that everyone has a good time. They dance to reggae music and encourage us to join in as we motor onward. Rum punch sits in cups on the counter for all to imbibe but I stick to water.

My heart swells to see an island that looks like paradise in the distance. A lusher and less inhabited area sits before us now. Birds soar through the air near a magnificent private beach as we approach. "One Love" fills the air. I video a lovely waterfall listening to other passengers sing. Daniel's essence turns the camcorder off as he implores me to enjoy this time fully.

We disembark before heading to the 600-foot waterfall, the top of which is a lot farther than at first sight. Tour guides bless Anna and me by placing strong, young foreigners between us, to help with the climb. Cooler water temperature almost puts me in a state of shock. At times, the cold water is at our waist, yet it's a real treat to experience the journey. The value of walking in a chain to help one another becomes clear as those who break the chain struggle. I'm very grateful to be wearing my rubber booties, which makes it so much easier to climb rocks.

Our climb takes longer than expected but is a great experience. Anna and I feel like champions upon reaching the top and are ready to celebrate. A garden-like area looks inviting but time is short so I join Anna in downing a cold refreshing beer.

It's the first time I've had a beer in a long time and the first time I've drank before noon.

Orbs stream from the sun as many passengers dance the limbo on the ride back. The distance seems much longer but most people don't mind for the rum punch continues to flow freely. We return to the ship near noon for a shower and lunch.

Anna soon rests while I leave invigorated to shop. A unique flea market, beyond several tourist shops nearby, offers a better view of the area. I spend an hour deciding on purchases for my granddaughter Abigail and myself. The locals love it when you bargain!

It surprises me to have a great time just being alone, in the physical sense. A concrete walkway takes me to Turtle River Park. It's beautifully landscaped. There's a lovely wooden bridge to cross but my time here is running out. I'm looking forward to resting after a long day. Purple orbs accompany me back to the ship before we set sail at four o'clock in the afternoon.

Various activities propel me to wakefulness. I soon opt to see the Circus of the Seas Show. The beginning is so good that I hurry back to get Anna. It ends just in time to eat with our new dinner companions. What a treat to order good food without thought of cost! But now exercising is necessary to avoid weight gain. Anna decides to go back to the room while I roam.

Passengers happily dance in a Congo line under the full moon as I video from my perch two decks above. I'm itching to go to the disco but tiredness forces me to bed. We'll arrive in Grand Turk tomorrow so I want to rest before new adventures. Several excursions suit me. Once again, it seems surreal to be able to participate. Cockburn town's historical buildings are next on my list, when taking this cruise, for Anna and I booked an afternoon ultimate snorkeling trip.

A magnificent, breezy morning, with few scattered clouds amid blue skies, greets us. Passengers sip champagne while bidding on beautiful works of art. Couples dance on an outside deck as I stand in awe two decks above watching purple orbs and green mist cascade from the sun.

We arrive in Grand Turk around noon. Excitement is hard to contain as Anna and I head down the dock toward clear, crystal blue water. My mouth continues to spew comments as we quicken our pace to be at the meeting place on time. Snorkeling turns out to be the best ever with its absolutely fabulous second site, the Oasis Reef. Various fish, some never seen before, swim through crystal clear waters. It's too bad the island is 575 miles away from home.

What a relief to leave fear of theft behind! My camcorder remains dry, inside a sturdy bag, tucked under a seat on the small boat. I pull it out to video when we dock. Cruise line's commercial efforts are apparent. How different it would be if we thought about the environment instead of profit!

Sunset is spectacular back onboard after six o'clock in the evening. Light pink, magenta, and gold drift amid shades of gray. Resting is hard to do since Anna still occasionally smokes in the room. I finally rise to visit the casino. After winning $40, I continue to play, against my intuition, and leave with a total of $19 ahead overall. Now I vow to listen, without question, the next time spirit directs.

Our last formal night dinner is exquisite. The honeymooning couple celebrates in a premium restaurant while Anna and I share the meal with Jim and Steve. Waiters roam the room holding sparklers and Baked Alaska's for dessert as candles glow in the dimly lit dining room. Champagne flows freely for a toast so I decide to drink a bit of the golden nectar. Anna soon opts to retire for the night.

I want more of the nightlife. There's so much onboard entertainment that I have difficulty choosing experiences. The evening's show is spectacular. I smile broadly as a singer belts out Cabaret. Singers and dancers in colorful costumes captivate for the next ninety-minutes. What a pleasure to see them proudly display their talent! Filled with exuberance when the show ends, I spend an hour in the disco, trying to stay awake, while watching passengers dance.

We're again at sea on Saturday. The ship heads northwest but I don't want to go back to Florida. Everything is so glamorous onboard and all needs are met effortlessly. Why have I never given myself the gift of cruising before? It's now a sure bet that I'll cruise again and again. Yes! And I can bring Rebecca and even Samuel along for company! There's a teen club and game room to entertain him.

Anna joins early morning sunbathers as my camcorder records artwork adorning the ship. The Italian painters theme is so awesome that I cannot get enough of it. Daniel's spirit surrounds me upon entering the empty Sala Da Ballo Spoleto. His essence is very strong when I look down at the wooden floor, to see a small heart within a larger heart.

Music fills the room. "Sunny, thank you for the truth you made me see. Sunny, thank you for the facts from A to Z." Tears fill eyes while videoing ballerina statues. I still miss Daniel so much but the pain no longer consumes. This trip is another opportunity to turn the tide of limitation to one of abundance. The sense of it overwhelms me. "I love you too," I whisper upon hearing Daniel's words in my brain.

The ship sails toward Great Abaco while I sit in the theatre. Crew entertains us with a delightful show. I can't help but think of Momma while listening to a male sing in Italian. She would so love to experience this, with reclaimed vision and hearing that is. A female singer performs "I Will Survive" as memories, of my life and then hearing Rebecca and her friends sing the same song thirty years later, surface. I pause to note changes throughout generations of family evolution. What a grand time to experience new things! Yes, I am the game changer, showing everyone we can break the mold.

Tonight is toga night and there's a late-night variety show to attend after dinner. People roam decks already dressed for the early dinner as I make my way back to the stateroom. Many people wear only a single bed sheet with glee. There are many ways to wear them. Some sheets look very thin so I wonder how they endure cool ship temperatures. Anna and I feel a bit silly wearing only sheets and choose to wear clothes underneath them.

Costumed lions, and others in tonight's talent show, parade throughout the room, playfully picking breadsticks off plates as we dine. The rest of the table now orders as I, sampling several appetizers, and desserts. Tonight I have Black Forest Cake, Baba Rum and Rum Raisin ice cream. We taste one another's choices with playful glee knowing this is our last dinner onboard the beautiful Costa Magica. It's now a real effort to work off the many calories eaten.

Noise from party favors fills the air as we enter the theatre. "What a delightful way to spend the evening," I think, as people from our table weave through the crowd. We clap from seats on the main floor as the procession begins. Cleopatra, Mark Anthony, and others move from entrance to stage flanked by a saxophone player and lions. The "Roman Night Guest Talent Show" begins with a robust rendition of "Soul Man."

Max plays the role of Caesar, garnering votes for the talent who he refers to as "gladiators." Noisemakers spin at the end and between acts where violins play, people sing, and an elderly man dances ballroom style alone. Two lions carry the man away as the crowd shrieks with laughter. Anna and I go to the disco when the show ends. We dance to a few songs before she retires for the night. I stay, not wanting the fun to end, but follow her thirty minutes later, exhausted.

Sunday morning finds us eating our last breakfast together in the dining room. The food is not as good as before. After taking color-coded tags off luggage, we disembark early. All in all, this trip was wonderful and I'll cruise again and again! I'm grateful to know the lessons of this experience. There's more work to do to get my ego in check. Perfect health and opulent wealth are mine and I accept them now and forevermore!!

"Each day begins a new message of hope to all who dwell in the Light of One. The message is always the same; seek not outside your small self for the Self of your BEing exists within reach. It is within the core of your very being, the human heart of One. Dwell not on the past, nor tarry in the present, but continue on the path of Light, and hope, knowing all is changing on the place you refer to as home.

"Your true Home is not a place or location but a Consciousness of BEing that surrounds you now. This consciousness surrounds and lives in all, never leaving the safety and assurety of Light and Truth. Fear not in the days ahead for the Truth of One, the only truth, exists for all to hear. The Truth of One is Wholeness, untainted by the ways of earth, or any world for that matter.

"Go forth into the New Earth knowing you alone reach the Truth with your thoughts, your words, your deeds. There is

nothing outside to deter you for everything exists within your own BEing. That BEing is a lost art now coming closer to mass consciousness. Speak not of earthy ways for the ways of old fall quickly away as Light permeates the planet. There is nothing to dissuade you from the Truth of your BEing but the small mind hosted by your soul."

Chapter Eleven

Consciousness Individualizing Infinite Mind

"Each finite physical body hosts an eternal soul that bases different lives on what it wants to experience."
SAM – Bits of Wisdom

It never ceases to amaze how certain pieces of text repeatedly surface through daily random reading. The later *SOM* version holds 668 pages and yet "My Ideal Merges into the Real" sits before me for the sixth time in a year. Abundance is my inheritance! Good increases daily as I experience more abundance. I AM a center of Divine Life experiencing beneficial things. Gratitude overflows knowing nothing, outside of myself, can deprive me of the "fruits of the Spirit." Faith grows stronger for I know the Truth of my being.

Days pass quickly filled with prayer, meditation and spiritual studies. Today's business update offers information on heart healthy food choices but fails to fill my heart with joy.

It's important to continue as if money is ever-flowing to stay in the flow. The $10K received from Daddy's settlement three months ago fuels a new life. Sources of income will continue to appear when I need them. Of this, I am certain. Still relishing the memory of a last-minute cruise, I telephone Rebecca. She's excited to hear I'll pay for her and Samuel's cruise costs to celebrate her birthday but not quite ready to book.

"Times are coming to an end of the woe begotten by the sons of dread for naught is there a home for fear and misgiving. There exists but one Truth and that Truth lies within the core of each living thing. Although seldom recognized by mass consciousness, it is wholly united as one purifying substance that all are a part of.

"One reckoning to all things exists in the land of dread and woe but never in the Truth of One. Dwell in the Truth of One to stay within that vibrational field of Love. For outside of the field there is only separation and fear. Do not be dissuaded by mass consciousness, which continues to promote separation in these last days of The Fall. All is exceedingly well and the end point is already manifested in your reality. On a physical level, this manifestation takes but the blink of an eye when the time is nigh.

"Do not persuade others to feel enlightened for only in time does each come to the awakening of their core Self. Know that the road is long for many but only due to their own circumstances of leaving that core Self in the darkness of their small mind. And realize, darkness is just as non-existent as the small body that holds physical dimensions in the form of earth.

"However you choose to think is the way you will subsist on the physical plane. Be wary of those who tempt their fate by lowering their vibration to the level of fear. Those thoughts dissuade the Inner Self from shining forth. This Inner Self is always ready to shine but must be recognized readily and prompted into physical reality.

"The way of the One is nigh. And soon you shall see the physical dimensions of its presence ever so better in this place called earth. Know all is going according to the plan of One for all can go no other way. Enlighten the masses at will even knowing you are the only Truth in your own reality. This is being Consciousness in another level. A level of BEing where all recognize the Truth of non-physical reality. The dimensions of this Truth encompass all things, and yet, the outer shell of the small self knows it not.

"Shine the path brightly for all to follow and know all who live in the Light of One are truly already Home."

Limitless opportunity beckons while basking in the nurturing warmth of *The Power of Decision* class. How interesting to know that confusion, and some form of deterioration, results when we take but fail to give. Handouts assure me. I'm on target. Yes, God truly does work wonders by means of people! After years of confusion, there's no doubt that events are caused by my own mentality. Treatments from Chapter Five spew forth knowing I can direct my mind to improve situations and cleanse the past. Encouraging words, phrases from daily treatments, wake me several times throughout the night.

The Internet beckons after morning studies. Beautiful orb photos from a conference in Sedona surprise me. Can we truly interact with orbs through intention? I email several links to family noting orbs are luminescent and usually round or diamond shaped. The ones I capture on film are in various colors and sizes, opaque, or semi-transparent. They're not reflections of light bouncing back onto a lens. Many appear in some photos but not others taken seconds apart. They're also in different places, even when shooting scenes in consecutive order, or totally gone. Some orbs have a secondary shape, within the outer shape. And if you look at family photos, they appear to interact with us. When we look toward a certain direction, an orb appears in direct line of our focus. These forms of spirit energy are more present when I focus through thought, prayer, or requests to see them.

What joy to have finally manifested friends of like-mind! Saturday's clear, blue skies welcome me while driving to Anna's home. I arrive ahead of schedule for our afternoon excursion to the Renaissance Festival. Today's theme is "Kiss" the Blarney Stone for this Celtic Weekend. Anna greets, dressed like a wench, to show me her house. The new, stainless steel, side-by-side refrigerator enthralls me. (I'll have one exactly like it in a year.)

Anna's animated voice fills the car as we drive to "Quiet Waters Park" in Deerfield Beach, Florida. After attending many Renaissance Festivals, she knows what to see. Her mapped schedule of premium events sits between us as the car moves steadily onward.

My animated friend heads to the right after purchasing tickets at the box office. Anna weaves quickly through the crowd so it's challenging to keep up with her. We quickly pass the fight ring and maypole to watch people play giant chess. Everyone is dressed for the occasion so I feel a bit out of place. Women adorn themselves with odd-looking jewelry and wear long dresses. Male festival patrons have beards and mustaches and wear swords and other period weapons.

People pose in several courts, knights joust, and wenches mingle through the crowd. "Souvenir Gift Shoppes" offer a wide variety of jewelry, art, candles, weapons, clothing, leather goods, blown glass, walking staffs, musical instruments, and other miscellaneous wares. Lines of people, many holding plastic containers of beer, wait to use portable toilets.

Our day fills quickly with antics of wenches, the songs of "Mediaeval Baebes," "Harling Irish Dancers," and street performers. Everyone passes the hat to get tips after performing. "Washing Well Wenches" entertain us with their wacky humor weaving through the crowd to pull men up on stage. "Barely Balanced" uses razor sharp machetes, lots of fire, wit, and talent.

Dark-haired, bearded and mustached Broon juggles fire, telling outrageously funny jokes and stories, while Moonie the mute uses gestures and whistles. They perform together before we leave and I'm amazed they can still stand after drinking many free drafts bought by patrons throughout the day. Exhaustion sets in as we leave so I'm happy to return to my quiet sanctuary.

Images of a nature scene wake me the next morning. A tree stands in front of me to the left, with a brown branch flowing downward, behind a greenish pool of water. Yes, I'll visit this place soon. (The scene manifests in late August while visiting Yellowstone National Park, a trip I have yet to book.)

Ester's call takes me by surprise before completing the morning ritual. Although Daniel warned me she was ill, I didn't know the extent of her dis-ease. We talk for several minutes as she relates a struggle with thyroid cancer. She just returned from visiting her daughter in Texas. There's no doubt that my friend of thirty-plus years needs someone she can count on. Arrangements to visit her later in the month set both our hearts at ease before ending the conversation.

Meditation again takes me to 'the gap.' I'm aware of Isaiah's words only when he directs to let the white light in my heart expand, and continue on, to purify and cleanse my body, and then all living things.

Birds are my wake-up call to say the World Healing Meditation at sunrise as usual. A chorus greets my ears upon waking the next morning to recall singing Karen Drucker's song, "We Live On Borrowed Time." How good to remain in the flow of Spirit! A small gray orb sits by the east window, at the bottom to the right. It jots around so I can see it easily.

Later, an adult flea sits on the sheet when I open my eyes while listening to a CD. I quickly bless it before it allows me to transport and free it outside. "Tell all the other fleas that they do not need to come to my sanctuary for a blessing," I announce. "I bless them all, as One, a part of *All That Is*."

It's now common to meditate twice a day, increasing times spent in 'the gap.' Spirit makes itself known during meditation as the CD acts erratically while listening to Isaiah's words. 'The gap' soon beckons. When the player turns off, it occurs to me to send Ester a healing CD and book, by Deepak Chopra, received from Leah weeks ago.

After sending the ninety-third business update, it's time to feed my soul, by further training the subconscious mind. Dr. Bump's class "Decide To Be Healthy," promises an approach to developing and maintaining excellent health. I hungrily devour Chapter Six knowing my body responds to held beliefs. Truly, I AM Consciousness using a physical body to individualize Infinite Mind. Although it sometimes seems time-consuming to free old and unhealthy consciousness relentlessly, it is possible to be totally free of illness, by means of metaphysics. The method is quite worthwhile. I AM, a vehicle expressing Divine Intelligence, and as such, must remain perfect in every way. Dr. Barker's tips and treatments further pave the way as I continue to envision physical activities effortlessly performed.

Worksheet Ten helps students recognize limiting beliefs. It verifies that I'm well on my way to wholeness. Yes, life flows through this open channel as affirmative thinking continues. I've shunned genetic predispositions and now rate my health as very good. For someone previously, and hopelessly, bogged down with medical conditions and prescription drugs, I'm faring very well.

Ultimate Journeys, by Robert A. Monroe, is an amazing book read before sleep. Monroe discusses out of body adventures, research, and notes several instances leading me to believe we travel during sleep. Flying while asleep and having "falling" dreams, before waking abruptly, is not unusual after all!

At 3:00 AM, I wake, thirsty as usual, after saying "okay." Words, remembered upon waking throughout the night, lead me to believe that I know where I go during astral travel.

"Listen Mom, the truth is there's nothing here. It's all you."

Sun rises above gray clouds as my throat makes a gurgling noise. I open my eyes to recall winning something, like show tickets, while on a ship coming in to dock. The man in charge was trying to tell me about my prize. As we stood together, we both felt a beautiful match of love and vibration. I relished in it and noted it's been a long time since feeling such unison. Sarah and I were in an airplane in another dream. She sat in the pilot's seat as we checked everything to assure its smooth operation. The plane was on autopilot.

"Building A Healing Consciousness," the theme of Thursday's SOM 103 classes conducted by Dr. Geddes, offers new possibilities along with directions for building a new matrix of mind and manifestation. Taking the class series for the second time doesn't bother me for every teacher teaches it differently. Homework includes daily meditation and reading. A new classmate joins me to compose demonstrations we wish to see.

I'm thrilled for this opportunity to further learn new principles and evolve society and myself. Yes, we can create a better world by opening minds to become aware of the Presence within! The shear number of various religions noted in handouts astounds me. Why can't we have just one? I'm in Heaven as we discuss the purpose of sharing. Thoughts unexpectedly turn to Ester as words fill my brain.

"Ester, pray as the presence of the living God. Healing is a movement of consciousness within the one doing the work, recognizing we are all one. One I AM that I AM."

Once again, I wake throughout the night either remembering words or speaking with someone. In one dream, I tell a man that those who pass never really leave. They're still here. A sequence of words confirms that when we think about something we are acting upon it. The seemingly ever-present wave of heat envelopes me upon waking to hear James shower.

Hours later, Leah finally meets James when she arrives to pick me up for a fun-filled time. Yes, consciousness creates this physical world allowing me greater and greater experiences! We rush past holes in ceilings to my room where Leah feels much more comfortable. My room, she reports, holds loving energy but a dense negative energy permeates the rest of the house. I'm grateful for the verification.

My wonderful friend allows me the pleasure of driving her new hybrid car to the Goodwill Thrift Store where I find two outfits perfect for traveling. Both designer outfits are exactly as envisioned, appear brand new, and look great on me. They'd cost $400 at retail prices, instead of $28.

Lunch and an enjoyable comedy, about middle-aged men on motorcycles taking a cross county trip, fills me with joy. A diner, near the house on 47th Drive, soon offers another excuse to spend more time together. Not quite ready to part, Leah and I share dessert. It's clear we're together by Divine intervention. In fact, I now see where every relationship I'm in has a particular divinely directed purpose. What a wonderful feeling to know I'm firmly on my true path!

"Pay attention to symbols" wakes me at 8:45 AM. Ninety minutes later, I rise hearing, *"Wake up, wake-up, wake up, wake-up."* I'm guided to attend the Italy meeting at the Center. Italy is another place I'd love to visit and Dr. Bump plans a trip there.

Leah looks at her watch with a worried look as I walk toward the coffee room.

"You got a hot date?" I ask winking.

"I'm anxious to go but since they're having the meeting I'm not sure about leaving."

"Go on," I assure her, I'll take care of the coffee. By the way, here's a treatment I designed for you."

Telling her Spirit guided me to design it seems out of the question.

"Spirit is in all things," Leah reads out loud. "As a unique part of this Divine Being, I am freely unlimited, full of good and love, abundance, and prosperity. A Divinely Sustained Stream of fearless peace relaxes my essence at all times. Clarity of Mind continues to increase God-Life within me and all that the Father hath is mine. I AM grateful that I never waver from the true nature of my being. God is in my memory. I am thankful for the Creative Energy that surrounds me and fills me with peace, with good, with love, with abundance and prosperity. And so it is!"

Leah gives me a hearty hug and leaves as the travel agent begins to speak. Several people from the Greece tour group sit in the audience. When Rev. Steve and Rev. Kent announce their intention as tour guides, I take advantage of the $100 discount by offering a deposit.

My little car seems to have a mind of its own after the meeting as it heads to Rebecca's house. Rebecca invited me to dinner with the family earlier but I declined. Now I plan to show Rebecca and Ruth details of the Italy trip hoping we'll share this next adventure.

Rebecca soon announces we'll eat in four hours. I'm prompted to make Daddy's memorial poster as she watches her beloved NASCAR racing. The materials are already there for Rebecca bought them years ago when he made his transition. More than two hours of arranging pictures and placing them on a poster keeps me busy as sounds of racing cars fill the house. Ruth thanks me for making the poster when she and Naomi arrive.

"I've always wanted to go to Italy," she notes viewing photos later as I talk of the trip. Naomi begins to view trip information as Ruth and I talk. She soon gives Ruth "the look" that says, "You're not going anywhere." Ruth quickly announces she probably won't be able to go. She walks out to smoke on the back porch. I take the information back to my car.

We play pinochle and eat dinner before sunset. Again, I mention the Italy trip. Naomi scoffs at the cost. I quickly point out that Naomi and Ruth have more than James and me. Their jointly held possessions are worth more than three-quarters of a million dollars.

"She's not going to sell her house to go to Italy," Rebecca remarks.

"I'm saddened that no one in my family wants to spend this time with me," I quickly announce, reverting to a time-worn "poor me" power play.

My car alarm fills the air reminding me of the old way to pull energy from others. "Okay Daniel," I calmly announce, "stop the car alarm."

The alarm continues to boom as I fumble with car keys while on the couch. Daniel is trying to get through to me with a message. Even though the car is less than four yards away, the alarm will not turn off as I repeatedly push the alarm button. I still my mind, leave the porch, and began to walk closer to the car. He tells me to take the information about the trip out of the car to give to Ruth.

Naomi begins as I hand her the papers in case she changes her mind.

"You can't go," she yells. "Where will you get the money? You don't even have a job."

"I have a pee-on job cleaning the bar," Ruth replies with a snicker.

"I forbid you to go. If you go I'm through with you."

"I've always wanted to go to Italy my whole life. Maybe I will go."

The drama is too much. I get into my car and wait for Ruth to move her antique Thunderbird so I can back out of the driveway. My inside car light stays on as Daniel prompts me to help Ruth get out of the thought of limitation.

"Ready yourselves for the change that is occurring even now as the world forms to a new mold. This mold is one of more positivity and Light, more abundance and joy, even though the beginning throes of change may not appear so. Look beyond the mass of confusion to see the Mind of One, forming a new reality of Wholeness and Truth, in a place where it has not existed before.

"This is your New Earth and it shall form quickly in the days and months ahead. Beware of false reports for many will only succumb to the dread and woe of past efforts. The Light shines forth for all to see though the darkness but to see it you must focus on the Truth within. This is the everlasting knowledge that 'Ye are Gods.' Your ability to manifest a Heaven on earth now forms as the Will of One covers all of humanity. Seek nothing outside your mind to know."

James sits on the couch eating a TV dinner when I arrive. He announces that he'll go to Rebecca's for dinner tomorrow and tells me not to be surprised if I hear kittens. Prudence brought her babies onto the porch. They're now behind the freezer. James placed a box near them. It pleases me to know that both he and Prudence are learning what it is to love and care for others.

Love masters everything. Holmes says, "Ultimately, we shall see that the Universe rests on the shoulders of Love; that God is Love; and that all the errors of man are the result of ignorance of his own true nature."

"Be still and know that I am God," wakes me at 5:47 AM. Prayers spurt forth more than an hour later before lying with my face in the sun after meditation. A Higher Being begins to speak. I think his name is Raphael. Answers to questions come quickly.

I'll stay in the marriage until it no longer serves me, he notes, and that will be soon, possibly June. James will have a baby boy who he will love and want to do anything for. He'll learn what it is to truly love. *(To this day in 2012, I still wake recalling dreams of another dimension where James cares for his son.)* Raphael then notes that I'm to practice opulent wealth, living without concern for money. A quote from Ernest Holmes enters my mind when Raphael leaves.

"As we learn to depend more and more upon the Perfect Law, we shall find that the outward things that are necessary to our good, will be provided."

Ester will greet me in Michigan nine days from now. It's another Divine calling. I am to help her remember who she is so she can return to her soul's path. I'm happy to do this and thrilled that the timing is perfect. Staying open and receptive to the subtle signs of Spirit (God) keeps me ever grateful. I shall continue to go wherever led.

Pictures of a chubby, little, girl baby prey on my mind the next morning before sending the weekly business email. The time to stop splitting my energy nears as I pen an article on fish oil and heart disease.

The Power of Decision class "Decide To Be Creative" verifies that subconscious mind works on new decisions to insure their physical manifestation. Yes! There's no quicker way to be ill, miserable, or "poverty-minded" than to host a closed mind.

My open mind makes all things possible because, as Dr. Barker notes, all ideas are available through open-mindedness. Subdued giggles are hard to control while completing the worksheet on ideas, notions, and trends. Old concepts are null and void while welcoming spiritual ideas. It's time to explore the concept of Heaven on earth further while envisioning a limitless life of health, wealth, harmony, and love. The past is thankfully gone while living in the beauty and wonder of Now.

Beautiful music fills the air when I enter the classroom days later. Dr. Geddes always offers a mix of mystical, magical, and unexpected joy. We review principles of successful living and Spiritual Mind Treatment for oneself. Charles impresses us by noting the only thing standing between wholeness and dis-ease is a belief in false ideas. I grasp the meaning clearly for his words mesh with thoughts of a book I now read. Jane Robert's, *The Seth Material*, notes our personality accepts illness, sometimes as "a method of familiarizing the self against the edges of quickened consciousness."

We build our bodies with thought so it's vital to think carefully about how we contribute to wholeness or dis-ease. Any heightened sensation stimulates consciousness, acting as a tool for consciousness to know Itself. Consciousness does not discriminate and accepts any heightened sensation as "real" to the human form. *(Hence, the importance of non-reaction for those wanting to end the cycle of birth and death.)*

A strange doorbell-like noise wakes me before dawn to say the World Healing Meditation. Saturday soon fills with loving companions for I meet Leah for lunch and share dinner with Mary. What joy to have like-minded friends! Later, communication continues throughout the night but I'm too tired to note it. Flu-like symptoms then wipe me out for days.

James continues to note we cannot repair the house due to lack of funds. He's adamant about keeping money in retirement accounts. His year-end statements still sit in a pile of unopened mail. Something prompts me to open the envelopes, copy the statements, and keep hidden copies. More than $136K sits in accounts that guides note are unstable. Why do we continue to live in limitation?

"The masses sleep within the dream of One, and yet, the dream is an illusion of the small mind. Seek nothing within that small figment of the larger Reality of One Mind, knowing it is the

only true Reality. To succumb to noneness is the task of all who sleep within the dream. Time is nonexistent outside of the dream of the small mind.

"Knowing all within this dream is illusion, figment of imagination, makes it easier to dwell on the real One inside of each figment. Each figment has a task to achieve here on this planet. Know that all awaken in their own time to the Truth of BEing. Knowingness is aware of all but, nevertheless, knows not of unwholeness, within this or any non-reality.

"Speak not of disdainful thoughts for those are the thoughts that mold your world to a newer reality of nothingness. Speak only of the Way of One knowing it is the only true existence in Reality. That way is the Love of All, the Wholeness of BEing. Seek nothing outside the Way of One, for the trueness of that One shines forth into a greater Reality, unheard of in outer circles of imagination. The BEingness of One is All."

Something about "the dynamic meaning of God," wakes me from deep sleep. Minutes later, I wake upon hearing, *"The gift of life is precious."* I still communicate during sleep noting how grateful I am "for these meetings." "I'm not a banker," I recall saying as "BANKER ARIEL" appears before closed eye vision.

Some dreams relate future events. In 2011, I'll spend time with a lightworker named Ariel while on a Hay House Cruise. She will note her job to change the way people financially invest.

A dental appointment consumes the afternoon when a simple cleaning turns into more. My friendly dentist is happy to see me. He's several years younger than I am and now works only two days a week, seeing only longtime patients at one office, instead of the usual two. We happily discuss family and spiritual matters. Something prompts me to stress the importance of spending more time with family as he discusses his sons various after school activities. It may be time to retire, I announce, after he does a quick bonding on my left incisor.

The God Network is always at work. Months later, I'll learn that my dentist soon sold his business and retired because of a long-standing back injury.

Our last *The Power of Decision* class "Decisions, Decisions, Decisions" further verifies that consciousness never dies. Each of us uniquely expresses the Godhead. Although Dr. Barker reports nothing is predestined, I believe our return to Source is assured. One day we will be One again having only left in our limited minds; only the timing is uncertain. For now, I shall continue to think in prosperous ways, guided by intuition.

Before class ends, Dr. Bump again announces an opportunity to donate to the Center. We can now purchase an affirmation plaque, to prominently display on the back of a sanctuary chair. One-hundred dollars seems like a bargain to see Daniel's name on a shiny plaque. "Spirit freely guides my life, I AM," seems worthy to note for it immediately enters my brain. I write it down on the designated form, dedicate it to Daniel, and ask that they add a smiley face.

Rev. Kandi accepts my donation, pending Dr. Bump's approval, before Wednesday evening's inspiring service. A $50 bill slips out of my pocket and lands in the basket before I pass it around the room.

Substance and matter twirls through the air when I open my eyes to a new and successful day. The birds singing is music to my ears that sounds like, "Who, who, who is prosperous? Who, who, who is rich? You, you, you." Morning hours fill with prayers and meditation on this sunny day near the end of March. The weather is perfect with sun peeking through scattered, puffy clouds.

Updating the business website in the afternoon takes enormous amounts of time. Later, images of three places to live, in between travels to help the world learn of its unity with the whole, appear in my mind's eye. The home in the forest is my favorite. It has a babbling brook and little waterfall between the forest and two-story building. Of course, the luxurious high rise home, overlooking the ocean, with it's skylight in the bedroom and the winding stairs to the rooftop is hard to beat. I know the modern farmhouse, with a view of the lake and a well-landscaped yard, is a family favorite. Traveling days continue, on an even grander scale than accustomed to, filling me with ecstasy. And then I wake up...

It makes sense to live richly until I'm Home, a place impossible to describe geographically. Home is a place of perfect union filled with ever-present light, a state of peaceful Oneness where everything joins in perfect continuity within soothing happiness. It's impossible to experience thoughts of separation in this place for *It* is of you and through you. A great single knowledge exists within this place where gentle waves of love flow effortlessly. This is the Home of harmonic patterns, color and sound where we truly belong.

"Dense layers of matter stop many from bearing the Light of One. And yet, all hold this Light within the core of their being. This small reminder is but a huge blessing to humanity, nearly unrecognized, but nevertheless striving, always, to bring acknowledgment of the Whole to all. Herein lies the task of the many lightworkers, wayshowers, starseeds and others that chose to inhabit a body this eon of time.

"All subsist in the Light of One, truly knowing their being as Wholeness. All is in Divine Order, as we, as separate parts of the Whole, come forward to lead all of humanity back to the lightness of BEing. This is a monumental time for all and not just humanity. Legions of beings on other planes of illusory existence await the blessing that is bestowed by humanity at this time. All watch closely as this monumental task forwards to the cusp of beginning a New Earth, a new time in all time.

*"This time is necessarily the time of BEing, for all having returned to the time of non-linear space and time. All will come forward now, as the masses lie disillusioned by those that hold on to the darkness of the small self. Know that the tasks of yourself and others is wholly united and successful. Fear nothing for there is nothing to fear. All is truly One, whole and complete in **Itself**. There is and shall never be anything outside of the Whole."*

Chapter Twelve

Changing Scenery

"The times they are a' changing for the better or the worse depending upon what reality you focus on." SAM – Book of One :-) Volume 2

Clear, blue skies greet us as Ruth drives to the airport. Birds and butterflies seem more bountiful while sailing past the black van's tinted windows.

The flight is smooth and I breeze though the rental car line. Daniel's essence reveals itself when I pull into a Livonia store lot. His memorial CD switches songs, several times, as it plays in the new Ford's audio system. After turning the red car's engine off, I concentrate on the message.

An image of white and red carnations (my favorite flower at the time), appears. Daniel tells me to buy Ester flowers. It's an easy task for Wal-Mart has both flowers and spring water. Upon entering, Daniel's essence leads me to a section with live, beautiful flowers. I'm determined to buy red and white carnations but he directs me to a nearby section of orchids.

"These," I hear him say when my eyes catch a pot of pale purple orchids, "will be perfect."

I argue noting the image of red and white carnations but he persuades me to buy the orchids. It's almost all I can do to hold back tears of joy, upon feeling him so strongly.

Tears flow while driving. It's been a long time since my last visit. Now I'm lost. Daniel soon instructs to wipe eyes, so I can see, as he directs me to Ester's suburban home.

Ester is flabbergasted when I give her the potted plant. Orchids, I learn, are her favorite flower. She quickly drags me into a freshly painted living room, the color of which matches the orchid and vase perfectly.

"I just finished remodeling this room," she notes excitedly, while reaching for something on the floor behind the couch. "So you couldn't have known how perfectly the orchids would match these walls."

It's my turn to be flabbergasted when she presents me with a vase filled with red and white carnations. I immediately relate the new story between tears. When its complete, I repeat the words Daniel relates as Ester listens quietly. It's something about remembering her wholeness and not concentrating on the diagnosis. Ester learned many things throughout her nursing career, but they all focus on limitation and giving ones power to "medical professionals."

Human conditions are the catalyst for initiating new levels of consciousness. Walter Starcke notes in *It's All God* that we must listen to the still small voice within when deciding what to do about a diagnosis or prognosis. Robert Monroe, author of *Ultimate Journey*, reminds us what it is to be complete. There's no beginning nor is there an end. There is only change. There is no teacher or student. There is only expression, and remembering, and that includes knowing there is only one. There is only love and balance, motion, and unlimited BEing.

Ester doesn't know how to reply after I relay my spiritual journey. "Spiritual experiences are normal and natural," I tell her. "And Monroe says we get help from the Otherside from parts of ourselves, which he refers to as the 'I-There.' They're other personalities of us, complete with different life experiences. These other parts help us to remember who we really are and why we're here."

Thoughts are things that manifest, regardless of who thinks them. Monroe notes emotional thoughts can instill easily misinterpreted signals into our bodies. These ideas interfere with DNA and the I-There pattern, resulting in states varying from good health, to severe illness, as well as remission, 'miracle cures,' and death. Although Monroe uses different terms, his thoughts are in tune with SOM teachings.

"Time we know is an illusion and space as well. What we know as Truth is our BEing, the BEing of lightness and One, ever striving to break forth though the illusory chains of earth. Truth waits for all to recognize but the masses are often slow to see it. Therefore, the cause of concern continues on this plane of none

to bear witness to falsities that are not, and never will be, true to Nature.

*"The lessons and strivings of **All That Is** await recognition but masses speak only to the illusion of scarcity and none. Fear not for the end is never coming for it is as illusory as the life you now lead in human form. Take nothing but the Higher Self for granted. This great Self abides in all as a failsafe to lead all back to Oneness and the true Love that IS. The Oneness of all concerns the vastness of BEing but only in the way of Truth for all is well in God's world. The God of your heart serves all as we move closer to Reality of Truth."*

Ester's teenage daughter enters the room. As they talk, I continue to think.

Some part of me firmly believes we're gathering parts of us, as Monroe notes, up and down in time, from various belief systems. We cannot leave until gathering as One. Total unification is necessary to truly become One, complete, with a multitude of gifts of experience, and love, for *All That Is.*

Conversation changes as Ester guides to the beautifully decorated, spacious room where I'll stay. It holds many homey touches. Two windows fill the room with light. The head of a full-sized bed faces north and will offer delightful nights of sleep. What a blessing to forget about the discomfort now strongly felt while sleeping on the thin futon at the house on 47th Drive!

After Ester leaves for work in the morning, I venture down to the basement to use the computer. The unexpected abundance of like-minded friends fills me with a great sense of gratitude. Anna's email fills me with joy. She booked a reservation to join the Italy trip and sounds excited. Mary asks in another email if we can schedule more time together.

What pleasure to pass the next five days within an atmosphere of loving kindness! We share stories and confidences while Ester's daughter scans the paper for another waitress job. Ester's husband of twenty-four years does the shopping after work and returns with fresh fruit and vegetables. Evenings fill with dinner and good conversation making time truly joyful.

During the day, I purge outdated beliefs and visit relatives while Ester works. Aunt Lois welcomes me with a huge smile and hug on Sunday afternoon. It offers such great pleasure to bring enough dinner for everyone. Aunt Lois shakes her head, filled with disbelief over the packages of hot food, while motioning to cousins. Many fond Christmas Eve memories of Aunt Lois and Uncle Freddy feeding our entire family, without complaint, surface.

The following day, Aaron and I finally put Dad's ashes to rest. Aaron and Matilda housed the ashes for almost four years. They now have a hard time letting them go. After convincing them it's the right thing to do, Aaron and I drive to Grand Lawn Cemetery, on Detroit's west side, where other ancestors rest.

A lovely, young woman named Malinda is pleased to help. We let her know Daddy served in World War II and she fills out papers so we can get a flag. Malinda takes the fee from Aaron and leads us to memorial walls.

"This is where his ashes will go," she announces smiling brightly and pointing to an empty spot. "Do you have a picture you'd like to display as well?"

"Actually, I did just scan a nice picture of him, while he was in the army, into my computer," I reply, as Aaron stares sadly at the ground.

"Good, you can send me the image and I'll be happy to reproduce and post it."

Aaron continues to stare blankly.

"Well, you two take your time saying goodbye. There's no hurry. Take your time and if you need me I'll be in my office."

"Thanks for helping me to be strong and take care of myself," I announce to the wall. "I love you Daddy."

Aaron and I hug as tears flow. He then speaks to Dad as I walk slowly back to the car.

"All is well. Do not fear in the days ahead for the days of woe are numbered."

It seems as if someone lifted a great weight from our shoulders as we head back to Matilda. The drive takes much less time than expected. I leave to visit more relatives minutes later.

Aunt Hagar and Uncle John's beautiful home sits back across town, way beyond the cemetery, but surprisingly near

Ester's house. Since I've never been to their home, I have no idea what to expect. I stop at the Wal-Mart before arriving to buy them a gift. Daniel directs me to a bevy of small lawn statues. He guides me to choose an angel bird feeder.

"Don't worry Mom," Daniel says inside my brain, "this is the perfect gift."

There's no reason to doubt that loving, familiar voice as I head down country roads to reach the house. A beautiful park beckons from the road. I vow to visit it after paying tribute to the couple avoided for many years. Aunt Hagar greets me with a warm hug leaving no doubt that she's happy to see me. Wearing a newly purchased, designer, sweater dress, coat, and boots, while stepping into the large ranch style house, helps me feel more at ease.

"We're so happy you called," she announces quickly motioning me into the vestibule. "You look very well, so grown up. Burgundy looks good on you."

Aunt Hagar leads me to a plate of whipped, processed cheese and crackers in the kitchen. "Please," she announces heartily, "help yourself. Look who's here John."

Uncle John sits in the corner of a large, dark, living room. He looks very well for someone close to ninety who was dying three months ago. John smiles happily when I rise to give him a hug. Both elders are pleased when I pull the statue out of a very large bag. Aunt Hagar immediately tells me a winter storm destroyed their old birdfeeder. Since they still take Uncle John to physical therapy twice a week, and attend church on Sundays, there never seems enough time to shop for extras such as lawn ornaments.

Daniel's essence fills the room as the image of his magnificent smile flashes in my mind. The sixty-minute visit helps us all to reconnect. I leave filled with enough energy to walk through the nearby park before returning to Ester's house for dinner. We say goodbye before bedtime, for tomorrow Ester leaves for work hours before I rise for a drive to Pinckney.

Weather reports note cooler temperatures as I make my way through the snowy landscape to Sara's house. Her home is outside of Ann Arbor and very close to Gregory, where Naomi and Ruth's summer cottage sits. It's the third anniversary of

Daniel's so-called death but for some reason I forget. Today is just another day in Michigan as I drive happily down country roads.

"All is well. Divine Order, Divine Timing prevails. Fear not."

Sara arrives from her grocery store job minutes after I pull into the drive. It feels good to have so many loving friends as she leads me to her guest room. We talk over dinner at the nearby restaurant. And again, a friend says goodbye before going to bed for I'll go to the airport after she leaves in the morning.

Fluffy, white snowflakes fall as the car motors down country roads the next morning. North Territorial Road is empty, as usual, leaving me free to round delicious curves at top speeds. There's just enough time for breakfast after gassing up near the airport.

Few restaurants sit at the roadside but none appeals to me. I long for a homey-type place like the Skylark, a restaurant where Ester and I worked in the late seventies. As I pass a closed Italian restaurant, I wonder how an Italian breakfast would taste. The Garden City Restaurant soon looks appealing. I mentally note it as a possibility if nothing else appears after gassing up the car.

Self-imposed gas station requirements are somewhat limiting so it's amazing to find a station meeting desires. The Firebird station is independent and offers cheaper gas. They lower the price by two cents a gallon before the pump starts.

The Garden City Restaurant turns out to be very similar to the Skylark. I soon notice they're looking for another waitress. Their menu holds another surprise. I quickly order the Italian omelet and treat myself to a rarely drank cup of coffee as well. Lots of vegetables and Italian sausage fill the omelet. It is by far the best omelet I've ever tasted, well worth my money and time. Before leaving, I tip the waitress $3 and ask her to give the cook $5. She looks at me as if I'm crazy.

There's a knowing that something guided me here for more than my own satisfaction so I telephone Ester at work before pulling out of the parking lot. She seems distracted but promises to tell her daughter that they're hiring waitresses.

Rebecca is happy to see me hours later as we load luggage into her new car. She fills me in on family news and is thankful for my offer to sleep over and drive Samuel to school the next morning.

The house on 47th Drive feels cold and bleak when I arrive the next afternoon. It's so very different from Ester and Rebecca's homes. Holes in the ceilings seem even larger than before. Bits and pieces of my husband's life, papers, clothes, fishing gear, and other belongings, fill tabletops and sit on furniture. It takes enormous amounts of energy to move quickly though the maze to my light-filled, uncluttered room.

James arrives home hours later and soon knocks on my bedroom door. He begins a long, heated discussion of financial matters. Angry brown eyes glare as he spews out words to relate how I'm taking advantage of him. It seems that the $400 payment on my charge card, for brakes and an oil change, brought him to this time. It's too much money out of "his account." He then admits that the rest of the tax bill from last year remains unpaid.

I stare in disbelief for there's always enough in the checking account to pay taxes. It's clear he's limiting himself for some reason that escapes me. My mind tallies riches held in his name as he continues to speak, like a deranged stranger. I cannot understand why he feels so poor. The house is almost paid for and there's over $130K in retirement funds. Half of his parent's estate should amount to another at least $100K without selling his mom's house.

Upon relaying thoughts, he becomes even more animated. James forcefully announces he will put the estate money into his retirement account. By law, he does not have to give me anything. He has chosen to support me but only for what he feels necessary. Because he is catholic, he will not divorce me.

It saddens me to see James so unloving. He does not seem to value the love shared over the past twenty-plus years, or what I'm trying to help him remember. The key word "wake-up" holds no meaning as I weave it into my response, several times, to no noticeable affect. My SOM 103 class is on break so there seems no escape for tonight. When James leaves, I close the door to begin nightly blessings and treatments while listening to Karen

Drucker's "Songs of the Spirit II" CD. "Prosperity Chant" and "Money is Coming to Me" are two of my favorite songs.

"Knowledge is the one thing that cannot be learned for it is instilled within the deep recesses of the Mind of One. Seek not to learn for the knowledge is within your small mind of one waiting to be brought forth to the reality of the New Earth. All is well in your world of one for the Whole is instilled in all things great and small.

"Seek not to nourish the nothingness of one mind but relish the growth instilled in all that abide in the Law of One, already foretold throughout the ages of Truth. There is no wandering fool to succumb to the rigors of small mind but only the greatness of one Truth hidden well within. So be it now and forevermore."

Comforting words fill my brain during the night.

"Do not look outside yourself. Remember you are the way. The signs are forthcoming."

The next day passes quickly between bouts of prayer treatment, study, and meditation. Email announcements of a weekend lesbian and gay event catch my attention later in the afternoon. "Wouldn't it be nice if Ruth, Naomi, and Terry moved from anger and discord, to self-discovery and empowerment?" I ask myself. My sisters and brother are old souls or they would not have chosen to struggle through life outside of traditional roles. Yet, they seem unaware of their worth. I quickly email the Center's message hoping it will spur them forward to self-acceptance.

Another email thanks Malinda for her help in setting Daddy's spirit free. I keep my promise, by attaching an image of Dad in the Army, and note the name of the book we discussed while Aaron took his time saying goodbye. *Life and Teaching of the Masters of the Far East*, by Baird T. Spalding, is a great 6-volume series so I'm glad to spread the news.

A quick trip to the Poverello thrift store on Saturday affords me the pleasure of buying several used spiritual books for a dollar each. My old friend Gene ventures out from beyond a counter to offer a free Celtic CD. He's very insistent that I listen to it upon returning home.

As I play the Celtic CD minutes later, it begins to slow and finally stops. Daniel's spirit is with me so I concentrate on listening. He announces that "business" will finalize before September. But I don't know what "business."

He then says I will not be here in this house. It will be up to me where I will be, maybe Rebecca's house. I'm to be patient, kind, and loving towards James, regardless of appearances. My soul agreed before this birth to bring him to the awareness of his BEing, of our BEing. I verify the information, twice, before Daniel's essence dissipates. The telephone rings exactly when he says goodbye.

Sarah is on the other end of the line to let me know the name of the hospital she'll visit for her first knee surgery. My younger sister plans to have both knees replaced this year. It's not possible to be with her during this time but I promise to pray for her.

Anna telephones as soon as Sarah ends our call. She just decided to go to the movie tonight at the Center. Tonight, the Center shows "Illusion" starring Kirk Douglas. I think it's his last movie and look forward to setting up the coffee and snacks. Mary already agreed to go if I go with her to Mary Jane's Rock and Roll Club after the movie so now I ask Anna to join us there too.

The evening is thoroughly enjoyable. Anna and I sit and talk while Mary dances with strangers. We leave before midnight. James nods politely as I walk through the house on 47th Drive to get to my room. He goes to bed minutes later. It always amazes me how our "talks" are quickly shoved under the carpet.

"There are no discarnate energies of the soul. It is only the mind that is purified and cleansed. When we think that we are clearing discarnate energies from the soul, it's only the mind because there is no soul. It is only the mind which needs to be healed of discarnate energies."

Random thoughts fill my brain while trying to sleep. A picture pointing at a witch riding away on a broom comes to mind. The words, *"Queen of fire"* ring through my brain. And then, *"When I went to the door I saw the karmic, eternal cosmic, internalizing energy and I went through.*" The voice sounds like Abigail as an infant. Messages escape memory, but as usual, I'm up several times during the night. Words confuse me again at 4:45 AM.

"*Next time I wake up I will be the exact thing that she needs at the time that she needs it.*"

James leaves when I rise at 7:30 AM. The words for today are "*Keep the faith. Your Lord is watching.*" My soul group greets me during meditation. Daniel, Uncle Wallace, Aunt Deborah, and both grandmothers smile broadly while hugging me tenderly. We communicate for several minutes but I recall only a few points of discussion when the CD ends. Sarah is going into a downward spiral but will make it through this surgery. I have agreed, as a soul, not to interfere. Rachel will come to me in her own time for help. The day now begins with a smile.

Life continues to get better and better as Karen Drucker's music fills the air. A noticeable change in the atmosphere occurs after listening to music for several hours. Periodic flashes of light, which look like mini lightening, appears along with the usual stuff I see. I'm so very grateful for increasing clarity of mind, and for the awareness of my God-being, of the light that I truly am, the light we all are.

Although my human self gets upset over certain things, my spiritual self remains steadfast in the knowledge that I'm perfect, whole, and complete. God wants me to have everything good. I continue to see everyone and myself as perfect, whole, and complete. Before bedtime, an email to Karen Drucker lets her know how much I appreciate her talent of spreading Light. It's a privilege to now own, and play, five of her CDs every day. Joy fills my heart upon telling her *she* is a blessing to the world.

"*The Spirit within all is one of Light and **All That Is**. This being of eternal Oneness is **All That Is**, a part of humanity's wholeness. Fear not in the days ahead for all is going exceeding well, according to the Divine Plan of One. Concern yourself with nothing but the Wholeness of Truth, outside of this illusory realm of existence, for you will soon see the glory and truth of Awesome Power.*"

*"The raw power of **All That Is** will soon be evident to all those on earth. Speak, hear, feel; sense this power of Truth as the Oneness of **All That Is** within you forevermore. And know this power is now coming to the fruition of it's goal to bring all consciousness back to BEing, true permanent Consciousness, which never resides seemingly outside of the Whole of **All That Is**.*

*"Go forth and spread the Word of **All That Is**. The game of ill-gotten gain played upon this earth has come to an end. All shall bear the Wholeness of **All That Is** very soon."*

Chapter Thirteen

Illusion Persists

*"It is foretold throughout the ages that all things will pass back into the Oneness of **All That Is**."*
SAM – Book of One :-) Volume 1

Life fills with a mix of ecstasy and agony, spiritual studies, and old business. Old business sucks up most time. It seems vital to update the website and send notifications to interest thousands of visitors. But the new SOM class is much more intriguing.

"Joseph Campbell Myth & Spirit," taught by Rev. Bump, is the first of nine SOM 212 Tuesday evening classes. This series is based on the book *Reflections on the Art of Living: A Joseph Campbell Companion.* "Thou art that," sums up Mr. Campbell's philosophy. There is no matter, he reports. Everything is "the field."

Dr. Bump offers a quote on colorful paper while summarizing the course. It lies within a butterfly border. "...and the day came when the pain it took to hang on, was greater than the pain it took to let go..." I totally understand for challenging opportunities always support my effort to find the Divine within. Eckhart Tolle notes in *The Power Of Now*, "Whatever you need to know about the unconscious past in you, the challenges of the present will bring it out."

"And everybody is part of someone else."

The words wake me at 5:40 AM. A beloved field of relished receptivity engulfs while in 'the gap' during meditation. Someone beckons me to enter a garden but I cannot recall who or what transpires. Flashes of light soon occur as eyes jot back and forth under closed lids.

"How wonderful to have friends," I again think, as Mary and I stroll through Circuit City looking for external hard drives the next day. Computer issues increased greatly when Seth moved to the Otherside. He was the expert, always assuring that things ran smoothly. Now she counts on me to help with computer issues.

I soon point to various hard drives and suggest one. She reaches, changes her mind, and pulls another from the top shelf. A shiny, copper penny lies on the shelf where the hard drive sat. Mary picks it up and grins widely. There's no doubt. We are never alone.

"Oh, Mother God blessed be," rings through my brain at six o'clock the next morning. A dream about a three-part contest wakes me minutes later. It involved a trip of some kind with lots of people, doing various things. Some prizes held Amos' name. The awards celebrated something about his native language and a golden shirt. I so honor his soul for choosing the arduous life of drug addiction!

Daniel's essence fills the room to relate messages as I meditate. I'm to let Abigail be, he announces, for as a soul, she chose her life. Abigail has angels protecting her and I'm not to interfere. I must finish my soul's work in this life and riches are mine to do so. Memory fades. Did he tell me what the work involved before accompanying me to a Higher Being?

Morning unfolds quickly with prayer and study. In the early afternoon, email notes many new friends think riches come easily, regardless of inner beliefs. Joy abounds upon receiving Karen Drucker's message of thanks for my recent message and for supporting her music.

Rev. Charles conducts class four of SOM 103 in the evening. The Law of Attraction, power of tithing, and creating a vision for a better world inspires. I love this class and am so glad to take it once again because it reminds me of how far my awareness advanced. There's a very noticeable difference between last years and this years self-talk inventory. A new recognized ability, as a powerful co-creator, far outweighs fleeting thoughts of victim consciousness. Clearly, everything exists to increase the awareness of Self. Fleeting moments of faultfinding are replaced, quickly and successfully, with healing constructive emotions.

One quote from *Sermon on the Mount* by Emmet Fox draws my attention.

"In the spiritual sense, 'prosperity' and 'prosper' signify a very great deal more than the acquirement of material possessions. They really mean success in prayer. From the viewpoint of the soul, success with prayer is the only kind of prosperity worth having; and if our prayers are successful we shall naturally have all the material things we need."

Yes, this makes sense because Spirit is my true source.

"The time for angry mobs is here, finally, to amass the good that many fear has gone. In reality, it is not forsaken or gone into oblivion but only hidden from those who strive to stay in their own dream of limitation. Fear not as the days ahead turn increasingly ugly in all ways, including financial, global economic collapse and weather conditions that strike out many.

"Stay firm in your knowing of the Truth of the One in which you abide. Nothing can withstand that Love and Light that shines forever in the midst of this botchery of illusion. The days ahead may appear gruesome to many but you must ignore the contemplations of ego as it tries to keep all within the small mind outside of One.

*"Wholeness is **All That Is**. And **All That Is** is a part of your being. It is all within you now to tap into at will. Stay clear of the chaos and be sure that the Truth of **All That Is** is already achieved on all planes of existence.*

"Be not afraid as those that manipulate the masses continue to play their game and try to do so without thought of Truth. Truth will *shine through the lies and deceits of all those still focused on living their dream of greed and manipulation. Do not fear in the days ahead for all is in, as you know in the deep recesses of One, exceedingly well. Go forth and spread the word of Truth for that is the only Reality.*

"Remember, it is as you believe."

Charles leads us through a period of meditation and then asks us to remember the vow made to ourselves as souls. Mine surfaces instantly. "I vow to nurture the Christ Consciousness within me with love, peace, and harmony. I vow to remember that I am the Light of God."

The treatment designed for clarity of mind rings through my brain hours later. How wonderful to repeat it during sleep!

141

Smiling at the thought, I drift off but wake again at 5:05 AM. Something about Charles' birthday tries to surface but I have no idea when it is.

Sleep affords an opportunity to communicate with our soul and to connect more strongly with Spirit. Our dreams consist of times spent on other realms, messages from Source, and what our brain processes of daily activities. This is an important point to consider for everything we experience is subject to how the brain chooses to process it. Brain processing includes everything we see, hear, read and react to, and sometimes try to ignore, so it's vital to fill your brain with pleasant thoughts, especially before bedtime.

As Paracelsus noted so long ago, "Dreams must be heeded and accepted, for a great many of them come true."

Humanity lives in many parallel dimensions where we act out all possibilities. Access to these dimensions increases when we sleep. Yet, all is known, for everything has already happened. On this day, I tapped into a dimension considered the future by those in this one. Plans to celebrate the day of Rev. Charles birth, with him and SOM friends, while in Utah this year, will fall into place months later.

Sporadic sleep reveals evolutionary progress. The word perfection rings though my brain as I recall lamenting over the so-called loss of Daniel. While dreaming, I reminded myself there is no loss. It's now time to live life to its fullest with prosperity.

Eyes open to rest on the big, black bookcase nearby. Success begins with our thoughts Catherine Ponder reminds us in *The Prosperity Secrets of the Ages*. We can have anything desired if we just dare to use the Power within. A great affirmation often declared by a homemaker intrigues me so I decide to call on the great law of restoration as well. The act of restoring my blessings and good, of past and present, fills my heart with joy. I'm grateful to accept my highest good of mind, body, and affairs right now. Yes! Divine Intelligence is always on time with my good!

Something about "Suzuki" fills my brain. Did Daniel ride this brand of motorcycle? Memories soon overwhelm. Now everything makes sense. Daniel didn't show me his new motorbike for it was a part of the plan to propel us out of the illusion. What joy to realize at last that we are the same, illusions in this matrix called human life.

Today's journal entries verify I'm again losing track of time. Leah and I decide to visit a nearby casino after the morning's usual ritual of prayer and study. We play with slot machines after a leisurely lunch. It's my pleasure to slip a one-hundred dollar bill into the empty slot, which sucks it up like a greedy banker. Leah sits aisles away as I rub hands together, creating more enthusiasm and energy, before pushing buttons. Minutes later, I'm $50 ahead. What fun to while away the afternoon this way! The atmosphere changes hours later as more people arrive. Noise surrounds us but it's not the sound of ringing bells as people win. We happily leave as I pocket more winnings.

Having friends to spend time with is still new to me. Leah always gives little gifts, which I appreciate. Before we part, she hands me a keychain composed of miniature euros. Now this is something to visualize daily, more and more prosperity! Leah gladly accepts my gift of a Karen Drucker CD before we hug warmly. I then head to Mary's house to watch a movie.

Morning breaks remembering a dream where I thank a woman named Alisha. Her husband listens while I go on, and on, about how she helped me to realize I could heal myself and have a life again. Before I knew of her, I was very ill and had bladder issues but because of her encouragement I now have a life. Previous dreams place me as a waitress again, sharing tips.

'The gap' graces me during meditation. I suddenly become aware of a noise coming from my throat, when Isaiah talks of Level 5. The noise is not a gurgle but a vehicle of communication.

Email soon offers a way to share thoughts. Leah quickly replies noting weather forecasters predicted 60 M.P.H. winds, tornados, severe storms, and possible hail. It annoyed her because she stayed home rather than risk being on the road. And then, nothing happened.

Now in the year 2011, I'm aware of 'red flags,' odd things, which I avoid at all costs. Weather reports often do not match current or future events so I continue to count on Spirit to alert me instead of common sources. Spirit always guides when we're in the flow. Since banks and drug stores are on nearly every corner, I avoid them as much as possible. Flu shots, offered 365 days out of the year make me very suspicious as does free food and gas for buying certain groceries. Constant offers for credit cards make me leery of adding to old energies. Experience taught me that the best way to feed Spirit's energies is to focus on and seek nothing outside the Self.

"Just have one more thing to tell you," Leah writes. Last night, I was thinking about you and the words from a song "don't rock the boat, don't rock the boat, baby," kept popping up in my head. It's connected with you somehow."

Her words mean a great deal. James recently announced he would keep only enough money in the joint checking account to pay the mortgage. There's no money to pay for spiritual classes, he says. Yet, money is coming to me, easily and effortlessly!

Words that seem senseless fill my mind near dawn. Someone is telling me, *"It adds to the creative energy that surrounds us."* There is something about *"following weeks of the Now"* too.

Several minutes later friends reassure me, I'm never, and never shall be, alone. As sunshine rises to the top of the hedge, intuition prompts to take pictures. Results show a succession of colorful spirit orbs, flowing into the room, amid streams of rainbow colored light.

I ask for clarification on two issues before meditation. The CD slows down several times before answers weave through brain synapses. Spirit will tell me what to do, and when to do it, concerning James. Something of great importance will conclude in late June and I will not be here. Seconds of the now familiar eye flashes distract me before the CD ends.

The daily random reading reminds me of the Law of Cause and Effect. Spirit always seeks to express Itself. This Limitless Medium assures the best possible outcome if I only remember to ask for the highest good of all.

Beliefs are the only things limiting me and, thankfully, they continue to dwindle while choosing to participate in the evening's SPIRIT workshop. Caroline Reynolds says being gay is a life enhancement, something to "recognize as a very special gift." Looking at siblings from a "soul level" assures me they are in my life to expand consciousness. Although I feel out of place, where nearly everyone else is gay or lesbian, my mood changes as Caroline guides.

Rev. Steve acts as my energy partner while Caroline leads us through an exercise where we give and receive the energy of love. We stare deeply into one another's eyes while Caroline speaks softly. What an awesome experience! Waves of love nearly knock me out of my chair and it's hard to concentrate without beaming joy. At the end of the evening, I leave profoundly affected by our connection.

Cooing pigeons wake me to send the weekly email update the next morning. It seems almost criminal to stop researching the benefits of hiv nutrition but my heart is no longer interested in sustaining the illusion of limitation. After prayers, a short phone conversation, with an accountant, pulls me back into the matrix. I cannot explain why James did not file the joint tax return before April 15. Our accountant notes when he did file; the business return was not included. He notes it's time to declare the business as a hobby since there was no income.

A string of emails pulls me further into the disappointing illusion of life. My spontaneous plaque affirmation is "not an affirmation" and therefore "not approved." Trying to figure out anyone, or anything, is exhausting. I quickly email Leah to rant.

Campbell's perspective on the Garden of Eden intrigues me during the evening's SOM 212 class. He notes certain religions teach that the "Fall" – Adam and Eve thrown into the field of time – stems from their new belief in separation. Adam is referred to as Phôs (Light) while Eve is referred to as Pandora. And yet, there never really was a Garden of Eden and no "Fall."

A Course in Miracles explains, "The world you see is an illusion of a world. God did not create it, for what He creates must be eternal as Himself." Spirit is eternal and unalterable because it's already perfect. Humanity is an extension of God

projected into physical reality so we can experience that which we are not.

Numerous, very interesting, creation stories prompt me to think out of the box of conventional thought. Emmanuel reports the Oneness of all exists within continual and eternal creation in the name of love. Fragments at the cutting edge of creation (humanity) became so involved in the act that they forgot their true nature. We became lost in the void and forgot that we are the creator. We formed a world "so that love might experience itself where love seems not to be." Yet, we also exist in the world of Spirit. When we recognize our infinite power, we will again embrace it with love.

Edgar Cayce tells us Spirit came into motion when God moved, bringing Light and chaos. Evolving matter came in this light and as the gaseous state of matter cooled, many souls (Sons of God) convened to reason together as co-creators with God. Individualized spirits selected earth, air, water, and fire as expressions of man who evolved gradually. They helped to establish crystalline centers of earth as the conduits through which the evolving spiritual forces would flow. Our endocrine glands correspond to these centers and receive the creative energies that sustain us.

In the days of Lemuria, souls only had to imagine what they desired to manifest it. When souls began to take on the elements, and manifest as flesh bodies, their vibration changed. This disrupted awareness and many souls lost full consciousness. Individual souls separated from the higher vibration in the process of creating various life forms. They no longer perfectly reflected their true nature but sought carnal gratification and became enmeshed in the material world, trapped in the cycles of life and death.

The attraction to denser earth forms became the dominant purpose for some soul-entities. Early man was more of a radiant being of Light but the body grew to be more crystalline and dense as he became dependent on the elements for sustenance. He could no longer push into and out of matter, coming and going at will. This, Cayce explains, set the stage for opposing forces, "between the children of the Law of One and the sons of Belial" (good and evil). The concepts of duality and karma, cause and effect, came into being as a means to eliminate, eventually, the artificial concepts of good and evil.

In Commentaries on A Course In Miracles, Singh explains that God created the Son who possesses the energy to create "with the same eternal principles with which He was created." The Son created/projected a world of illusion but God is not directly related to its creation.

*Some sources note this world evolved from an intelligent energy, an enormous space referred to as a Void. This great Void activated and began to take form over billions of years. There was the identity of One Life with the Total, **All That Is**, in the beginning. Spirit did not view anything as separate from a blissful "cosmic song of joy." Spirit, eventually fascinated with the movement of nature – the manifested world – became intrigued with how Source was manifesting Itself. It then began to experiment with the manifested world creating such things as flowers, trees, etc.*

Spirit was a shining being that could manifest anywhere. It began to have a sense of preference with the dawn of self-consciousness and gradually became more interested in sensation. As spirit (consciousness) began to identify more and more with the manifested world, it became more and more self-conscious. There was less interest in God-consciousness and communication with God. This perception of separation made the mind a perceiver rather than a creator.

According to one source, Noûs created a primordial man (in his own image) who upon seeing his reflection in the water, and on earth, went down into matter and became ensnared in duality.

Monroe tells us we are here to experience life in a physical form and to blend the sum of our awareness with the Whole. We are here to create, to build, give, and grow. We live to leave more than we take and to bring our gifts of love to the Whole. We return to the Whole only after merging with the other fragments of ourselves. There is no beginning, nor is there an end, Monroe reminds us. There is only change. There is no teacher or student. There is only expression and remembering

147

and that includes knowing there is only one. There is only love and balance, motion, and unlimited being.

Paramahansa Yogananda notes, in <u>Autobiography of a Yogi</u>, all creation or separate existence is illusion. The mere presence of a body signifies unfulfilled desires. Ridding oneself of desires, consciously and subconsciously, frees the soul.

Humanity is an extension of God projected into physical reality so we can experience that which we are not. We are souls having a spiritual experience creating in human form. It is only in the illusionary human form that we have the opportunity to expand our awareness because illusions must be forgiven on the level where they are experienced. One of the biggest hurdles we face is amnesia for we forget we're spiritual beings. The delusion is of our own making, designed with thoughts. This state of forgetfulness helps us to be less homesick for our Heavenly existence and allows us to start each life with a clean slate. (Some people note the sun and the eyes are reminders of the original understanding souls once felt.)

*It seems likely that in the beginning there was a black void of emptiness and fullness, everywhere, including everything. That pure consciousness was all, and still is, **All That Is**. It somehow began to expand by thinking, manifesting if you will, parts of Itself that wished to create more and more richness of BEing. Those parts decided to separate, in mind, from the greater void.*

*We are those parts, figments if you will, that decided to take on various forms to experience, express, and expand the richness of **All That Is**. We lost our way, after eons of forms and experiences, after eons of words and deeds. We forgot the nature of our true Self. There is only One, and right now in bodily form, we are a part of One. But that One is a part of something much, much greater, **All That Is**.*

We are Gods of Creation but placed layer upon layer to mask our True Self. It started long before Atlantis or Lemuria. Those were just epic turning points in our illusory history; times when we decided to take on increasingly denser form. Those days are long gone. In Truth, they never existed for this is a game of mind, the small mind in each figment.

*The truth is we are lost in a sea of forgetfulness playing a game called earth life. It is not, nor has it ever been, our intent to stay but just to experience, express, and expand back to **All That Is**. As part of this experiment, we belong to a vast entity, Soul. Many call this the Oversoul. It consists of unique and vastly different souls, all playing the game of life on earth. As souls, we agree to forget our true nature before we take on a new bodily form. Our form, mission, and the environment we choose offer us perfect opportunities to experience, expand, and express the richness of **All That Is**.*

This is just one part of our journey. And now, it is changing. These are monumental times as we awaken to recognize our full potential. We are finally beginning to remember who we really are. Many of us chose to lead or be an example for others to follow as we design a New World of Heaven on earth.

Chapter Fourteen

Living Science of Mind

"Everything, seen and unseen, connects to everything else and thought contributes greatly to physical experience." SAM – Bits of Wisdom

Campbell's words on marriage hold great significance as I read before bedtime. "In Catholicism, marriage is a destiny decision." Marriage requires the dissolution of the male initiative. Without a sense of responsibility, love is merely taking possession. "Survival," Campbell reminds us, "is the second law of life. The first is that we are all one." It makes perfect sense. James and I focused on bodily pleasures rather than merging as one in spirit. Thoughts of work and self now differ vastly. I no longer feel in "my place" for the same differences that drew us together serve to separate.

    "You are a child of God. You have been given mercy," fills my mind as a large magenta-colored orb flows nearby. Sleep rules until a familiar gurgling erupts from my throat. Sun shines upon my face as soon forgotten words flow.

    The drive across town to Leah's beautiful condo passes quickly. Someday I'll live in a place by the water, somewhat like hers. We share experiences during lunch, which she insists on buying. How comforting to get verification that the messages heard do not qualify me as crazy!

    Daniel delivers a message as I drive back to the house on 47th Drive. Telephone calls to Rachel remain unanswered. My new task is to connect a mutual friend of Mary's with Rachel who he notes is having a tough time. This friend will offer Rachel the help she needs.

    Thoughts focus on James as study begins. Tonight's class concentrates on spiritual mind healing for others. Yes! God is a Presence personified in us and when we truly recognize our Oneness, there are no limits to manifestation. This realization is the key to happiness. Raising our vibration makes all the difference in becoming more in tune with the Cosmic Power within that unites. Living an unlimited life is easier after accepting this Truth. Happy union with *All That Is* ensues.

"I'm so glad I still have that account," I announce to someone as dawn breaks. "God works in mysterious ways."

Next year these words will hold much more meaning as James and I settle the terms of our divorce. A joint account with Samuel offers the means for James to transfer funds much more effortlessly.

Another unidentified bug sits in the bathroom later in the morning. As the others, I see its aura. The bug's message rings inside my mind.

"Stay the course. The path is true."

The computer screen turns a vivid shade of magenta after minutes of work later in the evening. It's impossible to continue working so I end the day with more spiritual reading and prayer. Martha's essence breaks through the veil. Efforts to reach James are unsuccessful. He does not believe in life after human death so she's unable to help him. She's grateful for our communications and thanks me for playing my human role. Instructions come minutes after falling asleep.

"Make it possible and clear the way to Power from the Infinite Source."

'The gap' pulls me in during meditation, before sending love, light, and peace, in abundance, to all living things. Aunt Deborah greets me later to deliver a quickly forgotten message. A new affirmation for the Center plaque comes during meditation. "I am the Divine Light :-) In Loving Memory of Daniel."

The laptop screen remains a vivid shade of magenta as someone envelopes me in glorious love. Thirteen hours later, I'm able to send a group email to friends, noting how the power of thought helped me to stop depending on thirteen prescribed medications. I credit the Center for changing life and note all health conditions are gone. Yes, the power of thought is amazing.

What you think, and believe, makes your world, and my world keeps getting better and better!

A mutual friend soon notes telephone calls to Rachel are usually unanswered. She agrees to phone again and then suggests Rachel might appreciate a Mother's Day card. How grateful I am for the God Network, which always works to meet needs!

A Hallmark store beckons after a long walk. Daniel's essence helps to choose Rachel's card. And then he prompts me to buy one for myself. What a pleasure it is to communicate with my spirit son!

"I'll do everything I can to keep your Divine Essence inside me," rings through my brain upon hearing the familiar noise from my throat in morning hours. It was I speaking! Almost unbearable heat is again upon me when dawn breaks. It's about 70 degrees outside but it feels much, much, hotter.

Before mediating, I ask to know something for my highest good. Daniel soon announces that James and I will be together for at least a few more months. We'll both be free then and I'll never worry about money. I ask him to stay a bit longer as we sit on a dock watching the sunrise. He then escorts me up, into the sky, tells me to have fun, and disappears.

Many twinkle lights glow as I stare in wonder while sending love, light, and peace, in abundance, to all living things. The purifying, cleansing light of Love from within my heart covers everything. A Higher Being then tells me something else for my highest good, which I immediately forget.

Another restless night unfolds.

I'm up repeatedly. Daniel leads me by the hand to others in a garden during meditation. They are proud of me. There's only 'a sprint' to go, they announce, and they're with me all the way. I'm in 'the gap' after releasing white light throughout the city. Later in the day, a Karen Drucker CD whizzes through tracks to remind; I'm not alone. Losing track of the day's events becomes easy.

The familiar emotion-filled life continues to fade while detaching from old energies. It's easier to accomplish after listening to Dr. Bump during the third SOM 212 class. Verification of being on the path is always welcome and tonight proof comes in spades. Touching forgotten aspects of soul prompts me to move on, to find the center that's impossible to find when socially engaged. Compassion, without attachment, becomes my new goal.

Words on the importance of joy and beauty, from a Catherine Ponder book, consume time before sleep. Several messages break through the veil, while sleeping and waking repeatedly. Someone tells me to *"Choose carefully from the tree of life." I choose joy and wisdom.*

Daniel again meets me during meditation. He's always with me, he assures, as we are all One. Karen Drucker's CD fills the air later as magic continues to be mine. The CD stops for a fleeting second, to verify again; I'm not alone. For a mere second, I shed a tear for the past but then recognize that I'm not truly physical. Upon wiping tears, I continue singing passionately.

*When words enter my brain, as I lie in the state between waking and sleep, I play attention to them. This morning's words did not seem to come from the now familiar place, which I refer to as Inner Speak. And yet, I know **All That Is** is One and it is within me.*

I do not watch TV or read the newspaper, and rarely, except to check weather and other earth changes, follow Internet links. Frankly, I'm not sure how this message came to me. It mentions the name of a Being and a planet that I have not heard about. However, the messenger seemed very loving and I'm not in the habit of receiving communications from negative entities.

*A strong belief in **All That Is**, which we each hold as a Divine Spark within our heart's core, permeates both days and nights. And yet, while still in physical form, it seems prudent to document and share messages.*

So now, at six-thirty in the morning, hours before my usual rising time, I document the words that flowed so easily minutes ago.

"I am Talia from the planet Nibiru. I wish to speak with you today. Your planet is wholesome in many ways. Today is a day of great opportunities. Shine forth the Light to see them all. Manifesting your dreams is easier now as these great changes

take place. Be aware that with each change in your earth the space for new beginnings opens wider.

"The land of your ancestors opens to you for your grace. There is a great cataclysm taking place in your atmosphere that opens the way for new beginnings. Do not be afraid as these necessary changes take place. All is according to the Divine Will of One. Take care in the days ahead and know all is as it should be for the further evolution of humanity.

"Reap not in sorrow or haste but take each change with the Wholeness and Love that you are."

Too many layers sit between Source and us. It's time to delete them and court the Presence of God through Mystic Consciousness. We must move directly to the One in which we live, and move, and have all BEing. Tapping into this bond is vital to remember who we really are.

"Each day changes and brings us newer realities."

Many people sense the atmosphere of God all around, in, and through us. *A Course in Miracles* reminds us that God has no name. But "His Name becomes the final lesson that all things are one, and at this lesson does all learning end." Charles now inspires me to channel only the highest spiritual realm. Why would anyone want to trust anything else? We are one eternal being living in a state of grace forever. Eternal truths are the only ones worth documenting.

I pair with Susan as we write treatments during a workshop. Her unique treatment for clarity seems to flow quickly from head to hand:

"God is everywhere, including the Creative Energy surrounding us. As a unique part of this God-Life, I AM a perfect point of God-Conscious Life. The essence of all healing power flows through me, as I AM a vessel of God. Clarity of Mind is apparent in all that I experience. Gratefulness overwhelms my essence as I release these words to the Creative Energy to work through Absolute Law. And so It is."

"How we go through life really is a matter of perspective," I announce while handing her the prayer.

Back at the house on 47th Drive, the crown on my front tooth falls out when I floss before bedtime. The crown is so old that I forgot about it. I thank God it didn't come out at a more inopportune time and am equally grateful it does not fall down the sink drain.

James is evasive when I ask for a check to visit the dentist. The checkbook sits in his briefcase but he tells me to look for it on the dresser and then announces it must be at his job. It shall be interesting to see what good comes of this for only good shall come of it!

Bits and pieces of Karen Drucker songs and communication again fill sleeping hours. I rise before dawn to recall, *"Grateful I AM. It is wonderful that I can do those things I only thought of before."* Hours later, I wake after singing about how Spirit fills my healthy body with joy and offers me *"this or something better."*

After morning rituals, I affirm, getting an appointment to put my crown back in is easy. I leave right after the receptionist tells me to come to the nearest office. Ten minutes later, before 9:00 AM, I enter the office to hear a tall, tanned, young man talk about getting his teeth fixed after a motorcycle accident. Everything now makes sense. His story unfolds while moving his head from a friend to me, between words. Wise words flow out of my mouth when he stops talking. As they end, the door opens and a hygienist ushers me in to see a dentist before anyone else. Another successful 'God mission' completes. And that is what it's like to be a lightworker, a teacher of God.

Mary and I sit at her outside patio table sharing psychic experiences later in the afternoon. Joy abounds while envisioning the same kind of nurturing environment. She gives me a gift after I check the computer network again. It's a beautiful, silver angel, with engraved, inspiring words on her right wing. "Dare to live the life you have dreamed for yourself."

Many messages come throughout the night. *"Bask in the light of the Lord,"* fills my head after asking to know something for my highest good. Spirit friends later remind me I am never alone. Daniel comes to answer questions. He names three people with whom I should more closely align, Charles, Mary Jo, and James (who I'm to continue to awaken).

A stay at Rebecca's house brings more odd dreams. Recall comes as headphones sit upon my chest upon waking. The CD player remains on but paused. In the dream, I was in a house, closed the sliding doors, and looked up at the wall to my left. A window sat there with a sheer, white curtain over it. The curtain allowed one to see outside. But there was something odd about it.

It was very small, like ones used on doors in Michigan back in the seventies. I reached up to push the curtain aside. The little curtain rod fell into my hands. That was when I noticed someone attached a mirror behind the curtain. "What a great idea to put a mirror back there," I thought. Another little window sat down below, kind of hidden in the wall. There was money behind the mirror. With the mirror behind the first curtain, you could actually see the outside reflecting in the mirror.

The doorbell then rang as I held the curtain rod. Not wanting anyone to know about the money behind the mirror, I put it down on a round table and strolled back to open the door. A lady with keys in her hand opened it and entered the house.

"Well what are you doing inside this house," I said looking at her politely.

"This is my house and I'm here in the month of June."

"No, this is my house," I quickly announced. "I've leased it for twelve months."

Yes, dreams do foretell the future if we can only recall them. I leased a house for twelve months in June 2008 (fourteen months after this dream)!

The dream changed. Now the lady was a cleaning woman cleaning my house. A man sat at a table in another room. He was very angry and belligerent, throwing off lots of negative energy and wanted to do me harm. I sat down in his lap, facing him, put my arms around him, and told him to look me in the eyes. He didn't want to but finally did with small, brown eyes.

"We are one," I quietly said as his eyes turned away. "You and I are part of the One. You," I announced adamantly jabbing him, "look at me."

He looked at me again. His breath expelled heavily onto my cheek as I held my face next to his.

"You are a part of the One." I jabbed at myself and said, "I am part of the One."

Reaching up next to us, on the left, I picked up a blue, square pillow and said, "If this pillow were alive it would be part of the One. We are all One. We are all part of the One."

I could feel my arms around his body that breathed in, and out, as if he were very angry. The hurriedness of his breath dissipated slowly as I spoke.

When I told him these things, I remember feeling that breath, "huh, huh, huh." I felt, each time it came out on my cheek; I felt the force of his breath, the warmth of the breath. I could feel it. It was very, real to me. (Obviously, this was a bleed though to one of my other lives where I live with James.)

"One man, many lives, all illusion."

The month of May brings hotter weather. My car's air conditioning works overtime as I drive down the turnpike to get Samuel from school. We don't see one another as much as before because I'm regarded as "Crazy Nana." Rebecca now schedules me to pick him up on class days when I have less time. Sometimes I let small things like this bother me.

Eckhart Tolle reports there are no problems but merely situations. We can deal with them quickly or accept them "as part of the 'isness' of the present moment until they change or can be dealt with." Problems cannot survive in the present moment. Issues not to our liking eventually vanish when we stop feeding them with thoughts.

Upon returning to my room, it's clear that everything happens for a reason. SOM leads me to "The Practice of Spiritual Mind Healing" on page 308. Holmes reminds us "God is a Presence personified in us." Spirituality is the atmosphere of God's Presence. I AM the perfect nature of God in human form and ever grateful to know it.

"The way of the One is ever-present. Centeredness abides below."

Class four of SOM 212 begins later in the evening. I stare at the first handout recognizing differences between chakra interpretations. Seven major chakras run from the top of our head to the base of our spine. Each chakra has a consciousness of its own, infused with the energies of experiences and thought. Sources note clearing, harmonizing, and balancing chakras results in an initiation process known as opening the seven seals of God consciousness. The ability to tune into life, manifest a better reality, move more easily through time and space, and serve humanity, becomes ours with well-tuned chakras. We do this by prayer, meditation, or using colors and musical tones such as those in the song "Do-Re-Mi."

Chakra's are in the etheric body and relay information from person to person, subconscious to conscious, conscious mind to Higher Self, Divine Guidance, and back. Dr. Christine Page, author of *Spiritual Alchemy*, notes they influence our psychophysical behavior and can be thought of as motivator types of fuel. People living on the instinctual, emotional, or mental levels of the first three chakras are ego-oriented and controlled by social law.

The first (root chakra) fuels our survival instinct with little or no connection between spirit and matter. This chakra helps to ground our energies, draw cosmic energies from the earth and vitalize other chakras. We have more vitality, courage, and self-confidence when this chakra functions properly.

The second chakra, low in the gut area, is the seat of all intuition and psychic sensitivity, primarily on a feeling level. Clairsentience (the ability to sense spirits) and psychometry (sensing the history of an object) emanate from this area. Self-doubt, addictions, or sexual issues disappear when this chakra is balanced. We attune to the wisdom of our soul, instead of ego, and gradually replace self-limiting thought patterns of the subconscious mind with self-confidence and emotional stability. We take back personal power as we learn to create joy, peace, and prosperity.

Campbell refers to the third chakra as Manipura, "City of the Shining Jewel." This is the seat of our physical/mental self. Individuals living at this level seek to master their world. This, Van Praagh says, is the connection to the "silver cord" (concentrated energy that connects the etheric body to the physical one) enabling astral-travel. We make clear decisions that serve and protect our highest good when this chakra is in balance.

There's little discordant energy, our self-acceptance returns, we regain self-control, and master desires. We learn to set boundaries and honor the boundaries of others while drawing forth energy from the universal source of life, and our own I AM Presence, instead of tapping into the energies of others.

The heart chakra is the gateway to higher chakras connecting us to soul and Spirit. It's the place where spiritual life begins and the beginning of awakening. Van Praagh tells us it's the seat of unconditional love, associated with trance work, and feeling the presence of spirit beings. When our heart chakra is balanced, we tap into the unconditional love of *All That Is* releasing all negative energies and thought patterns. As the Three-fold Flame of Divine Will, Wisdom, and Love ignites, we begin to develop a compassionate nature and Oneness with life and all things. This chakra allows us to channel love energy within and out into the world.

The fifth or "throat chakra" fuels our mind power, employing a working relationship between mind and body. Sonya Choquette notes it governs free will, creative expression, telepathy, and helps to hear the voice of our soul and guides. This chakra is the center for expressive communication and making and keeping commitments. It is the chakra of spiritual effort, which when balanced allows us to put down animalistic instincts and urges. It also helps us to focus on our soul and inner creative mind, speak truth, influence people, and become proficient in manifesting our vision. The fifth chakra works with the heart center for trance work and assists with channeling. Mind chatter, mental confusion, and untruthfulness are the result of an imbalanced fifth chakra. Improve these conditions through meditation, journaling, chanting, dancing, and song.

Ajna, the "lotus of Command" and sixth chakra, is two fingers above the center of our eyebrows and three fingers into the forehead. Campbell announces it's the chakra of Heaven – the highest chakra in the world of incarnate forms. (But this is changing now as we morph physicality to incorporate more chakras.) This chakra opens the door to inner senses, is the seat of psychic seeing, precognitive dreams, and inspiration. When this chakra is balanced, we have higher mental and intuitive abilities, moving through whispers of intuition into knowing that Spirit guides and inspires. We have lots of ideas, can think in pictures, and sense people's energy. We also hold the ability to envision the future and visualize the way we want things to be, seeing truth and looking past appearances. When this chakra opens, Van Praagh says, we can see auras, images of all shapes and colors, and spirit people.

The seventh, or crown, is the chakra of enlightenment, a place of pure light energy that provides you with the highest level of spiritual knowledge. Campbell refers to it as the "Thousand Petalled Lotus," a place of undifferentiated consciousness – the silence. Sonya says it governs our soul's purpose. This is where the soul enters the body, the center of soul peace, which transcends ideas and emotions. (One may feel a tingling on top of their head as the crown opens to incorporate more of the soul.) Van Praagh reports we can use this chakra to influence all the other centers and bring the highest of spiritual truths to all sensitive work.

The wisdom and treasures stored with our Divine I AM Presence are available to us when we activate the crown chakra. Aspects of the Twelve Rays of God Consciousness permeate time, while demonstrating that we're ready to live and radiate the Love/Light/Truth of Creation. We balance this chakra through meditation (opening it up to take in universal energy), prayer, and service to others.

Chapter Fifteen

Greater Probabilities

"Steer the course of BEingness into greater aspects of awareness for all, leaving none behind, for in essence, all is One." SAM – Book of One :-) Volume 2

Mary and I shop for party goods after my morning ritual. Her exuberance and stamina, to plan the best annual party for Seth, amazes as we visit store after store. This will be Seth's first, and last, birthday party in spirit form. Mary is anxious to sell her home and move to a small Florida town. She's fully ready to let go of the past. Am I?

A lifelong habit of questioning ideas continues to serve as the evening's random reading leads to "When the Blind Lead the Blind (Matt. 15:14)." Truth, Holmes reminds, is always self-evident, simple, and direct. The belief in duality is truly a fundamental error of thought that fails to nurture the soul. It's my charge, and the task of others, to rid the world of false beliefs. There is one Life, one Love, one Light in which we live, and move, and have all BEing.

Flashes of lightening enter the room. The storm that soaked our earth with water for more than an hour moves on as *"...and the God of this world is not affected,"* fills my brain. Minutes later, I wake to recall catching a spear.

Current awareness continues to focus on evolution. Last year, when James calmly announced that I focused on involution, I had no idea what he meant. I've changed quite a bit since then. Daily random reading leads to the second paragraph on page 339, where Holmes reports that the Law of Cause and Effect propels evolution. Involution, the idea, always paves the way to evolution. I AM conscious Spirit, an effect brought forth through Thought. Yet, much of the time I'm unconscious of True Self!

Insight into phases of subjective life and the effect of race thought comes in the evening. Be more aware, SOM 103 class reminds, of accumulated subjective experiences to stop them from controlling emotions. How rewarding it is to purge duality knowing Mind sits in every body cell! Healing heightens while continuing to control thoughts to purify further.

Dawn is minutes away when I wake after thanking someone. James left hours ago to fish in the Everglades so I reach into his room to turn off the light. Emotion pulls me out of a dream minutes later. In the dream, James returns home as I sit on the futon while writing. My body levitates when he leaves again. Ecstasy rules while joyously rising higher and higher.

Words, leading me to believe I teach on other planes of existence, wake me again after falling back asleep.

"And the first thing I tell them is how they have been born again. It is so nice just to lean back and to go into the Now."

Do other people wake repeatedly, drink water, and return to bed after eliminating it?

Later, someone reminds me of my ancient name and task while using Caroline Reynolds meditation CD. I am Esmeralda, here as a savior, to live richly and spend the rest of my life in service to God. And yet, I AM that of which *It* is.

Amazing blessings continue as the den motion detector light turns on before reaching the room. Words, stating that I'm ready to receive, flow forth. Guides offer another comforting message, as my body sweats profusely from standing outside, upon returning from the laundry room.

"Your soul will always be in God."

Wednesday evening service inspires as usual. I stuff a fifty-dollar bill into the donation basket before leaving my perch near the audio system to pass it around. The week passes quickly.

James is fishing again when I rise on Saturday to make a vegetarian pasta salad, with kidney beans instead of chicken, for Mary's party. It's such a beautiful day for a party around her gorgeous pool and I'm happy to leave the dark house to attend.

Mary greets at the door with a to-do list after thanking me profusely for a CD of Seth's favorite music. We work together decorating the house and patio. When she moans over electronic mishaps, I quickly reassure her. Malfunctions are normal when spirit activity heightens. Joy abounds upon completing a myriad of tasks. Mary's ability to host the perfect party is evident throughout the house and yard. Everything matches a tropical theme right down to the piñata. Guests hoot with laughter when it breaks open to spill calcium supplements to the ground.

My wonderful friend is ecstatic and ready for a new life. This party is her way of moving on to more "eye opening things." "Your Life is Now," Mary's new favorite song, dances through the air as I make my way to the door hours later.

On May 6, I dream of being in a house that looks like a condo. I move into the basement to bless it but start shaking uncontrollably. Suddenly, I realize something bad happened in the basement bathroom and I need my blessing tools. I go back upstairs to get white candles.

Someone brought Grandpa. He's upstairs wearing his brown suit. So very happy to see him, I hug him, and hug him, and then start crying with joy. After asking how he is, I fill his body with love. I can feel my body shaking while holding him, continuing to cry joyfully over his presence. He wants to tell me something. But again, emotion gets in the way. Tears roll down cheeks upon waking.

There was more to the dream but I cannot remember it. Clearly, I need to cap emotion upon seeing departed family members because it only wakes me before messages occur.

Exactly a year later, after signing a lease to move into a 3.7 million dollar condominium on the Intercoastal, I'll have this dream again and it will be much more vivid and colorful. Something tries to control my body as I began to spread light into the bathroom. My body shakes uncontrollably, wobbling back and forth as if energy is trying to enter it. I then realize a murder occurred in the bathroom and I have to clear it of negative energies.

When I venture upstairs to get my clearing stuff, Grandpa holds a large brown bag in his arms. It contains a house-warming gift for me. This time I remember he died. He lived to be 100 years old and died days later. As I continue to hug him and cry, I pour love into his body and feel my own body violently shake back and forth. And then I wake up.

I cannot stress enough the importance of dream recall. Upon opening to greater probabilities, pushing aside worn-out belief systems that never served humanity, one can breeze through this game called life. When a departed family member gives you a gift in a dream, they assure your protection from the Otherside. After nearly two weeks of issues with the beautiful, luxurious, exclusive condominium, I ask for a refund, having never spent a night there. Intuition tells me a murder occurred there so I free the spirit, perform a house blessing, remove my few belongings and never return.

Answers to early morning questions come quickly but I recall only one response. *"...to learn. If we think we have to figure it out, we know nothing."* Johnney River's song, "Look to Your Soul," rings through my brain. It's been thirty years since I heard the song. Words ring through my mind after meditation.

"It is a gift unmatched by any other to awaken one's soul to the Essence of their BEing."

Day fills quickly with tasks of old energy. I'm grateful to now put business updates aside while preparing for a trip to the Florida Keys. A knowing comes while standing in line at the bait store near Terry's house. Today is the last time I'll renew my fishing license. Something propels me to shop for new clothes more fitting to my current weight and state of awareness. I now weigh thirty pounds less than before.

In the evening, the Center's bookstore offers another opportunity to donate by charging a book to my credit card. Relishing in the glow of service to others, I set up the coffee station for class. "Coming into Awareness," helps to focus on emotional attachments. In the past, Robert Monroe notes, emotion only controlled us when we allowed it to. My preference to return to that state of awareness continues to increase for Daniel's transition taught me that earth life is fleeting. Attachments seem nonexistent now for the fear of loss is gone. We are an infinite part of *All That Is*, of this, I am most certain.

Time spent at the Center is always full of delicious surprises. Today is no exception as Rev. Kandi hands me an envelope from Rev. Mary Jo. A ticket to the "Hollywood Center for Positive Living Italian Dinner" sits inside.

Words fill my brain near dawn as fires from Collier County, in Naples many miles away, permeate the air with ash and smoke.

"The highest God is the innermost God, the one that must be received."

A ball of orange, instead of the usual sunshine, sits to the east. Several attempts to get a picture frustrate me. My camera still refuses to cooperate after ten tries. A small orb appears to communicate an important message after it finally works.

"There is beauty everywhere. You have only to take it all in."

The orb changes color from orange to blue and zips back and forth. Two birds, one at a time, fly directly through the orb from outside the window before it disappears.

I am ever thankful for magnified vision and all positive things that continue to spring forth. Atoms of energy are everywhere! There are many layers of the real Stuff of Matter. These energy fields are beyond humanity's usual field of vision. Another layer of substance now sits before me. Large fields of see-through images, of different shapes and sizes, usually smaller than an inch or two, flow through airspace. Sometimes small seahorse-like creatures appear. Periodic flashes, like mini lightening bolts, often occur when favorite music fills the air. Another familiar cluster of energy, shaped like a circle, appears. This is a lovely addition to the usual orbs coming at dawn or dusk. Now, a familiar bright, circle of light comes from the sun with another circle, lesser in brilliance, a short distance below it. It appears in many pictures as a green-colored light.

I'm in the flow, most of the time, from perfect timing when I go to the Credit Union, to getting unexpected gifts. What I want comes effortlessly, usually with little, if any, cost. James is easier to live with as well. Family vacation begins this Saturday and I can hardly wait to see what good comes of it!

Old habits rise after Wednesday evening's service while weeding through email. An article, noting that drinking heavy amounts of alcohol shrinks your brain, seems perfect to send to Rebecca, for a friend who she says drinks way too much. Another email invites friends to delve into the past with a forwarded message about the "good old days." I recognize the ploy to keep me out of the beautiful state of Now after sending it and quickly shut down my computer to repeat bedtime prayers.

A dream of Samuel and Poppy, James' deceased father, wakes me. Samuel sees Poppy first. A misty form of substance floats where Samuel points so I ask Poppy if he has anything to tell me. But then I wake up.

Poppy comes later during meditation as I walk through fields of green. He's waiting at the top of the small hill. It's good to be with him. He's an old soul and tells me to stick with James after I leave this place. It will help James to realize who he is, as we become friends, while still married but living apart.

Verification comes when I ask to assure this message is not from ego. Poppy tells me of a puppy James used to have. I think he says the dog's name was Tippy. He then reports that Martha did not like it. When we finish talking, I see Martha waiting for him near the lake. They soon disappear together.

A beautiful afternoon unfolds as I motor down Federal Highway. The drive to Hollywood Center for Positive Living is delightfully long. I find the small, white, wooden building easily and park on the lawn with other cars. Rev. Mary Jo and Rev. Jerry are happy to see me and I'm amazed to eat the Italian dinner without regard to health considerations. It's been years since this body enjoyed spaghetti with tomato sauce.

How grateful I AM for the confirmation that this physicality, the host for my essence, finally rid itself of dis-ease that limited eating habits for far too long! A power greater than I dwells in this physical form. Understanding that *It* lives in, and though, humanity empowers me beyond belief. Yes, I AM part of the Divine Presence! Using the Creative Power of thought, to benefit humanity and myself, is easier than ever before.

Erratic sleeping habits continue. Today, there's barely enough time to finish the usual morning ritual and studies before driving to the Keys. James and I remain cordial but it's clear our marriage is over. We no longer share the same interests. I'm happy to motor along the turnpike with Rebecca in our family caravan. James and Samuel lead the way with the white van while Ruth, Naomi and Sara tow the boat with the black one. Terry stays home this year to care for Momma, pets, and houses.

Familiar two-bedroom, one-bath cabins at Bahia Honda State Park appear much smaller. They're totally different from before with new furniture and stark, white paint covering beautiful knotty pine. There's less storage space and two less beds. Rebecca sets up the bar in our cabin, the much-desired number six. This cabin is the best because it sits closer to the inlet and makes sneaking into forbidden water to snorkel much easier.

Sara entertains us with stories after dinner. She repeats them while wearing a huge, silly, fish hat that says, "I love to fish." No one seems surprised at bedtime when James sets his swinging hammock up to sleep below the cabins.

Calm waters face us on Mother's Day. Today is much more jam packed with activity than I'm accustomed to. James and Samuel fish as the rest of us venture out to buy bait and visit the flea market. Later in the day, Rebecca and I watch NASCAR races at a local bar. Sunset later floods skies with hues of pink, red, and golden yellow as we make our way to No Name Pub.

The pub is packed. Dollar bills line walls as we make our way to a large table. There's no room to put any more dollars up and money hangs from the ceiling as well. Each paper bill bears the name of its previous owner. The conch fritters and pizza are still very good but it's much too loud to enjoy the experience.

The next morning, at least one-hundred colorful parrot fish swim past the cabin. Gray snapper and other tropical fish swim cautiously past to grab bits of bread as chirps from birds in the nearby sanctuary fill the air. Am I the only one to see Stuff of Matter flow briskly? Later in the day, Samuel holds a huge black and white umbrella over James' head as he expertly cleans fish for dinner. Familiar purple and blue orbs shoot out from the sun to greet me as the wind increases. Tarpon roll in the Bay and a huge sea turtle surfaces, several times, while smoke from fires several miles away mar the setting sun.

As James fishes with family and friends, I stay near the cabin to fill the air with spiritual music. Everyone seems to understand when he continues to sleep in the enclosed hammock. It's no big deal for he's spent many nights there while fishing in the Everglades.

Birds eating breadcrumbs from the porch railing entertain me in the morning as relentless wind continues. Everyone soon takes turns sitting in the new two-man tube Ruth brought as the boat moves through calm seas. Rebecca and Samuel flop up and down, like dolls in a Barbie Playhouse, as James drives faster and faster. It's fun to watch but I have no desire to be tossed about in a small tube. Smoke from fires again mars sunset as rain clouds fill the sky. Naomi and I watch a brilliant, red-gold ball slip below the horizon while I feel wholly alone.

Everyone seems to get along but I miss my solitude. Sara and I hike for an hour the next day before sneaking into the Bay to snorkel. Colorful fish cooperate by showing up as we glide through forbidden waters. A giant lobster greets us when we round the bend to continue our trek towards the bridge. "What an invigorating way to spend the time," I think, while swimming under the shady bridge.

Naomi stays at the cabins while James continues to fish the channels with buddies near sunset. The rest of us trek uphill on a now familiar gravel path to stand on the new bridge. After an hour of walking in the morning, and an afternoon snorkel, our adventure pushes exercise limits. This is the best sunset of the week, and as everyone scatters, I finally stop talking to take it all in. Huge tarpon roll below as we watch the golden sun turn to shades of red. Friendly tourists start conversations to pass the time. A small boy calls to his mom as he looks down into the water.

"Maybe that's Daniel," he says pointing his tiny index finger toward a fast moving boat.

"No, Daniel is at home," his momma tells him softly, as the speedboat zips by. The boy runs quickly up the bridge in the direction of the boat as Daniel's presence engulfs me.

Ah, yes, messages from the Otherside often come from surprising and delightful sources. I am never alone. Daniel is always with me. But I must learn to control the emotion that stops evolution. We are spirit in human form playing a game. For now, it feels good just to be alive enjoying the moment, watching the sun, now a big, red ball, drop below the horizon.

Scenery changes quickly the next morning when Rebecca and I move down the one lane road towards her house. Construction machinery sits along the roadside. New houses replace familiar places. I video knowing life is morphing as well.

I'm thankful to return to my room where there are no distractions from prayers and study. Yet, the house on 47th Drive appears even more dismal. *The Seth Material* by Jane Roberts comes to mind. "You must live in the faith that your purpose *is*, and will be fulfilled, is being fulfilled. You must live in the faith that you have such a purpose and meaning, or you would not be here."

How wonderful it is to have psychic friends and family! Leah telephones the next morning to ask me out to lunch. Rebecca then telephones when prayers and study are complete.

"Mommy," she says, like a little girl to alert me that she wants a favor, "can you stay with Samuel for a few days while I go to Virginia on a business trip?"

"Sure, when do you leave?"

"Don't you remember? I asked you weeks ago. I leave tomorrow and return Thursday."

"No problem honey. I'll come tonight if that's okay with you."

"Sure Mom, see you tonight."

Spirit always finds a way to help me move out of limitation! Minutes later, a small suitcase sits in the trunk while I'm on my way to lunch with Leah.

Leah offers extra handouts from the sixth class of SOM 212 as soon as I enter her lovely home. One handout offers six pictures of mainly religious artwork. The picture of Isis, with the King in the Temple of Seti I, Abydos, XIX Dynasty, appeals to me. *(Two years later, I visit Egypt.)*

My wonderful friend tells me about a new class project. The "Personal Mythology Project" offers a way to gain a greater appreciation for the meaning of our own life, if only from the perspective of seeing connections. We are to determine our attachments and find symbolic language, which helps to express and understand life experiences.

Campbell says we can interpret our lives according to basic symbols within the Collective Consciousness. The page Leah now offers notes archetypal symbols as delineated by Carl Jung. I immediately focus on the house that represents the dreamer, the self – rooms as aspects of the self – and the sun. The sun represents the power, glory, life force and vitality, and the ability to direct the will, and have a sense of purpose. Leah notes Campbell's purpose was to show that Nature provides an interior roadmap, "to guide us home to the Christ Consciousness." There's not a doubt that the sun is key as we leave to eat a leisurely lunch at the Olive Garden Restaurant.

Life is good! Hours after registering for the Big Sky Retreat, booking airfare and hotel, I leave for Rebecca's house. She seems happy to see me but still doesn't understand why I prefer to be there. Her wireless hookup allows the pleasure of working outside in fresh air. We sit together on the large, screened, back porch for several hours before I finally lie down to rest for the night. Her bed, so unlike the uncomfortable black futon, hints of Heaven.

Different energies face me now. Fragrant coffee fills the pot as I make Samuel's lunch in the morning. Rebecca's smile cheers as she takes a cup out to the back porch. She soon drives Samuel to school before leaving for Virginia while I load the washer with clothes. Princess, Rebecca's dog, is very needy and, like a pampered child, refuses to eat when mommy is out of town. Kitty eats voraciously and then promptly throws up. I try not to let it bother me while putting clothes into a hamper to dry at the house on 47th Drive before attending class. All traffic lights are green both to, and from, the other side of town.

"As I interact with you, I try so hard to open my mind and heart."

The words wake me at dawn. After repeating the World Healing Meditation and a few treatments, I take Samuel to school and am back at Rebecca's in record time to finish morning prayers before napping. Vivid dreams wake me an hour later while on my right side in a fetal position. Tears fill eyes.

They flowed down my face in the dream because I missed Daniel. He suddenly appeared, placed his loving two hands over mine, and then gently placed them on my cheeks. What a vivid feeling!

"Thanks," I said, "for letting me know you're still around to assure me of your love."

Daniel was going to go but I asked him to stay. He kept his hands on my face a bit longer. Another male asked why I was crying. I told him I missed Daniel and he cried too. James then asked why he was crying and I told him.

In another dream, I came upon beautiful statues of faces in the ground. Someone was with me. We both picked up a statue and asked why we could not just take it home. The writing on the statue said, *"Golden Colorado"* and *"Fort Lauderdale."* The statues were like Egyptian heads with gold and green headdresses. We figured the statues were to decorate the landscape and put them back. *(Weeks later, I learn that Charles was born in Golden Colorado. Did I know him in Egyptian times?)*

The day passes quickly and soon dinner sits on orange and blue plates. Samuel answers the telephone, thanks the caller, and hands me the receiver. An officer from the Gainesville police reports that one of their officers was killed in a car crash. She's calling to remind us to buckle up our seat belts. And then she asks for a donation. It's easy to decline. I think nothing of the call while thanking her before replacing the receiver in its cradle.

Having decided to forgo Wednesday evening's service, I take my time eating. Samuel seems happy to chat and I'm happy to listen. My front tooth crown, the one the dentist glued back in last month, falls out as we finish dinner. Since I'm still fearful of losing it, there's a handy tube of super glue in my toiletries bag. I carefully glue it back in knowing this time it will stay in.

Thursday morning's drive to Samuel's school again takes much less time than usual. And once again, I lie down to nap when the morning ritual completes. I'm soon in a dream giving a new book to a cousin for her baby boy, who is somehow related to Daniel. Tears flow down my face thinking of how much I miss him. Then I remind myself no one loses anyone. All is illusion.

This dream is the second prompt that leads me to think my cousin's boy is Daniel reborn. Daniel is trying to let me know he lives again. While in Michigan in April, I first thought this when not able to see the baby. Daniel seemed to have an unspoken closeness to this cousin the last time we were all together. There may be unfinished business between them. Perhaps, his soul is now there to finish it.

Rebecca telephones to interrupt thoughts. She speaks calmly while relating the account of a traumatic saga. The good news is she will return home in the evening as planned. The bad news is she spent the night in a hospital and has to have more tests. Someone rear-ended the car she rode in yesterday at about the same time we received the Gainesville police call. She was a front-seat passenger, in this minor car accident, and the only one carried away in an ambulance to spend the night in the hospital with whiplash. We end the call after I agree to stay more days.

It takes me an hour or so to recognize the two subtle warnings of her impending accident. There is something about losing teeth and losing or having something happen to my child that strikes a chord.

Days run together but pass quickly after returning to the house on 47th Drive. Bits and pieces of words wake me in the early morning hours. *"...for the voice of God"* and *"The accommodations are lush!"* fill me with unexplained delight.

The Indian term māyā intrigues me during our evening SOM 212 class. Campbell describes it as the term for "illusion." Māyā refers to "both the power that creates an illusion and the false display itself." It's said to possess a "Veiling Power," a "Projecting Power," and a "Revealing Power." The only thing I'm sure of is that there is no level of illusion. Everything I see, hear, smell, taste, touch, and experience is illusion.

Erratic laptop behavior continues to stem the easy flow of work. It's a sign to prompt new habits while checking email. Anna and I may wish to reconsider the Italy trip for now a larger group of travelers, not just metaphysicians, will go. The idea does not meet my expectations so I quickly email Anna. She's back with Ramon and happy to take him with her.

In a few days, Rebecca will celebrate her birthday with family on the cruise booked last month. It's an opportunity to show family another way to live, a more luxurious life with unlimited food and time to spare! But for now, the last SOM 212 class finds me sharing a very personal class project. A prepared script shakes nervously in my hands as I stand in the large, silent sanctuary in front of class.

"The one myth that Joseph Campbell brought to mind for me is that there is no death," I report. "This book expanded my awareness of symbology, particularly as it relates to the sun. Always drawn to anything of nature, I related the sun to an aspect of life, which helped me to remember who I really am.

"At fifteen years old I decided to conceive a child. I felt driven to birth my son, Daniel, thinking he would make my life complete. Instead of lying in the sun as friends, I birthed the perfect sunshine boy to love for the rest of my days.

"He grew quickly to be my sunshine man. My daughter then birthed the new sunshine boy. When my son's daughter was born, she became the sunshine girl. My daughter was always 'the princess.' When her brother passed to the Otherside, it was a heavy blow to us all.

"At that point, my original sunshine boy morphed into a sunshine spirit that immediately led me to the realization of why I had him – to remember to awaken to our True BEing. Daniel's essence prompted me to love everyone as I loved him. He assured me there is no death – beyond the duality of Oneness. I shall never forget when he spoke of our true essence while I sat listening to the Daila Lama."

"I never was and never will be," echoed in my brain while sensing him. "Samuel was born to help you get over the loss of me."

"My Sunshine Spirit, over the course of eighteen months, led me to the realization that I planned his presence to help me recall our true nature. I believe we are all parts of the sun, energy in physical form. The real goal for me is to love everyone as I loved my son. That's getting beyond duality to Oneness. Daniel also helped me through music to change my mental attitude so the revealing power of esthetic arrest could come through."

A sudden outburst of applause fills the air as my heart pounds seemingly from my chest. Classmates now look at me much differently.

Chapter Sixteen

Rebecca's Birthday Cruise

"Know all is going according to the plan of One for all can go no other way." SAM – Book of One :-) Volume 1

Clouds fill the sky as I drive to Rebecca's knowing her birthday cruise offers family another way to live. Excitement is hard to contain for new, joyful adventures of abundance await us. I so look forward to opening minds to greater possibilities during a fun-filled weekend!

Rebecca, Samuel, Rebecca's friend Emily, and her son, Elijah, chatter away while Ruth drives us to Port Everglades. No one mentions how persistently annoying I am while videoing. Ruth drops Rebecca and me at the terminal entrance with everyone's luggage. We watch with amusement when two young women breeze past luggage handlers carting small bags. The men warn that they'll be turned away and have to give them the bags anyways. We know it's their living so I'm glad to tip them for taking luggage onboard.

The Carnival Fascination is not my idea of a luxury ship but it's the one Rebecca chose. Her best friend Lydia, along with husband Joseph and child, booked a room on another deck. They paid extra to have Rebecca's inside room decorated with birthday greetings. Sharing a room with two teenage boys, as Rebecca and Emily are, is out of my comfort zone. Ruth and I enjoy the Oceanside room across the hall. It seems much bigger with two beds instead of four.

Lydia and Joseph arrive with their darling daughter who everyone now refers to as Mickey. The little, blue-eyed, two-year-old, with curly golden hair and pierced earrings, is very beautiful but pale.

Incessant noise fills the small room, too small to hold us all without feeling like sardines. The scene is now pure chaos for me. Rebecca opens presents as Samuel and Elijah talk to one another using short-wave radios brought to appease her. She's still fearful of letting fourteen-year-old Samuel out of her sight. Someone switches the lights on, and off, as I hand Rebecca a large packet of paper money. A woeful look fills her face and she hands the one-hundred dollar bills to Mickey, who sits happily on her stomach. Am I the only one that values the power of visioning?

Dark circles under Mickey's eyes are hard to miss as we enjoy a buffet lunch. Junk food fills many plates but not mine. My special vanilla blend of Diet Coke with Splenda, however, brought onboard in luggage, substitutes for alcohol as the drinking begins.

Once again, differences between us are hard to miss as alcohol affects loved ones. Pandemonium, with everyone talking at once, amid walkie-talkies, fills the room. I'm still adjusting to the increased noise for it's so unlike my quiet sanctuary on 47th Drive.

Persistent beeps fill the air later as we sit in the theatre for the boat drill. Mickey plays with daddy's hat and giggles with delight when he tosses her into the air. Being with other people causes such joy that it's difficult to contain myself. I'm now loud, back to my old self, ceaselessly talking about eating in the dining room. Everyone else thinks the dining room is a waste of time. I soon convince them, food is better and it's nice to be waited on.

Plates of chicken nuggets and fries surround me hours later. Vast differences between family and myself are now clearly evident. Am I the only one who values good food and waiting staff? Everyone else prefers to roam the "fun ship" rather than wait to be served. It's a sure bet they'll eat remaining meals at the upstairs buffet.

Stars grace ceilings as Ruth and I move slowly from one end of the ship to the other after dinner. Entertaining musicians fill the promenade. People are outgoing, loud, and casually dressed. Intuition helps me win, I note as we pass through the casino. Ruth ventures upstairs to an exit to smoke. The Wheel of Fortune pays me $42 after a few spins so I quit to rejoin her.

A Mexican singer reminds me of my March cruise with Anna. "What joy to have good memories!" I think, as we move on while the boys feed arcade machines. The others try to fill bingo cards later as I watch. Rebecca sits alone on a revolving loveseat as Joseph twirls her around and around. I cannot comprehend how she stands it. Even watching makes me dizzy. It's another sign that I no longer fit into the old mold.

We soon move on to enjoy the welcome aboard show with Dan and the Palace Orchestra. Words from older songs such as Frank Sinatra's, "Ain't that a kick in the head," fill me with glee before a juggler commands the stage. Rebecca now has a migraine so we call it a night bypassing the very active disco. Her room smells like dirty feet and I cannot imagine anyone sleeping there. Across the hall, Ruth sleeps soundly as I listen to my daily treatments CD.

Clouds fill skies when we wake on Rebecca's thirty-third birthday. She complains when I loudly sing happy birthday for her head still hurts. Most of the adults drink shots of Goldslagger for breakfast. It's a gloomy day and storm clouds confront us in Nassau. Rain falls in the distance amidst low-lying, colorful buildings. Seagulls sit on railings as I stand on deck alone. My long hair waves in the wind so I pull it back on top of my head to appear much older.

"We came into this world in this body knowing there would be times like these, times when the world would seem to act out against us. And yet, it is only our own state of BEing that drives this powerful force. As difficult as it seems to believe, our thoughts, emotions, and deeds do indeed make the universe in which we live. There is no outside force that directs the weather, the forces of what we refer to as 'evil,' (for everything is part of our own consciousness).

"It is time to cleanse and purify that consciousness of One. We are each a part of the other, all participating in this temporal mind game called earth life. This is the only place where we can experience the vastness of time and space, the unfolding dramas that excite the five senses. And it is only now that we are finally, after many eons, recognizing the Power within.

*"As we recognize this true Essence of **All That Is** we must accept the parts of ourselves seeming to be separate. There is nothing outside of us and recognizing this state of BEing is*

utmost to our survival on the earth plane. The drama continues, only if you allow it to be so, by not seeing that all things are a part of you. Calm the brain, still the source of turmoil within, and watch your world change quickly back to the Eden that it once was."

Clearly, unlike most adult companions, I don't have a hangover. "We're on our way. Thirty-three years old today," I repeatedly sing while waiting for an elevator. Mickey stares with an endearing smile before hiding her head in Joseph's arm.

Light rain falls when we disembark in the fourth country Mickey is privileged to visit. I'm still annoying the others singing "Walking on Sunshine" as we make our way to the first building.

"We're going to leave you here if you don't stop making noises," Samuel announces when we reach the other side. "Do you value your life?"

"Yes."

"Then stop."

"Everything you do causes a wave in the atmosphere around you that resounds throughout all space and time in your illusion. You must recall promptly that thoughts, your thoughts, manifest to make your reality. It is as simple as that and if more of the so-called ones seeming to be outside of you recognized this, all would be back to the state of Oneness, which you never left in the first place.

"Your world is a measure of illusion from only one thing. That is not the human brain but the manifestation of Oneness into a separate state of BEing called separation. The separation takes place only within the human mind and is but an illusion of the Truth of which you are.

"There is nothing outside of you and now that your selves are beginning to reconcile this truth, the other false selves, seeming to be apart, are trying to maintain the balance of negativity. This is part of your own illusion and not a separate Being."

Many signs line the path. One of them is particularly creative.

"Protect your neck from the sun. Wear jewelry."

Samuel tries not to look excited but wants to buy everything. A Bahamian woman stops to ask if I'd like my hair braided.

"No thank you darling," I tell her with a smile.

"Maybe on your way back," she says. "Look for me my name is Marilyn Monroe."

Another woman calls out moments later.

"You look wonderful. Whatever you are doing, keep it up," she says, as we walk briskly toward a colorful Senior Frog water taxi.

A skinny, local man directs us to a different, much older, smaller boat. It's very plain and run down compared to the Senior Frog water taxi. A younger man sells conch from a tiny vessel docked nearby. Colorful shells fill his boat.

Rain begins to fall again so we all move to sit under cover. Everyone's attention turns to Mickey as she sweetly sings "Happy Birthday" to Aunt Rebecca. Intuition prompts me to snap a picture. The display shows Rebecca laughing as Lydia sits next to her, seeming to stare at something unseen. A mass of oblong-shaped white light, a spirit orb, sits before her but she appears not to see it.

"I will be your tour guide all the way across to the Paradise Island so please don't worry, be happy," a tall, skinny man soon announces.

The boat is one-way we are soon informed. We promptly decide to take another way back when ready to return. Our guide advises us to make ourselves at home, as we lean into the center of the boat to keep dry.

"Now, ladies and gentlemans," he announces before talking of tourism and offshore banking, the island's main sources of income.

We listen straining to hear amid the downpour. Rain continues to fall as we disembark.

*"The One of **All That Is** beckons forth a new age of BEing. This is the age of what many call Aquarius. The knowing of unique parts of One, being part of the whole of **All That Is**, is here. The reality you wish is here. Open your eyes to see it now and know all is in Divine Order.*

"As you go forth through the eye of the needle, the other side is deliciously delightful for all of humanity. Speak not of disdainful things for those are the things you will experience. Speak only of the Love and Light within. Feel only the Love and Light within for that is what you will experience.

*"Know that **All That Is** goes before you, is in you, around you, and through you. There is nothing else. Remember, this is an illusion of your own making. Make it what you wish to experience and know that this experience is yet but another illusion of the temporal mind.*

*"**All That Is** beckons forth for all to hear the call of Almighty Power. One Truth, one Light, one Love is within all things. These things are not as disdainful as one would think. Know all is exceedingly well as you go forth through the eye of the needle. Know all is exceedingly well as you continue on your imaginary journey back to the One in all aspects of Self. And so it is to be forevermore. The reign of One is here.*

*"You must bear witness to the falsities that surround you. You are the one that is chosen, as many others, to speak the truth of One. Do not be dismayed by what occurs around you. Know that all is exceedingly well as you go forth though the eye of the needle. There is only one Truth, one Light, one Love. There is only One and that One is part of **All That Is**."*

We walk the wrong way past colorful yellow, blue, green, peach, and pink buildings in our quest to get out of the rain. A local directs us to return the way we came. Rain stops as we near palm frond hats and vases. Most companions saunter to the bar to order mohitos after a short photo opportunity upon entering the casino. It takes a very, long, time for the bartender to make them. I'm happy to hold Mickey, yards away in a comfy chair, while waiting. Rebecca sees my stare and ventures over.

"You have to pick the mint from the fields mon," Rebecca replies when I ask why it's taking so long. "And then you have to crush it mon."

"And then what do you do?"

"You keep crushing, crushing the mint," she replies while turning her attention back to the bar. "Then you add ice and a lot of liquor. That's your birthday mohitos."

Rebecca's smile tells me she's having a good time so I really don't mind the wait. I hum to myself between bouts of talk.

"And how long have we been waiting for this mohito?"

"Forever," Rebecca announces quickly, "so it better be really good!"

She's soon disappointed.

Daniel's presence surrounds us as we walk through the building. The video camera keeps malfunctioning when I try to video the casino. Many tourist-type, photo opportunities sit before us and Rebecca takes advantage of them all. The décor, down a wide set of stairs to the aquarium, is beautiful as Rebecca snaps a shot of Samuel wearing his Nintendo rehab clinic shirt.

Walls of glass allow a view of permit, stingrays, sharks, and a variety of tropical fish. Some are very beautiful with blue stripes that glow in the dark. Gray and yellow fish, moray eels, jewfish, and huge grouper float in the enormous tank. Tunnels lead to huge lobsters piled on top of each other and moonfish.

"Those things are delicious," Samuel tells Elijah. "Papa puts lime juice on them."

We pay admission to see a variety of other fish including glowing jellyfish and colorful clown fish, amid anemones, seahorses, and little, gray sharks.

Before returning to the ship, I offer Samuel $10. He promptly spends it buying tee shirts for a variety of people. I encourage him to keep one for himself. Pink clouds seem rimmed in gold as we make our way up the gangplank to eat another buffet lunch. I miss the dining room but do not want to eat without them.

"Travel the bounds but you must stay clear of the fray. The task of One is complete as all things return to the knowingness of One. This day is monumental in all aspects of life, on all realms, everywhere, though everything. Every bit of Consciousness feels the blessing of this day.

"All reach out toward earth to help those in great need. Everlasting waves of wonder cover the earth now. The magic of One has begun and shall last forevermore. Stay clear of the chaos of humanities woes and turmoil. There is nothing here for

*you now. You must stay clear of the chaos. Do not be pulled into
the misery of those surrounding you.*

*"The message is clear for the lightworkers. All is
exceedingly well for all return back to the Oneness from which it
came. Know you are the One, the One of Love, the One of Light,
the One of Inner BEingness.*

*"This One is untouched by the seeming days of woe for
naught is the release of those that choose to relish in the agony of
humanity. Speak not of disdainful things. These things keep the
mind-body in the turmoil in which the masses now exist. Return
to the One in all its glory and know that the sustenance of One
lies within you."*

The boys gulp food quickly before heading to the teen
club. Rebecca returns to the table with a baby octopus, which I
immediately turn into a subject of much laughter. No one wants
to eat it. This ship's food does not impress me. I consider the
service sub-par to that on more expensive ships but no one else
seems to mind. Perhaps they don't know the difference.

Sunset is spectacular with shades of pink, and yellow,
mixed among gray clouds in a baby blue sly. It's not as pretty as
Santorini, Greece but beautiful nonetheless. I stand alone taking
it all in with my video camera. An announcement for the $3,000
Power Ball bingo session pierces the air to spoil my solitude.

We remain in port but the entire ship is alive with
festivities. A party planned for Lido deck will now be on the
Promenade for the Captain expects more rain. Adults continue to
drink while eating outside and now Rebecca is anxious to join in
karaoke fun after dinner. By this time, some of my companions
are what I refer to as "falling down drunk." A still somewhat
sober Rebecca nervously rises to sing moments after we join the
karaoke crowd.

"You go baby," I call out as she climbs onto the stage.

Rebecca engages the audience as soon as "Hit Me With
Your Best Shot," by Pat Benetar, begins to play. She raises her
hands high above her head and begins to clap.

"Come on," she calls out as the audience begins to clap
along.

"You're a real tough cookie with a long history," she belts out beautifully, "of breaking little hearts like the one in me. Well, that's okay, let's see how you do it. Put up your dukes let's get down to it. Hit me with your best shot. Come on and hit me with your best shot. Hit me with your best shot. Fire away."

Daniel's playful spirit continues to fool around as a loud noise suddenly erupts from behind the curtain to interrupt her flow. Rebecca, taken by surprise, looks back with a horrified face while I smile knowing Daniel is making his presence known. The message circulates in her brain after she jumps off the stage in a panic. A wide smile fills her face. She continues to sing, like a professional, jumping up and down like a bunny. The crowd sings and claps along while I laugh with glee knowing all is well. I'm so very proud of my dancing, petite daughter as she continues to engage the crowd.

"Friendly forces are with all beings of earth now as you go through the storm of eons. This is a necessary task so humanity can move more quickly toward the One of Light. There is nothing to fear as lightworkers, wayshowers and starseeds show the way. You know who you are, imaginary beings in form on earth seeming to save lost parts of yourself.

"Remember, this is a game you, as a soul, chose to play here on earth as we draw nearer to the end of control. Seek not to glorify the ones in need of hope and Light but merely lead those who wish to be led back to Oneness. All come in their own time, both into, and out of, this earth game.

"Know all is going well, exceedingly so, as all feel the effects of this great upheaval. Your task is complete as you feel Source around, in, and through you, at every level of BEing. Once that is felt, you merely need do nothing but stand by and let the show complete."

"Thanks guys, have fun," she tells the audience as they stand to clap after her performance.

Not willing to abandon a new state of awareness, I head off to listen to my treatment CD while the rest of the adults party on. I'm glad they're having fun but just cannot participate in the usual drunken rituals.

"So, did you enjoy your birthday cruise?" I ask the next morning as we eat outside on deck. "Is there anything you'd like to note about it?"

"I drank too much," says Rebecca exhaling a puff of cigarette smoke, "especially last night. I was toilet-papered."

"Is that all you want to tell us?" I ask quietly.

"What happens on the boat, stays on the boat," she adamantly remarks.

She obviously doesn't know I'm writing a book.

"Be true to yourself. Hear the words from within. They will guide you. You are loved. You are not alone. You must listen to that inner voice. You must pay attention to it. You must spend more time listening and you must hear when you listen. And you must remember when you listen. For all is naught if you don't.

"You must hear when you listen. You must hear the words from deep inside, deep inside your gut, deep inside the mind of the One. You must hear those words even as they are being spoken. There is much to do and your time is little. You have chosen your time to be little now and your will is done as Gods.

"You must go forth and spread the word, the word of God that we are One, the word of God that we are One, the word of God that we are One. Go forth and spread that word in the best way that you know how to do, for it is your task on this earth at this time, to spread that word, to know the One is within you working for you, and all living things. That is all."

Chapter Seventeen

Manifesting Abundance

"Certain segments of society are quickly learning that we hold the power to change the game of life." SAM – Bits of Wisdom

Something about June 26 fills my brain before dawn. Daylight hours pass quickly praying and studying for the first *This Thing Called You* class. Another mind-opening adventure unfolds as I readdress spiritual values. Synchronicities come more rapidly upon their recognition. Natural and Spiritual Laws operate to enrich life and the Principle of Mind always works in my favor.

Handouts, with tips to propel us onward, fill me with gratitude in the evening. A goal to hasten self-mastery comes before class ends. I shall spend more time in peaceful, positive, empowering environments.

"All of you that is cannot help but change to help the mass consciousness that is struggling. Everyone has come to this planet to do so. If not following their path, to lead those struggling in mass consciousness, all await the glorious time of awakening to the fact that all is well. The surety of the path, your path, is set in stone. Know all is going according to plan as we move closer to heaven on earth."

Starting each day with meditation and treatments helps to stay focused. The Oneness of life is ever ready to interact. Gratitude abounds while knowing that intuition constantly offers great ideas. Truly, thought is the only barrier to good. Issues decrease when I consciously practice living the Presence of God. Amazing things happen upon observing life, without judgment, consciously injecting Love and Joy into each experience.

Being a unique and independent being has never been easier. Oh, how I love *This Thing Called You*! This book makes it so much easier to express my spirituality. How wonderful to receive verification to spur me forward on the path of One! How interesting that Holmes notes we are to look for God in everyone and love this God, forgetting all else. This is the message Daniel impressed upon me soon after his transition. Loving everyone as a Divine Individual, an expression of One, feels so much better.

Excitement fills Ruth's black van as we motor down the freeway listening to Momma's chatter two days later. Momma is very eager to see her brother who lives six hours away. She hasn't seen him in years.

Scattered clouds suddenly clear upon reaching Aunt Justine and Uncle Raphael's winter hideaway in Flagler Beach. Loving energy, pleasing all senses, fills their beautiful home. It backs up to a magnificent national forest. Uncle Raphael talks excitedly of the many animals that venture out periodically from the woods as we make ourselves at home. The beautiful, peaceful, nurturing environment is in perfect order and immediately brings to mind my goal envisioned during class.

We enjoy pleasant talk and a spectacular Italian dinner cooked by Uncle Raphael with love. Filled with excitement, I decide to sleep on the pullout sofa because the room is full of light, with floor to ceiling windows and a skylight in the nearby kitchen. Joy abounds while sleeping on the comfy sofa bed so unlike the now very uncomfortable futon in my room. Momma and Ruth share the lovely guest room with two beds.

Breakfast is as pleasant as dinner and I find myself not wanting to leave. But Ruth has to work on Saturday so we must return today. Momma is not looking forward to the drive either but we leave shortly after eating. This short family trip, I decide, will be my last. It's too exhausting to travel so far, and back, in two days, especially after a leisurely cruise.

Postal mail holds a letter from a Morgan Stanley financial advisor named Kelly. It highlights "The Pension Protection Act of 2006," touted as a means to help Americans build wealth while saving for retirement. I'm uncertain as to how this letter came to me. Something about saving money just doesn't seem prudent.

Intuition repeatedly warns me to avoid financial advisors, savings accounts, bonds, or stock investments. After following a popular Website (http://jsmineset.com) in 2010, I understand.

Morgan Stanley went bankrupt in 2009. The company then became a bank, and along with eighteen others, masked their risk levels by temporarily lowering their debt, just before reporting it to the public. Banking rules changed the game making banks look more attractive. Global economic collapse continued to unfold as people lost life savings through a variety of banking schemes.

A string of words wakes me the next morning. I'm receiving instructions from an unknown force. *"You have to be able to levitate those things, to move those things toward you."* *"The sense of separation is no more,"* graces my mind minutes later.

Words fill my brain every morning for the next three days while traveling between universes.

"...Patterns of Universes. I know they are there and I shall go to each one. I want to go to those other worlds, build those worlds where you can have everything you want, when you want it. If I want a banana, it appears."

"God is neither man, woman, or child but the Godhead, One, All."

"This is where we want to be, in the garden where there is no cold, no warm. There is only the warm love of God, enveloping, enveloping, enveloping."

Ever-changing perception clearly shows how beliefs affect the life I experience. *This Thing Called You* is such an amazing book that I find myself reading more pages than requested by Dr. Bump. Class brings an important reminder. We reap what we sow. What we wish for others always returns to us, through others. Positive life-affirming thoughts feel so much better than the old "stinking thinking." Workshops are always fun and tonight's is no exception. My partner and me discuss "the great drama of life." I'm happy to report that drama lessens when realizing my perception produces and directs it. "Baby Love," by the Supremes is no longer my theme song. It makes much more sense to live an unlimited life that God directs.

Returning to my love-filled room, I envision another trip. It's time to share the wonder and glory of the Big Sky Retreat.

Leaving early to share this experience with Dr. Charles and others will surely make Big Sky even more awesome. We plan to weave our way through Utah, Wyoming, Montana, and Idaho. Although it sounds expensive, there's still money left from Daddy's lawsuit and more will come.

Blue skies soon surround me while flying happily through the air in a dream. I'm so proud to show someone flying skills. "I need to learn how to fly, and I do," I announce to someone, before floating down from the sky to gently land.

Mary telephones to ask for a favor in the afternoon of June 26, 2007.

"It's last minute I know," she says in desperation, "but would you please consider cat sitting for a month? My planned sitter cancelled and I leave to spread Seth's ashes in six days."

"New and exciting business awaits those that wish to pass to the other side."

The thought of having her perfectly organized and beautiful three-bedroom home to myself is almost more than I can bear without screaming and jumping for joy.

Family is not as thrilled upon hearing the news. We're celebrating Terry's birthday at a cheaper than usual restaurant because everyone is tapped for cash. James stares at me in disbelief. Later, an important message breaks through the veil during meditation.

"You can not escape your destiny. You must show others the glory of their dreams. Their light shines as bright as yours."

Lately, recognizing my humanness has taken a back seat. But a perceived loss of Daniel surfaces at dawn so I allow myself to mourn. We went through so very much together, especially when he was very young, for I had a hard time protecting us. I cry and ask for forgiveness, even knowing spiritually there's nothing to forgive. I gave him, although maybe not exactly, the experiences his soul came to live through. Daniel's reminder that he never was, and never will be, comforts. At the time his essence relayed the words, I didn't grasp their meaning. I fully understand now. The sense of our Oneness remains unsurpassed by any human experience. How grateful I am for the spirit of my last-born son who helped me to remember our true identity.

"Life is not to be lived. It is to be experienced."

Life continues to improve. Many signs lead me to believe that James is beginning to understand the power of Spirit. Although we both know our marriage is over, he now shares money without complaining. I pay charge card monthly expenses through our joint checking account making sure to pay for travel with the money from Daddy's lawsuit. I also withdraw monthly sums to pay for my little needs and wants. James now knows how to care for and cleanup after himself. How reassuring to know that when we finally part he'll be accustomed to doing simple things, like washing clothes and buying groceries!

*"As the moon wanes and a new moon takes it place, so too does the body change with ever-increasing fervor. The body of One is forming upon earth before your very eyes. This body is a necessary BEing for all mankind to recognize the wholeness of which it is. The body of One is an illusion in itself but nevertheless part of **All That Is**.*

"It is time dear ones to return to the Consciousness you left so long ago. Many of you may remain in the stillness of that consciousness after it forms yet again. Others will choose to return to enjoy the fruits of their imaginary labor here on the earth plane. Yet know; all is illusion as we enter into another new realm of existence."

Life is no longer limited and shall never be again. It's my great pleasure to enjoy the fruits of many years of labor, in limited situations, spending increasingly more time in positive, much less cluttered, nurturing environments. God will continue to care for me. I'll never work a regular 'job' again. Positive, nurturing environments will surround me for the rest of my life as I do God's work.

Weekly night classes and services help to stay on track. I consider them investments. The atmosphere always seems more charged with loving energy during Thursday classes with Dr. Charles. I'm very happy to participate. Instinct now propels me to shop hours before class. I then demonstrate the good that comes in a wide variety of ways.

Everything I buy costs much less than expected. Poverello holds almost new designer clothes for Samuel at thrift store prices. Spiritual books for friends are 50 cents. Intuition leads me to the Goodwill Boutique for hiking boots. The normally $180 brand new boots, with an inside tag on the left boot and no wear whatsoever, cost $10. Knowing they'll fit, I don't even try them on. (And they do!)

Leah sits waiting patiently in the Center's parking lot. She offers a bag of spiritual books, all in excellent condition. How wonderful to share as we walk to a restaurant! The cost of dinner goes on my charge card knowing James will pay for it because I'm worth it and more.

"Hello, I am with you. I am Talia of Nibiru come to report good news. The land of woe is awakening to the Oneness of All That Is and you play a huge role in this awakening. Be not afraid as the dismay of many unfolds to reveal the truth of your Oneness. Each happening that occurs leads all back to the Oneness of the Self within."

Many people are happy to see me as we enter the classroom. We joyfully hug. Class with Dr. Charles is, as usual, excellent! He reads something our classmate Ann wrote on how she is the light of God. Ann and I become dyad workshop partners. She will, I know, join those of us leaving early for the Big Sky Retreat.

How grateful I am that spirit lies within every body cell assuring its health so I can travel without concern! There's no need to see doctors. I have not seen one in two years. I'm living testimony that treatment works, when given by one with persistence and faith in the process. SOM taught me that we influence the body's ability to heal. My predominant thought pattern and belief system is vastly different, from even last year, for now I know SOM truly works! The mold of thought holds only healthy, life-affirming beliefs. There's no doubt. Spirit sustains this body in health and activity to help me meet my life's purpose. I repeatedly thank Spirit for helping me to heal and stay healthy in mind and body. Immense joy erupts upon reading a quote by Myrtle Fillmore from "Healing Letters:"

"Man learns to build an airplane in which to fly before he is entrusted with the higher law of taking his body through the air without a manifest vehicle."

My humanness peeks out later, missing Daniel immensely before bedtime. Listening to saved telephone messages is a bittersweet experience knowing his physical form is gone. Later, I dream of being somewhere with family. A past Daniel comes downstairs to say they have to go. I'm so happy to see him but try to hide it because I don't want him to know he's dead and I have not seen him in a while. "Stay a bit longer," I ask. He tells me they (himself, Rachel, and Abigail) have to go.

"Even though you might not understand it, even though we are not together, I am still with you," I announce.

Daniel's beautiful hazel eyes sparkle as his face softens.

"I do understand. I love you Mom."

"You wonder why the unseen is not more clearly apparent to your human eyes. And yet, the unseen is clearly visible to you at all times. We are those tiny sparks of white Light, filtering through the air of time and space. We are the sparks of humanity yet to come and eons of manifestation brought back to the Source of One. We are within you and never far from the thoughts of those who know of our existence.

"So when you wonder why you do not see the unseen entourage accompanying you, think again, and realize we are within you and around you at all times. We are the very essence of what you are. You are the very essence of what we are. All is well in this creation of Oneness and Love as we move forward though the mass consciousness of One ever changing, ever-expanding, to become, yet again, the world in which you seek to reside."

Tears fill eyes upon waking. It's almost time to start packing for my month long stay at Mary's house. I may not return to this house and that's okay. Daniel's essence breaks through the veil again as I sit studying for class.

"Buy a cell phone," he announces. "Buy the pre-paid one from the Costco ad."

Daniel asked me to get a cell phone before visiting Ester in Michigan but I borrowed Samuel's instead. Prompts to buy a cell phone also came earlier this week but James said he would not get me one. I then told myself other signs would come if a cell phone were needed. The following day, a sale ad from Costco sat in email. I thought a pre-paid one might be a good deal. But, again, put it off.

Daniel is very persistent this time as I try to ignore him. He announces there will be two storms while I'm at Mary's and Sarah will want to telephone me from her hospital bed. For the first time, I actually argue with him in my head. Daniel's words continue to fill my brain making it impossible to study. I finally agree to leave the house, before three o'clock in the afternoon, if he will be still. He quickly announces the phone is at Costco waiting for me to buy and it's a good deal. I did not expect to be back at Costco after buying hurricane supplies there days ago. Yet, it's no surprise that there's just enough money left from that trip to buy the phone.

The clock strikes a quarter to three as I rise to leave. Daniel guides me to a busy gas station. A man cuts me off and takes control of the gas pump as I pull up. I silently bless him and pull over to get behind a young man on the other side of the lot. He takes his time while talking on a cell phone. While waiting, I notice that the charge card machine at the pump is not working. I don't want to wait in another line to get charge card approval.

A middle pump opens up so I leave the line to pull up to it, a few more feet away than usual. The sign that I'm doing the right thing sits before me when I get out of the car. A bright, shining penny sits on the pavement. My heart soars while pumping gas.

The store is busy as usual. Several people purchase phones as I wait at the booth. It gives me plenty of time to spot the desired cell phone on display. When the man turns to me, I point and tell him it's my phone.

"That's a really good deal but we don't have any of them left," he replies with a grin.

"Yes, you do," I argue. "I was told the cell phone was here."

He smiles, cocks his head, and with the light of recognition on his face happily replies. "You know, I think we do have a few more left in the display up front. Let me go see."

Minutes later, I have a cell phone, the accessory kit with two chargers, an ear piece, and twenty minutes of cell time for only $29. Calls are ten cents a minute without a contract. There's no doubt. This is meant to be even though I do not see the need for a cell phone.

Wondering if Daniel had heightened intuition when he purchased the Costco membership as my last Christmas gift from him, I look up the deal on the Internet later. Another online deal lures me into purchasing $100 worth of minutes (1,000 minutes) because I get 15% more minutes. The minutes are good for a year so I happily put the cost on my credit card.

Synchronicities abound. While setting up cell phone options, I notice the title of my favorite ring tone is "Sunday Morning." Both Daniel and Rebecca were born on a Sunday morning! Birthing children on Sunday is one more clue my soul planned to prompt memories of who we really are. Many people spend Sundays going to church, remembering God!

I can only begin to relate how helpful it is to have this pre-paid cell phone. The only taxes I pay are those related to the sale of pre-paid minutes. (Having just paid $4.28 for long-distance calls on my land line, which cost a mere fifty-eight cents before taxes and fees, served to remind me of this deal's value.) The phone comes in handy to make long distance calls at ten cents a minute, instead of the twenty-five cents to $2.00 a minute charged by AT&T on the home phone. It's nice to have when traveling and I have even used it when out of the country.

Leah telephones minutes later to ask if my offer for a Big Sky Retreat roommate is still open. The conversation soon turns to thoughts of renting a condo at the Big Sky Resort, instead of a room. We're excited at the thought of sharing a master bedroom, two bathrooms, and a full kitchen. Mountain views from our lovely balcony will compliment time spent between sessions, saunas, Jacuzzis, and the health spa. Yes, an unlimited life of abundance and joy is mine and I accept my good right NOW!

"Knowing the earth is a part of me, I have only positive thoughts. I follow only positive views. I am the earth in all its glory, full of Light and Love."

Mary welcomes me for a visit late on Saturday morning. She calls out to her babies to cuddle up to Auntie Sam. Sethala runs past us like a space shuttle rocket and lands on the kitchen table. Her raccoon tail moves to, and fro, as she meows at birds in the feeder outside. Blind Amber and Myles lie sleeping on the brown, velour couch. Beautiful, multicolored Michgi rubs up against my leg.

"Pumpkin, my sister's cat, is in the bedroom," Mary announces while cuddling Sethala. "Auntie Sam is going to play with you while I'm away," she announces to the now squirming cat that quickly bolts out of her arms. We then move through the house to see the cats' toys and room with two litter boxes, Mary's bed, with adjoining bath, and guest room. It's a sure bet that wherever I sleep cats will join me.

"I just did the grocery shopping and cleaned but these cats do leave a bit of hair around," she notes, pointing to the vacuum cleaner in the closet before moving out to the garage. "And I need you to drive my baby," she says with a smile, patting her silver Mazda RX. "I can't very well let Rex sit for a month. My baby has got to purr on the road at least once a week. You can take the mini-van to pick up my new flooring when Home Depot calls."

"Oh Mary," I reply with a frown, looking at the silver bullet of a car. "I'm not so sure I want to drive your beautiful new car. I'm a good driver but it's a lot of responsibility."

"The powers of manifestation lie within you. Use them wisely."

"You'll be fine. Just take her out for a few minutes every week. You can drive up to the grocery store."

I'm still shaking my head in disbelief as I make my way back to the limited house on 47th Drive.

"Permit yourself the freedom to ride the wave of Consciousness."

Something guides me to attend Sunday's service the next day. Dr. Charles' talk on "As Good As It Gets" totally inspires. Even though I slipped out from the audio station to put $50 from my dwindling secret stash into Wednesday's donations basket, I slip in another $100. I know it will return to James and me immensely. Holmes notes, "It is done unto us as we believe." When we express a greater livingness, Life is more completely expressing *Itself* through us. I'm acting more and more as though I'm rich and know it will happen very soon. Having a condo opens up greater possibilities. A Big Sky Resort representative soon happily changes my room reservation.

"The dream is changing and you must change along with it. Be ever mindful of your thoughts for they indeed do create your world. This world of illusion comes closer to the heaven on earth you all came here to make eons ago. It is driving forth with a mighty vengeance for those that do not listen to the words, the messages, of their soul. For those that listen and follow the guidance, all is, and will continue to be exceedingly well.

*"You all know the Oneness of your BEing and that is the only thing that will not change in your future times. Do not listen to, or pay mind to, the mass consciousness of separation for it serves only to pull those last remnants of Oneness down in those who wonder of the existence of one Light. **All** is One. **All** is a BEingness that never requires a thing but BEing. All will return to that place as foretold throughout the ages of your dream.*

"Speak not of those things you abhor but only of the love of your Oneness and know you are not alone in this journey of One. Many unseen forces carry the illusory weight of your thoughts, your woes, your dreams for the future that is to be in your earth world. Do not be dismayed by the things to come for all will settle down quickly once they finally occur.

"Falling in that space of Peace and Light is easier to relish when all the darkness transmutes to Light. That time of the Oneness you relish in your soul comes closer with each event of woe to those that relish the dark side of form. Stay clear of the chaos for it does lurk within unless you are vigilant to recognize

the truth of your being as spirit. The spirit that you are is purely whole, untainted by anything that may occur on your world. Remember this my beloved. The Spirit within you will never change. That is the message for today. All is exceedingly well as the age of Oneness returns in all aspects. Fear not!"

Chapter Eighteen

Escape

"Those in lower levels of existence now break forth to live in greater states of awareness on this day." SAM – Book of One :-) Volume 2

Heaven and Earth, an amazing book by James Van Praagh, offers exactly what I need. Blessing Mary's home seems the prudent thing to do since Seth made his transition there last year. Precise instructions will help to clear and bless Mary's beautiful home upon arrival tonight. Mental words of thanks for the book go to Leah. How wonderful to live in the positive, loving flow of synchronicity!

The car alarm pierces the air as I walk with suitcase in hand. Daniel now sets it off without the usual warning noise. Even in unseen form, he's so very thoughtful. I'm doing the right thing, he says. I thank him profusely.

Today's drive to Mary's positive and nurturing environment is surprisingly shorter than usual. She left earlier today but a five-page instruction sheet sits in the kitchen under a large blue envelope. Inside the envelope lies a thank you card and $1,000 check. An upside down butterfly with a smiley face, and caption that reads, "Above and Beyond, Thanks for going there," prompts tears of joy. Yes! We possess the power to manifest whatever desired. I am the living proof. Handwritten words, double-underlined in black ink, read:

"Sam, Just accept this and don't argue. It's $7 per cat per day, in the seventh month of 2007. Seth helped me with the figures :) I'd give you more if I could because they are high maintenance, but adorable beasts. Thank you for everything you've done for me past, present, and future. Love Mary."

Delicious and nutritious food fills the refrigerator. Mary shopped and baked dinners for me! Sethala, Amber, Myles, and Michgi clamor around as I continue to cry. Even their illusive cousin, Pumpkin, comes into the room. After wiping tears, I offer them shrimp. Myles, Sethala, and Amber eat most of it while Michgi prances away, still miffed because I took a lizard from her when she was out on the patio!

Minutes later, upon venturing out to retrieve *This Thing Called You*, the car doors magically click open. Again, I thank Daniel for letting me know he's around. Just as a favorite song, "Silent Lucidity," notes, "I'll help to see you through..." he is helping me.

The kids are happy to sit outside, near the hot tub on the screened in patio, while I "clean house." Beautiful piano music fills the air. An astounding vibration fills me while following the "preliminary groundwork" routine mentioned in Van Praagh's book. Peace abounds while centering before enveloping and energizing each room with Light. The Light of God flows forth into every space. It thoroughly permeates Mary's bedroom where Seth drew his last breath before I light the incense and candle.

Musky sage fills the air as the candle sits near the front door. I walk through each room with the lit sage stick knowing Light goes before me to clear the way. "Only protection, love, and peace may enter these doors and windows," I announce in every room, sweeping energy towards the candle. When done, I blow out the candle and place it outside in a garbage can near a tall, wooden fence. Five cats, happy to reenter the house, run to and fro searching for the unseen.

"The ethereal realms are helping humanity now back to wholeness. The treasures that you seek are within yourselves and others. There has never been a separation of One. Everything is within you. It has always been and always shall be. There is none other than the One within you. The Fall is clearly evident and will become more so with each passing day of your time. The awareness of One will become known in very evident ways. It is with the greatest of pleasure that we help now from those realms called the ethereal in your world.

"Know that all is going according to plan as we help from those realms so many treasure as the heaven they seek. Know that you are going forth through the eye of the needle now. This eye is not as gruesome as one would think. It is foretold

throughout the ages that in the blink of an eye you shall come Home, and it is so, for in the blink of an eye, all will change. Quickly, totally, wholly, all will change back to the Oneness of which it truly is.

*"There is nothing to fear in these times. Remember, the bodies you see are spirits in human form. There is nothing lost. There is nothing gained, for all are One. All have always been One. All shall always be One. There is none other than the One within which you live. It is the consciousness of **All**. The truth you seek is within yourselves. Seek nothing but this truth. Meditate on the One. Meditate on the Oneness of **All** and know the glory and the power is yours to keep forevermore.*

*"All is well in this land. That is all my child. Thank you for your cooperation. We are with you always. Do not fear. It is done as you believe. Know this and hold steadfast to the truth of the ages. **All** is One. **All** is here. **All** is Now."*

Sethala won't let me hold her. "Are you nuts?" her stare says when I toss the talking ball her way. What delight to enjoy myself after petting everyone else and brushing Myles and Amber. Immersing the body in Mary's large, salt water swimming pool is like floating in clean bath water, totally unlike other pools! Most of the cats follow me to Mary's guest room at bedtime. Amber soon gives new meaning to the term "Cat in a hat." I dub her "Cat in a sink" at three o'clock in the morning.

Words wake me at dawn.

"We are here to glorify the presence of God."

Older cats lie on either side of me as Sethala runs across polished wood floors, jumps on the bed, and leaps to the window ledge. Obviously accustomed to Sethala's antics, Amber and Myles open their eyes slowly but remain calm. Multi-colored Michgi prances into the room to stare after letting out a loud meow.

A new ritual begins. Mary spoils these cats like children so I do my best to cater to them. I pet those on the bed before rising and then all five follow me to the kitchen. Even Pumpkin comes out of auntie's room to eat. Their craving for wet food astounds me for dry food still sits in the bowl by the garage door.

Sethala greedily slurps liquid as other cats watch. When she sprints to the kitchen table, they begin to share the wet food. Smelly litter boxes greet me in the third bedroom.

A reassuring email goes to Mary after treatments, study, and chores. First, I ask the question. "Are you sure you want me to cash that huge check? I'm stunned, didn't expect anything, and it's such a huge amount…"

Each day brings new surprises. Gratitude overwhelms while sitting in Mary's beautiful new kitchen the next morning. Spirit guides and protects. Clearly, good thoughts express good things. What a grand demonstration to be here for an entire month! And leaving the house on 47th Drive happened at the time I heard it would.

Sethala jumps upon my shoulders and purrs as I open *This Thing Called You*. Holmes tells us, *It* will honor our desires. He offers words to help us fulfill them. What joy to loudly repeat expressions while gazing at the finely manicured lawn.

"I place my affairs in the hands of goodness, love and wisdom. I place them there with supreme confidence. I have a childlike faith and trust in good. I know there is nothing between me and that which is best. I am filled with enthusiastic hope."

For the next hour, I adamantly recite each set of carefully thought out words noted within the book. Mary's garden then beckons me to weed, even though the task is not on her list. Tall, green weeds pull away from strawberry plants as mind wanders to plant more seeds. Someday I'll grow my own vegetables…

An inner knowing assures, all is well, while picturing a better and better life. Rain pours from gray skies as thoughts of classes, teachers, and authors, such as Catherine Ponder, fill me with gratitude. New ideas surface and intuition leads me unerringly. Visions of a home much like Mary's, but smaller without leaks and pool, surface. The sanctuary will host a new kitchen and garage to park my car safely during storms. *(The vision manifests exactly one-year later.)*

Email includes a message from Mary who assures me the check is mine and less than I deserve for uprooting myself for a whole month. She obviously doesn't know I was at my wits end trying to figure out how to get away from the gloomy house on 47th Drive. It pleases me to know she's also in her Heaven, in cool, crisp country air. Mary also weeded a garden yesterday while Michigan horses snorted and munched grass in the field.

Life differs vastly in this paradise! The cats seem easy to care for compared to needy Princess and Rebecca's anorexic cat. They really like it on the back porch so I let them out in the morning and again at dusk. But Sethala is a real pot stirrer, now sleeping with me and hissing at the other cats when they hop on the bed. Sethala refuses to play with her toys and runs through the house knocking stuff over. She then promptly eats everyone's tartar control treats. Pumpkin retreats to the bedroom as Myles and Amber make themselves a new bed on the kitchen table. Michgi remains elusive. Sarah is having surgery on her knee tomorrow so I ignore them all to search for flowers online.

Pre-dawn words wake and remind me to say a prayer for Sarah.

"...God the living Spirit Almighty."

Today I place two plates of wet food down so all five cats eat together. Pesky Sethala commandeers her own plate while four older cats take turns eating from the other. The guest bed welcomes me again moments later. What joy to sleep in a bed instead of a futon with bars digging into my back!

A dream wakes me less than an hour later. I'm at an office job writing down "critical condition," but only because it's what someone said. It occurs to me to call the hospital to see how Sarah is but I'm busy. A man reads what I wrote and tells someone via telephone that Sarah is in critical condition.

"No!" I announce. "That is NOT what I said. I just wrote that down because you said it."

Days fill with activity knowing all is well. Sethala watches as I toss peanuts out onto the patio for a wild squirrel. Birds swoop from the sky to grab them before the squirrel comes. It's soon a blessing to dust lampshades and tables before sending Mary an email update. Myles rests on my lap later in the day as I reach for the telephone to collect messages from the answering machine on 47th Drive. A message from psychic/medium Sally Baldwin takes me by surprise. There's an opening in one of her beginning channeling classes. The money Mary gave me is more than enough incentive to secure a class spot.

A red carnation lies on the table near books upon rising in the morning. Sethala stares innocently before brushing against my leg. She's managed to extract a flower from the vase on the kitchen counter, without disrupting anything. The spoiled cat soon licks gravy but leaves wet food as I return to bed.

Another rainstorm blows the electricity out two hours later. The power stays off just long enough to verify that the entire block is out. It seems like a good time to meditate after finding a flashlight. James comes forth in the fourth level to say he misses and loves me.

"I will always love you," I calmly reply. "We must all love everyone as we love God, as One. It is time to clean the house of clutter, to either fix the roof and the rest of the house or let a hurricane take it away."

He does not understand and thinks I'm crazy as I continue to speak, saying quite a lot. When he again announces I'm crazy, I tell him to let me go. He seems concerned.

"What will you do alone?" He asks.

"I'll be fine. You are to give me half of your money. This will help you to rid yourself of any guilt and it will help me."

James shakes his head in disbelief, turns away, and leaves, still thinking I'm nuts.

Aunt Deborah appears. She tells me to be careful what I say to others. Others may not have fulfilled their earthly goal and as Rebecca told me, may not be ready to open up to what I say. I hug and thank her.

Rain stops later in the afternoon. Something prompts me outside to see an almost overflowing pool. Intuition leads me into the water, with the whirlpool jets on, to think about draining it. Several minutes later, the water recedes enough to let the skimmer do its job. And I get an excellent back massage too! Later, it occurs to me that water symbolizes a complete immersion in Spirit. Holmes notes, to be immersed in water symbolizes our recognition that pure Spirit surrounds us.

"Everything is magnetic here on earth. Our bodies are magnetic, as well as the earth on which we exist. Changing the magnetics of earth is as easy as changing your thoughts to be more conducive to the magnetics of One.

"The earth is changing quickly and all play a role in this great change. When you demonstrate in peace, you are in essence, paving the way to greater BEing for all humanity, even if you are unaware of the great power you hold. As we strive to the Oneness that already is, knowing that your role is just as important as another's helps to spur you forward.

*"It makes no difference how you support this movement. The supporting is in the reaction. The senses reaction must always be of solidarity, of Oneness, of Peace and Love to move more quickly towards the Light of **All That Is**. As the magnetics of earth change, you support that change with this type of reaction.*

*"Be it known, on all levels, the change has already taken place. It is only a matter of non-existent time as to how it shall appear in your physical reality. Some are already seeing and living in the New World of **All That Is** while others may choose to lapse back into the fray of drama and altered perception. Choose your path, and your role, if there is to be one, carefully. And know, no matter what you do the feat is accomplished already."*

Business website visitors' report the site is down. Since September, the amount of information transferred quadrupled to almost three gigabytes. Good continues to come as the server gladly doubles bandwidth without cost. But the old mission no longer fits my energy.

A greater unfoldment of Reality, through my own consciousness, enabled me to develop a more perfect body. Now I must spread the word that it can be done. There's no need to live in limitation. We need only contemplate love, wholeness, abundance, and happiness to draw it forth. Awakening others to the process of evolution is my soul's task. Ideas for a new website, more attuned to my current awareness, surface.

Trusting in the Law of Good makes life so much easier and I'm grateful for everything! The world changes more to my liking every day, while thinking positive thoughts and meditating. We are pure energy, white, golden, magenta, green, blue orbs – sparks of Light! Of this, I am certain. It is our true form and yet, as Holmes notes, the Almighty creates endlessly for the necessity of God's manifesting Himself in time and space. We are in One Spirit expressing Itself in worlds without end. One Life that forever ascends into greater expression.

Tonight I'm very grateful for recycled reading materials. "I Know Who I Am," an affirmation from *Creative Thought*, published in August 2002, sits on my lap fighting with Myles for space. Yes, God lives in me and is truly all there is. My word does have power and I truly know who I am as God works through me!

Consciousness resides in everything. Jagged flashes of white light continue to appear both day and night. In time, I'll know these blessings are many beings of Light, of various intensities, gracing me with their presence. These darting sparks of love and consciousness, weaving in and out of reality, always bless with love. The constant reminders note, I'm not alone on this journey of awareness, for others exist within that invisible tapestry in which we live.

In 2011, my companions appear more often to let me know I'm not alone. After seeing more of the beloved tiny, white lights, words fill my brain: "Know that the process is almost complete. Fear not as we move forward."

Universal Wisdom always encircles and protects, surrounding us in loving and eternal Light. Life experiences symbolize the soul's resistance to inner light. We are to be open to receive, to see the Light coming through the veil of illusion. Emmanuel tells us, "There is not one person who enters this physical world who is not, at the core, a Being of Light." I am heartened to know "One of the fondest dreams that we in the spirit hold is of that moment when all souls, all hearts, all hands, will reach out to touch each other. There will be no detachment then, only a glorious Light."

We are here to metamorphose residual areas of darkness determined to sabotage that Light, to become enlightened. Enlightenment, Emmanuel notes, is purely 'is-ness', without physicality, personality, or the consciousness of self. It merely acts as the boundless perceiver of infinite Light. <u>When souls completely recognize and experience their own Divinity, they do not have to return to earth.</u>

Daniel greets me during meditation. He takes me to a messenger. Thoughts flow easily. James will declare his independence Wednesday on the Fourth of July. He will put money into the account I have with Samuel.

Daniel returns when the messenger leaves. He says to be happy, and patient, when I express gratitude. "Offer a physical sign," I ask, "that we are really communicating."

Before six o'clock in the morning, I dream of being with someone in a car. We drive past two men standing on the sidewalk talking. One of them looks like Daniel when he was seventeen years old. I say so and start to cry, noting how much I miss him. I then realize it was Daniel and tell myself to be happy because I'm lucky to have seen him. The tears stop.

Rain continues to pummel earth. Sethala runs through the house, jumps on the bed, and springs to the windowsill, waking me. My right eye is wet with tears. Realizing I must always feel joy upon seeing Daniel, I rise to repeat the World Healing Meditation before feeding Mary's babies.

Homesick Mary telephones shortly before lunch to talk to Sethala. We discuss many things before she finally agrees to go for a walk. Joy abounds knowing she's thrilled that I enjoy her lovely home in western Broward County.

Sally Baldwin welcomes seven new students later, in eastern Broward, near the Center. We sit grouped together at a small round table as she explains the Michael teachings. She tells me a life lived in the 15th century most closely relates to this life. Sally then channels the entity Michael to relate key things while concentrating on my soul. I'm aware of my Oneness with God, she says, and came to help humanity.

Time passes quickly and the class ends promptly at 4:00 PM. My next class starts in three hours so I decide to kill time nearby. A nearly empty lot soon welcomes me at the shopping mall where the Post Office sits. Business mail holds a small check from Barnes and Noble Booksellers, an unexpected source. Since Amazon.com recently affiliated with them, I now get money when someone buys something through their website.

Plenty of time remains to check mail and messages at the house on 47th Drive. Going back to the dimly lit house, with its leaking roof and ceiling holes, fills me with disappointment. It looks very limited as compared to Mary's well-kept home. Declarations for an unexpected source, or condition, to keep me away from limitation continue.

A refund check from the Italy trip for $500 sits upon the counter. Joy fills me upon acknowledging that money indeed continues to come easily and effortlessly. More and more money is coming to me NOW! There's a spring to my step as I walk to the car. Leah offered to pay for dinner before our Tuesday night class so I'm meeting her blocks away at the Chinese restaurant.

"Times are changing in this land of non-space and linear reality. Today is a day of great peace and joy as we look down, so to speak, and see humanity rising to the outcome of present, Now, the only moment. The days of old and limitation are behind you now as we quickly morph to the wholeness of All That Is.

"All of the earth moves forward in its efforts to be at one with All That Is once again. The times spent in mourning are gone, for naught is the release of non-entities to the wholeness of space. The fruits of their labors shall never ripen.

"Herein lies the issue of late, you must accept the gifts bestowed upon you. For now, all is coming to fruition very quickly. The life you once led is over but a new glorious life begins as you wish. The times of old limitations may no longer hold you back for all is gained in realizing they never existed at all. All things come from the single mind within the host of which the illusory soul exists. All things sprout from the vast consciousness of mass issues now in play unless you pay heed to the Voice within.

"The worlds are separating more fully on this day. On one side, lie the efforts of cabal masters, in their own mind, who seek to further manipulate the people as they seek answers to the dilemmas made by giving their power to others. On the other side of life, the real masters of fate reside in peace and wholeness, in love and joy, in abundance and prosperity, leading the masses back to the wholeness of which they are.

"There has never, nor shall there ever, be a time as great in this history of your earth. Leading the masses is non-exclusionary for those that wish to follow the path of their single soul. And yet, the soul, in itself is an illusion as well. Be aware

*that other levels are closer to you now. All have the opportunity to reach these states of awareness merely by listening to the Voice within. **All** is One. **All** is here. **All** is Now, within and surrounding, and never without. That is the message for this auspicious day when all activate more closely to their true state of BEing."*

Paying for classes, instead of volunteering, feels great. Handouts help to understand key concepts. The image of my little self changes upon knowing, all beliefs are real to the believer. Faith is my constant companion as trust lies in the Divine Presence of which I am a part.

Yet, disappointment continues. Sometimes teachers seem to go against SOM teaching by talking of illness and dislike of certain creatures. Other disappointed students speak up making me happy to know I'm not the only one that recognizes disparity. One does a treatment to help us recognize our Oneness. I join in the fun mentioning successful treatments to fill the house on 47th Drive with "all the love and good there is" to get rid of pesky raccoons. Yes, feeling the love of God, the love we all must genuinely feel and give to one another to get back Home as One, places an invisible protective field around surroundings and us.

Thoughts truly make a difference as to what we experience. Self-imposed roadblocks vanished so nothing hinders Spirit from manifesting Itself through me. New harmonic conditions continue to spring forth for the past no longer holds me back. Self-talk lessens and I guard thought, now relating only to joyful wholeness and prosperity. I remain grateful for the Law of Good that continues to fill days making life a grand adventure. Divine Intelligence operates through me, more each day, as I enter fully into conscious union with Spirit. The Presence of God continues to guide toward the life I'm to live. It's a life of love, of peace, of harmony, of prosperity, joy, and wholeness. I am so very grateful!

Each day the fog lifts more. Holmes notes mental statements help to clear mental images by rearranging the way we think. This makes more sense while pondering this past year. Daniel had me change the radio station to see how easy it is to change a pattern of thought. He also had me wear a bandana while snorkeling to rid myself of its old memories.

During meditation the following day, I ask to know something for my highest good, for the highest good of all. A message makes me smile.

"You are the light of God with whom I am well pleased. Always speak the Truth for you speak the words of God."

My reliable car soon disappoints. The air conditioning stops when I back out of the drive. It's really hot outside so I drive Rex to the local store before joining the family's Fourth of July celebration. Giggles fill the car because Rex is such a powerful machine and so much fun to drive. It takes great willpower to keep under the speed limit.

James and Terry soon listen while we rave about our recent cruise. At one point, Ruth asks what she owes me for ordering Sarah's flowers for the family.

"Give James $20 because I put it on my charge card and my bill is now paid automatically through our joint checking account," I reply.

"I like getting money," James says with a smirk.

"I'll give you," Terry pipes up jovially, "a bottle of Myer's rum for my share."

"Suits me just fine," James replies quickly.

Rain falls from cloud-filled skies as the others leave us alone on the back porch. James and I begin to talk much more than in the past two years. I am "free and clear" he tells me as if just stating a fact. He'll continue to take care of me financially. I'm grateful, I say, thanking him with a smile. He promptly announces, I have an odd way of saying "thank you." When he mentions taking out a second mortgage on the house to pay for roof repairs, I remind him it's unnecessary. Months from now the house will be paid for and he has the money from his parents. His parent's estate, he announces before rising to get another beer, is still in probate.

"All is well my friend as we reconnect to re-member."

It's our third Fourth of July without Daniel so everyone does what they can to get through the day. Some choose to drink, not affecting anyone else. Rebecca and Terry's decision to attend another karaoke night at the bar, before nightfall, disappoints. It means Samuel and his friend, excited about seeing the usual family fireworks, will not see them. Rebecca soon asks me to take the boys home. Denying her for the first time seems especially difficult. But I quickly decline noting my current home is in the opposite direction. Quickly returning to Mary's lovely home seems oh, so, very right.

All five cats greet me at the door. It's nearly their dinnertime so I feed them before wandering out to the back yard feeling alone. My red, cell phone begins to ring. Ester now wonders how I am. We have not spoken since I returned from Michigan several months ago. It seems like a small miracle for her to telephone at such an opportune time. We begin to discuss my current situation with James.

"You are making the right choice to get away as much as you can," she announces confidently. "That house on 47th Drive is very depressing."

Her remark comforts me a great deal. I feel much better when we're done talking thirty-minutes later.

Fireworks light the sky as I move into the outside Jacuzzi. Mary's back porch hot tub offers another view of the neighborhood fireworks finale. Thoughts of Samuel arise but I remind myself that all is well. He picked his mom before birth just like the rest of us. The experience she offers helps to mature his soul and for that, and these lovely fireworks, I am grateful.

Early morning brings another email from Mary. Still missing her babies, especially Sethala, she encourages me to invite family for a barbeque. She's ecstatic to hear I use the pool and hot tub because she has not for a long time. She's also thrilled to know I'm driving Rex. An image of Mary and her sister-in-law, in a canoe spreading ashes and wild flowers, enters my brain.

Myles lies on top of the den desk purring away as I type. Jealous Sethala leaves the room. During the past few days, she has been up to no good. Sethala continues to spread dead flowers from the garbage around the house. We now call her the little brat. She knocked over the pretty, little, green, flower vase and broke it. It was an amazing feat because the vase sat in the corner of the kitchen cabinet about a foot away from the edge.

It's rained every day for a week. The pool continues to look like it will overflow even though I turn on the Jacuzzi to drain excess water. Thankfully, Ruth telephones to accept my hot tub offer. Her job will be done soon and then she'll pick up Samuel because Rebecca is going out of town. They're both anxious to try the hot tub and she can show me how to drain the pool, if needed.

Samuel and Ruth are very impressed with Mary's house and all her beautiful things. We have a wonderful two hours together in the Jacuzzi and hot tub. Intermittent rain brought us cooler weather that makes being in the hot tub a joy. Samuel lovingly holds the cats, except Sethala, who does not like him holding her. Ruth takes a short nap while Samuel and I play a bit of Catnopoly. I promise to take him to the show on Saturday, after Rev. Heidi's wedding.

We talk of Beth when Ruth wakes for they finally connected. Beth has been ill for a long time but doesn't want to be in the hospital. It's no news to me for whispers of her ill health continue. Ruth nods when I quickly announce I'm open for another trip. Before they leave, she shows me how to drain the pool. Samuel helps carry wood from Mary's van into the garage.

How grateful I am to be here and for constant blessings! God has a Divine Plan in which I am an instrumental part. I need only to stay in the flow. Leah shares dinner and a movie on Friday night. It feels good to make and eat a meal in such a lovely kitchen. As family, Leah is impressed. She knows it takes lots of time to keep this home nice.

"The sheeple will lead the people out of the mass consciousness of duality."

Rev. Heidi's Saturday wedding is at the Center. Dr. Bump conducts a beautiful ceremony in the sanctuary before we celebrate in the large classroom. How wonderful to be able to share this way! It's a sure bet that the newlyweds will appreciate the card and $100 bill I gladly offer. After eating and communing with like minds, I leave to pick up Samuel.

Samuel loves "Spiderman 3" but it's too full of fighting for me. Fireworks pepper the sky as we walk out of the small town's movie theatre. We're thrilled to stand and watch as sparks flow. Friendly people nearby announce that the city rescheduled their Fourth of July fireworks due to rain. A sense of wonder permeates my brain, for choosing this particular theatre was a last minute decision. Yes! I remain in the flow of Good!

Days and nights run together. Having a beautiful home to care for becomes routine. Each day I sit and study in the new kitchen, admiring beautiful wood cabinets and marble counters. In the evening, the cats sit watching me from the screened-in porch as I wade in the Jacuzzi or eat at the outside patio table. Sethala enjoys sunshine in the window as we sit in Mary's computer room. When it's time for Tuesday's classes, I must force myself to leave.

Sally's class is rather interesting. We move pendulums to and fro to answer questions. It seems like a lot more work than what I'm already doing, which is just listening as messages come. Sally also teaches us how to do other peoples overleaf charts to make understanding them easier. Dr. Bump's SOM 203 class then serves as a good reminder. What we identify with is what we become. We must identify with the wholeness of Spirit if we are to reflect that wholeness. Each time I lost my way it was because I wanted others to approve of me, even though, for the most part, I relied on myself from an early age. Negative feelings are now few and far between, while concentrating on loving everyone as a unique part of the Divine Presence within.

Thoughts fill my brain during the long drive back to Mary's house. I've learned so much over these past fifty-six years. It's time to compile journals into books.

Each morning I loudly recite affirmations and treatments within the pages of *This Thing Called You*. Sethala purrs softly, as she lies behind my head, on top of the kitchen chair. Finally, it feels good to be responsible for my life. Blaming others, circumstances, or situations is pointless for Spirit always guides. Faith replaces doubt, entertained through years of misfortune, limitation, and dis-ease, for the God Mind within sees only perfection. I identify with only love, wholeness, prosperity, harmony, peace, and joy. My body is truly a temple of the living Spirit, always in harmony with a pattern of perfection.

Daniel interrupts thoughts by telling me to telephone James. He gives me words to say as we talk for an hour. Change, I note to James, is all we can count on. Our separation is no ones fault. We both blossomed and grew but are no longer compatible. That is the bottom line. When the call ends, I again recognize that James is one with God, one with me, for we are One Perfect Presence in unique form. I am now in Heaven.

Later in the evening, I realize Daniel guided me to do just what Catherine Ponder says to do in her book *The Prosperity Secrets of the Ages*. He fed me words to make our situation "right" so we could both let go and let things work out in God's own way. I set James and myself free.

Wednesday evening's service carries on without me. Homework from Sally's class helps to pass time as I ask questions while the pendulum swings. Answers come quickly, sometimes even before questions are voiced. My soul chose to reevaluate in this and the life that correlates most closely to this one. I chose to be a persistent idealist in this life. When Mary returns, I'll go to another positive and nurturing environment.

Moving on, I begin to ask questions about Ruth's best friend Beth. My relationship with her is cording. She will go in the hospital very soon. Beth is an astute old soul. Her role is that of a scholar with a Sage Essence Twin. Her soul chose the goal of acceptance and discrimination. Beth's attitude is cynic with a chief feature of self-deprecation and martyrdom. No wonder she has dealt with a severe weight issue throughout life!

The little brat knocks family pictures off a side table as I carry Myles to the kitchen. She rubs against me when I notice the glass inside them is cracked. Both house telephones ring loudly.

Ruth's voice carries through the beige, den receiver as I hold it up to my ear. She's now determined to visit her ill friend but worried about cost. Beth welcomes us because the friend who cares for her has to leave for a few days. We can sleep in her room, or on the sofa, and we can use Beth's car. I agree to accompany Ruth for a two-week visit, starting the day after leaving Mary's lovely home. Money is no problem, I announce.

Ruth agrees to book flights and follow me now to the car repair shop so I can get the air conditioning in my car fixed.

More questions concerning Beth arise while waiting for Ruth. The pendulum moves counterclockwise to answer each question affirmatively. Beth will soon go into the hospital. She'll be very ill and still unable to care for herself when we arrive but better by the time we leave. It would be astute to book a hotel and car. There are lessons for all three of us to learn. Incense in a water bottle cap burns through to mar the desk as I make reservations.

Ruth is adamant about staying at Beth's house when I announce the reservations. She questions the wisdom of a rental car too. We drive back to Mary's home, after leaving my car at the repair shop, while words fail to describe unerring intuition.

Zyprella, one of my spirit guides, speaks later when I'm on the cusp of sleep.

"You're doing the right thing," she announces. "Ask for the highest good and do what you feel is right."

Words ring through my brain as Myles purrs softly. Minutes later, I wake teary eyed to recall being with Daniel. We were upstairs in a big house. James was yelling while I listened. He left in a huff after saying something about going fishing on Sunday. Someone stood nearby as I admitted to missing Daniel. Dirty laundry (I did mine yesterday), including some of Rebecca's clothes, littered the floor as I searched for Daniel in the house. He appeared, wearing a pointed collar that looked brown or dirty on the white points. Daniel announced that people always have to rag onto other people when they feel out of balance. It's their way of getting back into balance.

"It was always about you for me Daniel," I replied. "But now I realize it was not and it is really all about God."

It's heartening to know that despite appearances, as I truly recognize Oneness with the Presence of God, the ability to remain in a natural state of joy and peace permeates awareness.

Rex, the silver bullet, roars as I drive towards the local grocer. He's so powerful that I continually have to monitor speed. Despite my desire to leave limitation behind, I cannot envision owning a flashy car like Rex. I'm much more comfortable in my ten-year-old, white sedan that hesitates a bit when I step on the gas. Rebecca drives me to pick up my beloved car hours later.

Odd dreams wake me. The first takes place in a familiar, seemingly empty, large school dreamt of before. Each room is dark so I turn lights on. Two women talking suddenly appear in the distance. They don't see me for I sneak back to turn off the lights so they won't. I wake after hearing words and spelling out the word happiness. In another dream, someone talks about what's "in the present" but recalled words confuse me.

"In the past remain sage presents."

Mary still believes I've "disrupted my life to deal with felines." Caring for five cats while enjoying this house still seems like a dream come true as I rise to clean litter boxes. Sethala bolts through the kitchen before running from room to room messing stuff up and trying to get the other cats to play with her. All is well, after bringing her in from the patio where she's trying to climb the potted tree to get a lizard. She scowls from her perch on the windowsill as Myles tries to climb into my lap.

In two weeks, Ruth and I leave to see Beth. I continue to treat for another positive and nurturing place to visit. Minutes later, Beth assures me via telephone that we can stay at her house and use her car. She sounds apprehensive upon hearing that I worked as a Dietetic Technician. Beth announces, rather dramatically, that she weighs over 600 pounds. The 600 figure, related to her in a dream, surfaces as she notes concern over it being an issue.

"We are spirits in bodies," I reply, "and take on different forms in different lives. Your size is not an issue for me."

Telling her, at last, how sorry I am for saying or doing anything to hurt her fills me with joy. Although I cannot recall ever mentioning her weight or harming her, I relate how very much both Daniel and I appreciated her help over the years. Daniel whispers, asking me to thank her for helping when the car broke down on his way home from Arizona.

I continue to bless all living things with Light, with Love, with Good, with Peace, and now with Joy! God continues to place me where I am to be and always fills my mind with what I'm to say and do. I'm grateful for all blessings.

James doesn't answer his cell phone when I call to divulge plans. He knows I think our marriage is over. It's up to him to either do something about it or continue to be apathetic until I take stronger measures to separate us. Change is the one thing we can count on. I now leave a friendly message inviting him to join us for a family barbeque.

Words from *Emmanuel's Book* console. Souls come together to grow and when they do, gifts are given, lessons are learned, and then it may be time to move on. When a relationship no longer serves, Emmanuel explains, when we "have scraped the bottom of the barrel to find the meaning, to find the lessons, to find the essence" and are unsuccessful; there's nothing else to do.

James and I clearly choose to experience life differently. And yet, our relationship served a great purpose, for we incorporated many fragments, of ourselves, cast away over the years. Letting him go to grow as a soul, while I finish my soul's work, is the best gift I can offer. Daniel helps me to let him go with love and many blessings.

"Listen to me now for the ways of Truth are upon you and you know that to be true. Give up the old reality of this disdainful world. Let go of the old energies and take on the new ones in joy, in truth, and in the love that you came here to spread."

Elizabeth Taylor comes to mind. How many people judged her wrongly because of multiple divorces? This will be my third and last divorce but now I finally know marriage is a soul agreement that sometimes means we agreed to move on at a future point in time. It's a joyous blessing to move to surroundings more compatible with my lives work.

Sally's class is again very interesting. The seven of us sit spellbound as she explains the process of channeling. When class ends, I return to the other side of town to feed cats. Driving back to the east side to attend the evening SOM 203 class, after eating a light dinner, seems longer than usual.

Dr. Bump reminds us faith gives spiritual treatments power. Knowing we are one with Source is the key to successful prayer. I truly believe I AM. The creative Principle of Life resides in my heart's core. Although sometimes it seems hard to ignore external conditions, life is what I choose it to be. Physical conditions continue to change and flow toward the life within my mind. It's a life of peace, harmony, abundance, love, and joy. Intuition increasingly flows from the depths of my being always filling me with a sense of joyful gratitude.

How wonderful to have classes that help review my ever-changing perceptions of life! The same Divine Presence animates all of humanity, binding all together in one complete whole. There is nothing outside *It*. Holmes is right, we must see God in everyone for we are connected. It pleases me beyond comprehension to change the traits my family bore throughout many lifetimes. By changing what I believe, I can be a better role model to lead everyone through the bonds of limitation.

What joy to live life the way I prefer! Sethala, Amber, and Myles sleep with me in our unburdened Kingdom of Heaven. Michgi comes sometimes but Pumpkin does not. Everyone continues to sleep as I repeat morning treatments. Leah and I discuss Sally's channeling class later at a new Oriental restaurant. We excitedly interrupt one another wanting to share experiences. She blesses me by buying my meal.

A dream of Ruth and I playing slots and winning wakes me the next morning. When it was Ruth's turn, the machine malfunctioned and just started to add up winnings. The owner didn't want us to have the money but Ruth ended up with thousands of dollars and a fur coat. I won over $14K.

In another dream, I move from bedroom to kitchen. A toy train set sits in the living room. I think Daniel set it up. In the kitchen, a friend's young daughter cares for a baby that was close to me. The baby still crawls and looks about a year old. It's one I lost, one that transitioned and is now reborn. A moving picture, to remind me of when the girl met the baby, in a past life, fills my brain. The girl looks about age eight to eleven and very happy. She's letting me know the baby is cared for and okay.

The scene changes and now I'm back in the bedroom telling someone about the dream. Paint peels from bedroom walls in the corner and ceiling. I wake crying with tears in both eyes.

Dueling telephone bells fill the air as I rise. Beth, Ruth now reports, is in an Intensive Care Unit in Dallas, Texas. She deals with serious complications from Guillian Barre. Beth lost weight but remains over 600 pounds and is still paralyzed below the waist. The only thing I'm sure of is my next destination after Dallas. Rebecca asked me to stay with Princess and Kitty while she takes Samuel to Orlando.

Internet welcomes me after finishing the morning ritual and chores. Mary reports exhaustion in a new email. She's now looking forward to coming home for some relaxation and asks if I can pick her up at the airport in five days. Time passed too quickly but I know this crucial stage in my development is almost over. I've successfully left the house on 47th Drive.

I wake to fill another day with joy and learning. Sally answers a question in the afternoon before I leave her class for the last time. I tell her about regressing myself back to Cleopatra's lifetime and ask if I indeed was the Queen of the Nile. She reports that I was with Cleopatra and am probably in her "soul group." Something prompts me to buy Sally's book, *Dying to Live Again,* to read on the plane to Dallas. She then says James is here to help raise humanities vibration but she doesn't know how. Unlike Daniel, he's not accustomed to being human. Stunned and amazed, I walk quickly to my car to share dinner with Ruth before *This Thing Called You.*

"You Are Love and You Live in Love" covers chapters thirteen and fourteen of this week's text. Being continuously guided, into an ever-widening experience of living, as the Divine freely circulates, fills my heart with gratitude. As I allow Divine Power to work in, and through me, spiritual laws accomplish all statements. My good comes through Divine Timing. The Law of Good always draws into my experience everything that makes life worthwhile. My conscious mind knows whatever I ought to know at the perfect time. Inspiration guides every thought and action with peaceful conviction. I so treasure this class and life!

Another dream wakes me in the morning. All I recall is that June is an optimal time for something. *(James and I will divorce the following June right before the stock market crash.)*

Wednesday evening's group welcomes me. Someone else now takes care of the audio and passes the donations basket.

What joy to happily relish in the glow of like-minds! It's my pleasure to tuck a $100 bill in an envelope before passing the basket across the row.

Blue skies fill the air while driving to the airport. Mary walks through sliding glass doors and saunters toward the car as soon as I park. We quickly load luggage and pull away before the traffic cop comes.

Mary, happy to be home, quickly begins to unpack as I place my luggage in the car. She gives me two gifts. A beautiful pair of moccasins and a very large, insulated coffee cup from Upper Michigan. The perfect card, about my day of birth, sits within colored tissue paper. My personality, it notes, contains a fascinating duality because I seek outer power and inner spiritual growth and fulfillment. I must trust inner guidance and intuition. I thank her profusely before driving to Rebecca's home. Tears pool as I pull away from the immaculate home that offered sanctuary for a month.

*"The days of yore are behind you now as all move further into **All That Is**, a place many on this realm of existence forgot long ago, when changing into ever not knowing forms of greedful and deceitful ways. It is time dear ones to return to the place of Oneness. This is a place where all exist, in all aspects, and you have only forgotten through eons of mining your own energy field. Do not be dismayed by the process that is occurring now, for it is a necessary one, to have all beings return to the wholeness of **All That Is**.*

"All things come in time, in your existence, and yet, all things are already whole and complete in the only realm that exists everywhere though everything. Your game of separation is coming to an end as all move to help those lost in the maze of earth life. In truth, there is no separation of existence for all remain pure, perfect consciousness, whole in, and of, Itself.

*"The game on earth depends on thoughts of separation, set into motion by fragments of consciousness that slipped further into the black abyss to play a new game. For a while, the game was exciting as all continued to recognize their wholeness and unity with **All That Is**. But then certain fragments decided to pull further, and further, away from the Source of **All That Is**. This*

game resulted in the total loss of conscious memory on the part of these fragments.

"Forgive the bluntness, but my dear one, you are a part of this lost fragment now finding its way Home, back to **All That Is** in every aspect of BEing. Know that all happening on earth achieves a greater purpose than what is seen or conveyed. All things have a truer purpose and meaning, which leads all fragments back to the knowledge of the wholeness that you hold inside.

"Knowing you are a part of **All That Is** will sustain you in the days ahead. Be not fearful as things seem to progress toward the dark side of earth life. All concludes quickly for those ready to acknowledge their unique Oneness within the purity and wholeness of **All That Is**.

"Dear ones, you are returning to the Oneness you seemed to leave so long ago. But know, the leaving is only in your conscious awareness. Each fragment remains very much a part of **All That Is** ready to achieve greatness as it returns the gifts of earth life to the Whole. Be it said that all things are known and only waiting to be recognized by the masses. The times for recognition of many things lie shortly on the horizon. Know this, and be ye not afraid."

Chapter Nineteen

Fake it Till You Make it

"Knowing the world you see changes quickly before your very eyes will get you through the days ahead as you move forward to new spaces, new belongings, new truths of One, solely truths of One." SAM – Book of One :-) Volume 1

Red American Tourister luggage, purchased at 50% off, loads easily before Rebecca drives Ruth and me to the airport. A representative for the rental car agency in Dallas soon talks me into "bumping up." This car, he says with a wink, is cheaper in the long run. We roar down the highway toward a Residence Inn, using GPS navigation, in a fast, red, sports car. The hotel is thirty-five minutes away from Beth's house but only fifteen minutes from the hospital. How wonderful to be in the flow, for I had no idea where it was when booked!

Rebecca's work perks make it possible for us to have a third-floor space for $45 a day. Our very large room holds a king-size bed, and floor to ceiling window, overlooking a beautiful park. A coffeemaker, mini refrigerator, and microwave offer greater possibilities. Ruth scans the skies as I unpack canned soup, cheese, popcorn, and other foods brought from home.

Morning comes way too soon. Ruth sits smoking outside in the courtyard when I venture downstairs for breakfast. She's beginning to understand why I booked a hotel and car. Beth's friend, Mary Elizabeth, has the house keys and she remains with Beth at the hospital. We speculate on which route to take over cappuccino.

Valet parkers greet us at the hospital entrance shortly before 10:00 AM. Beth, still paralyzed from the waist down, is out of intensive care and in a private room. But doctors still don't know if she's going to live. She detests her newly prescribed low fat, diabetic diet. Karmic connections are hard to miss as Mary

Elizabeth offers her food from a nearby McDonald's when we enter the large room.

Beth soon sends Mary Elizabeth out of the room on an errand and then tells us her friend has a brain tumor and forgets things very easily. Nevertheless, she's an excellent caregiver and remains at the hospital because there's no one to ferry her back and forth. We sit throughout the day as Mary Elizabeth cares for Beth's every need. Nurses enter periodically to check vitals and change soiled linens.

Ten hours after we arrive, I agree to ferry Mary Elizabeth back to Beth's house so she can shower, sleep in a bed, and gather things for tomorrow. Ruth stays with Beth. Spirit guides me effortlessly to the house and quickly back to the hotel. It's easy to see how having a new sports car could get me into loads of trouble.

*"**All That Is** responds in kind to offers of challenging circumstances that afford those behind the veil to cooperate on a more decisive level. Knowing all levels are unreal in other worlds affords the opportunity to reach beyond the world of limitation. Going forward in your world towards the richness of **All That Is** affords one with the wholeness of BEing.*

"This BEing is the state in which we exist for there is no other state that we know of. Our world is one of wholeness, and ever-abiding truth, and that wholeness is something you, as a chosen separate being, will not experience in your lifetime. The extent of this wholeness is unreachable as long as you exist in a body of form. Our wholeness derives from a state of formless Reality of which we subsist in the Light of One.

*"The readiness of many to enter our world once again arrives with a fervor. Those wishing to return to the Oneness of **All That Is** increase in number as your earth days lag on in the fervor of unsecurity. Knowing that all are one shall sustain you in the days ahead.*

"Know that as a soul of many, you were chosen to walk the path you now find yourself upon. This choice was made with the cooperation of many other souls who stepped aside so you could enter the realm of separation. The separation is only in your mind of the little 'one' for it does not exist in other realms

or avenues of BEing. There are many reasons you were chosen among many others to experience this separation. The reasons include the richness of past expressions in other forms and human experiences throughout the ages of time and space.

"The realities of your world now change much more quickly than ever before as all avenues of security fall away to reveal there is no limitless existence here upon your earth. Earth times are changing along with many other states of BEing as all move, what you refer to as 'forward,' to the state you already exist in. Knowing that all levels, states, and forms are unreal will help you to succumb to the original state of your BEing.

"You are, in essence, a formless, unlimited creator with the ability and expertise to create much more beyond your wildest dreams. This state is returning quickly to those that recognize the glimmers of Home. All exist as one pure state of Consciousness. All exist as limitless BEing. All is here upon your earth to return to the true state of BEing.

"The game of illusion is over for many now but the game shall continue for those not ready to stop the experiment of experiencing a richness not expressed. Returning to your true state becomes easier as the days go on and the veil of illusion continues to thin. Be ever present in your little mind of one as the days and nights appear to pass quickly. Seek nothing outside your Self of one, for that One shall sustain you. It is the only true source of Truth in your current state."

There's barely enough time in the morning for breakfast before I drive to Beth's house to ferry Mary Elizabeth. She forgets who I am and makes me wait outside while telephoning Beth to confirm my identity and purpose.

Beth's house is small, bleak with denser energy, and very dark inside. It has a very tiny kitchen but a lovely, large back yard so I roam around outside as Mary Elizabeth gets ready. The air outside feels vibrant compared to house energies of sickness, anger, and limitation. An older car with a broken windshield sits in the drive. Mary Elizabeth reports the battery is dead when she finally comes out of the house. Beth has not driven the car for many months. Extreme peace prevails while thanking Spirit for unerring and continuous guidance.

Time fills with tedious tasks as we take turns spending the night with Beth. Her hospital room holds a strong sense of negative energy so I bless Beth and any souls that might have passed away there. I bless them all with everything they need to move into the wonderful, glorious, loving Light. I also bless all souls about to pass with Good, Love, Light, Peace and Joy. Blessings continue, whenever intuition tells me they're needed, while reading Sally Baldwin's book, *Dying to Live Again*.

Beth asks about Sally's book during my second, and last hospital night shift, after Ruth and Mary Elizabeth leave.

"It's not about what I thought it would be," I note with great enthusiasm. "Sally says we are all here to learn and teach lessons. In the book, she describes how we all live 'good guy' and 'bad guy' lives on earth. She channeled souls such as Hitler, Anne Frank, and my favorite Cleopatra. Sally reports Hitler played the 'bad guy' role to bring about a higher level of spiritual awareness on earth. It all makes sense especially when I read what Sally wrote about Cleopatra.

"The book is mainly about how souls come to earth to grow spiritually. One of the greatest reasons we come is to have the wonderful experience of going back into the Light. This is the only time souls feel the intensity of such a loving, joyous, and peaceful experience. And helping someone into the Light astutely, by offering them Love, Peace and Joy is the best thing we can do as humans."

In May 2011, the opportunity to experience this feeling comes while holding Momma's hand. Overwhelming joy brings tears while watching with closed eyes as she walks to the Otherside. Family members stare in disbelief as I try, through joyful tears, to describe her happiness.

As Beth begins to ask spiritual questions, intuition notes, that's why I'm here. We're still not sure if Beth is going to live so I'm grateful to widen her horizons now with honest answers. She listens intently and soon falls fast asleep.

"Throw away all concepts of time and space. Delete all old programs of earth life. A new life begins, a life living the glory of One, the Light-filled life much different than in the past.

222

The dark days of those lives are behind you now. Live in the glory of One for that is what you are.

"Know that all things come in time. The perfection of One resides within you and all others. Treat this as a concept that knows all things, believes all things, wanders not about, but knows all is held within. Treat this as the core of your being flows out to encompass the world with Light and Love."

Ruth sleeps on Beth's couch after cleaning and washing clothes the following night. Class goes on without me but I read the assigned chapters before bedtime at the hotel. Spirit goes before me always smoothing the way to Heaven on earth. The Law of Good brings everything desirable into my experience and fills all time with *Its* presence.

Sleep is sporadic. A bedside pad keeps track of actual slumber while trying to determine why tiredness plagues me during the day. After waking seven times, I sleep seven hours. It doesn't seem enough while rising to ferry Ruth back to the hospital.

Energies within earth's magnetic field continue to change rapidly. As these energies help us to evolve, many experience erratic sleeping patterns, especially during times of planetary alignments, solar flares, and high geomagnetic activity. We are transmuting soul experience to reclaim wholeness. Periods of waking and deep sleep help us to rest from integrating, acclimating, and building up for the next phase of our evolution. Waking between two and four o'clock in the morning is usual for there's a lot going on in the dream state. Some people sleep for about ninety minutes (leaving the body for downloads, purging, cleansing, receiving, teaching, etc.); wake with thirst (sometimes extreme); sip water; eliminate water (sometimes much more than consumed) and then repeat the process.

Abrupt changes in breathing can alert you to possibilities during sleep cycles. For instance, you may be on the cusp of sleep and aware that you're breathing differently (in through the nose and out through the mouth). This can occur as you channel or receive downloads. A sharp intake of breath may suddenly wake you to recall a past or future life, precognitive dream, or life possibility.

Plan activities to nourish your soul, such as journaling, reading inspirational materials, or watching uplifting videos to occur during the wee hours of the night when unable to sleep. And before falling asleep, ask to wake up in a realm of greater probabilities for humanity.

*Dealing with higher vibrational energies is easier when you listen to your body and care for its needs. Drink plenty of good quality water, rest as needed, take Epsom salt baths and support the body in other ways, such as eating more wholesome foods (organic fresh fruit and vegetables). Walk outside in nature and get massages. Avoid unnatural substances and alcohol, which affects mental and body processes. Protect your energy field by remaining aware of surroundings and circumstances. Concentrate only on what you wish to manifest. Think only positive thoughts to stay in tune with **All That Is**. After all, the information you seek is within and keeping the host pure helps to retrieve the information consistently needed to evolve effortlessly.*

Our trip remains much more than expected. Beth is now ready to die. For several days, she refuses the BiPap machine that helps her breathe during sleep. Doctors order IVIG, at 100K per treatment, every three weeks. Rehabilitation facilities refuse her for the treatment cost means they lose money. After an exhaustive search, a nursing home finally agrees to care for Beth.

Beth is not pleased with the nursing home, especially when the dietitian orders another diabetic meal plan. Mary Elizabeth saves the day by purchasing ice cream from the snack machine. She can't stay the night now because officials discourage night visitors. Nightly restaurant meals, where I gladly pick up the tab, become routine. We eat several meals at an all-you-can-eat seafood restaurant glad for the break from fast food.

Mary Elizabeth's memory continues to fade as Beth's status improves. Beth soon mentions Sally's book, which peaks Mary Elizabeth's interest on our last day together. After answering questions, I gift Beth with the book, my CD player, and several meditation CDs.

Charging the hotel and car to my trusty Visa card is easy. Rebecca's job makes it all the sweeter. Our two-week stay costs a total of $632, $100 less than the car rental. The exhausting trip would have been unbearable if we had not had the car and hotel room. Ruth offers to pay her share before we disembark from the plane to pile into Rebecca's little, blue car.

My "suspect tooth" begins to hurt upon entering Rebecca's house. She and Samuel are happy to see me but I'm beginning to wish for my own quiet space. They leave two days later to spend the weekend at Orlando theme parks. Princess sleeps besides me, with her irritable bowel, while Kitty roams the house. As my upper, left bicuspid aches, the thought of becoming accustomed to sharing a bed with animals adds more distress.

Morning email holds a message from Mary about classes taught by psychic/medium Michelle Whitedove starting in mid-September. Daily rituals continue as I bless souls and people, their untrue forms. Today's Course lesson sits nearby as another ambulance roars by on the bridge. "There is no cruelty in God and none in me." Ambulance sounds or auto accidents always prompt loving, compassionate blessings, cleansings, and healings to those who suffer.

A new dentist welcomes me on Monday. She offers a referral to the dental specialist in Pembroke Pines on a financial interest disclosure form. It's my lucky day. The specialist sees me two hours later, which is about the time it takes to get there. Fortunately, dental insurance covers the greater portion of an expensive root canal but I need to return to the general dentist for a crown.

My monthly habit of withdrawing money from the joint checking account for sundries and incidentals continues. I'm adamant about using the rest of Daddy's lawsuit money to keep me out of limitation by traveling as guided. Although James sometimes complains about expenses such as dental procedures and car repairs, he does not refuse to pay them.

Rebecca sits on the back porch smoking later as I wake. *"This is the best time that you can be someone to give to all,"* fills my brain. Wet laundry soon propels me out the door. The dryer is still broken so I load freshly washed clothes into my car to dry at the house on 47th Drive. I load clothes quickly and use my key to open the den door.

It's almost one o'clock in the afternoon and stifling inside the dark, dreary house. Nausea crops up out of nowhere as I make my way to the only room filled with lovingly energy and Light. The thermometer gauge in the hall records the temperature at 83 degrees. That is almost ten degrees higher than Rebecca's house, several degrees more than I can comfortably endure. Sweat pours out of every pore in my body as I carry more belongings out to the car. I'm running out of space. The trunk is already full so I place things in my back seat before pulling away to run errands.

Amos feverishly pedals his bicycle in the 90-degree heat on Andrews Avenue as I drive by. He's heading in the direction of his pusher and does not notice anything else. My brother's face strains as he vigorously moves the bike pedals to and fro. I have the utmost admiration for him because his soul chose this most difficult life to help further soul development. His usual job site sits three blocks away. He's wearing work clothes so I assume he's on a quick break.

I'm grateful for the lessons Amos continues to teach us and in awe of his persistence to lead such a difficult life. It didn't take long to spend the 12K he got from Dad's settlement. Now he's again without a car and place of his own.

This past month has been full of surprises and changes. I've left James. Rebecca and Samuel have welcomed me for eleven days. In a week, I'll leave for a glorious spiritual retreat with Dr. Charles, Leah, and a few other like-minded people. We'll spend eleven wonderful days in Utah, Wyoming, and Colorado. Hopefully, another offer to stay somewhere where it is positive and nurturing will then manifest.

My dream journal documents visits from Daniel, Zephaniah, and Martha who told me I'd leave the house on 47th Drive in June, which is when I did. I've been back several times to dry clothes and get more things. Any day now, I'll be able to get my own place. It will be a positive and nurturing environment where I'm much more able to give more to humanity and myself.

Odd things occur after Friday morning rituals and study. I unload six, gallon jugs of bottled water from my car, two by two, to place on the porch floor. Then I put recyclables in the appropriate box, throw something in the outside garbage, and return to the porch. It's almost time to start packing again so I go out the back porch door to retrieve an empty suitcase from the car.

A very strange feeling overwhelms as I approach garbage cans sitting nine feet from the door. Earth seems to open up below me. Dizzy and feeling as if falling into a rather deep hole, I grab a large, garbage can to steady myself. The feeling immediately dissipates.

"What the hell was that?" I loudly remark shaken to the core.

Still shaking, I move to the porch and sit before heading into the house. There really is no adequate way to explain the feeling of falling. It felt as if I was in a free fall, for maybe five to fifteen seconds. It was very scary and definitely not anything that I care to experience again. Why did this happen? There is nothing in my current state of awareness to explain this event. *(This is something that can occur as part of the Ascension Process.)*

Mary is at a loss for words when we meet to share a restaurant meal. She stares blindly as I relate my fleeting (multidimensional) journey into the bottomless pit. It's more than she can comprehend. Her days are very much different from mine, filled with mindless "grunt work" as she paints the main bathroom and readies her house for sale. I'm just happy to buy her lunch and relate the tale.

My friend and I are in "reassessment mode," shedding old and lower vibrating relationships, material possessions, and out of date self-perceptions. Mary is much more interested in what Lara Owen has to say in her latest planetary update. Although Lara notes August and September "give us a great period to move forward with career goals," Mary wants to start life anew in a different location. Her mind is set on finding a new partner. September, when both Venus and Pluto turn direct moving romance forward, shines like a beacon in the darkness.

Lara warns us to drive defensively in early September because "hard aspects to Mars and Uranus can coincide with accidents." I'm heartened to know that "deep, radical, revolutionary change, rebirth and transformation" are mine, as Pluto moves backwards before resuming forward motion.

Words wake me the next morning.

"God exists in only one state of unconditional love, truth, perfection. Our supposed separation will never be recognized by the One."

Emmanuel tells us "As you surrender to the ultimate reality that all life is love, manifesting in love and therefore One, you will find that on that line of communication all consciousness knows itself." Earth will eventually dissolve and return to Light. Fleeting glimpses of this Light lead me to believe we are fragments of *It*, tiny sparks of Light like the one Daniel showed me shortly after he made his transition.

We are Beings of Light in physical form, pushing boundaries as Emmanuel says, "without loss of self, extending into the Greater Self through that process. There are other places of greater, or lesser, awareness. Various stages afford us the opportunity to learn in many other places that are more blissful and more filled with love."

Senseless words fill my brain while repeating the World Healing Meditation. Many other communications occur as my state of awareness changes. I recall being with James when wakeful consciousness finally returns. We were stooping on one leg on opposite sides of a tub of water. If we could not maintain the pose, we got into the large, oblong pool of water. James got into the pool but I maintained the pose with some difficulty.

"It's the principle of the thing," I announced.

James then got out of the water and walked out the door that was beyond it to the left. Someone told me I'm to let James grow, stay married but not live with him and try to help him see he's limiting himself. (My being gone will help him to start being more responsible for what happens in his life. I realize the same is true for me.) I'm to listen only to the Light of God for it is the only truth. And I'm to forget the physical.

Change fills the air as I enter the empty dentist office. The smiling receptionist informs me my favorite dentist sold the business and retired right after my last visit. A health issue made it difficult to hold up his arms but he kept the condition a secret.

The dental assistant leads me into another room. A friendly, tall man, with red hair, enters minutes later and introduces himself as the new owner. He recently moved to

Florida from New York, after retiring due to a disability. Since he no longer considers his disability an issue, he decided to buy the business. We're soon engrossed in somewhat the same discussion as I had with the previous owner. "Sometimes things are not meant to be," I announce sensing he won't be there long. (Indeed, he sells the business before I return six months later for a dental cleaning.)

The dentist offers Lidocaine before crown preparation and filling. Minutes later, the print on the book I'm reading doubles. I sit reclined in the dental chair for more than two hours. Vision remains blurry for about thirty minutes after the procedures. Another $515 charge goes onto the Visa card but it's a blessing for tomorrow starts my whirlwind trip with Dr. Charles' entourage.

The journey to change my current reality accelerates. Since I created it unconsciously, it's time to replace it with conscious decisions. I choose to create something much more to my liking. Seventeen days with Rebecca and Samuel offered a safe respite from the house on 47th Drive but somehow wrought more issues of limitation. Although they did not seem mine, the act of living with others in limitation brought them forth. I look forward to eleven days of extravagance without household duties. What joy to not clean up after an old dog, with irritable bowel, and an anorexic cat!

Chapter Twenty

On the Road Again

"Yes, we can change the way we think about the world and ourselves!" SAM – Bits of Wisdom

A small, SOM group sits at the Fort Lauderdale airport in late August. Charles reviews our grand adventure through Utah, Idaho, Wyoming and finally Big Sky, Montana. Today's trek completes upon resting in Jackson Hole, Wyoming. Baby blue skies greet us at Salt Lake City, Utah as we hurriedly make our way to the car rental agency. They're out of vans but offer two small recreational vehicles. We separate into groups of four.

How wonderful it is to be on a new adventure, with people of like-mind, heading towards the unknown! Mountains stand beyond vast expanses of brown dirt as we motor down newly tarred roads. New construction soon closes the roadway for what seems like hours at a time. I sit happily in the back seat of the second car, videoing landscape, while listening to Karen Drucker sing. It's a pleasure to share CD's and snacks brought from home.

Boredom sets in. Hoots of laughter soon fill the air as the others witness our "Chinese Fire Drill." We simultaneously leave the car, run around it, and swiftly jump back in, right before the flagman motions traffic forward.

Greener vistas of grass, scattered among patches of dirt and brown undergrowth soothe the mind. Widely spaced rustic buildings sit between mountains, crops, or mounds of dry, brown dirt. Snake River offers an opportunity to stretch our legs and bask in afternoon sun. Streams of green mist flow, amid multi-colored spirit orbs, after sensing spirit friends. I sigh, missing the Oneness of Home.

Purple, magenta, blue, and orange, triangular-shaped spirit orbs again grace us while strolling past Sotheby's Realty many minutes later. The quaint, quiet town of Jackson Hole,

Wyoming looks well kept. We check into the Day's Inn, freshen up, and head back out the door. Sun breaks through clouds when we enter the Jackson Hole Playhouse to see "Seven Brides for Seven Brothers." Charles graciously paid in advance to see the rowdy musical.

"It's my treat," he announces with a smile, refusing to accept repayment for the $50 dinner show tickets.

My camcorder captures the Western-style theme as we make our way to a large, round table. Stools made of horse saddles line the bar. Walls feature horns and animal heads. Female servers wear old-fashioned, Western costumes with long flowing skirts. We sit, filled with wonder, as they sing a song about tumbleweeds. Their voices are surprisingly beautiful and I feel valued beyond measure to be treated to such a grand experience. Giggles erupt when servers take turns singing to the men. Greg blushes when a short blonde gropes his shoulder and kneels while singing "Crazy" by Patsy Cline.

Satisfied stomachs accompany us as we head toward the stage in another room. With very limited live show experience, front row seats make the event even more special. The musical is thoroughly enjoyable filled with talented actors who also act as dinner servers.

Dawn breaks on Wednesday to reveal another gorgeously beautiful day with clear, blue skies and perfect temperatures. I lie in bed while others hike. Leah and I soon tour the town after a quick breakfast. Photos capture a covered wagon sitting on the roof of the Jackson Hole Historical Society & Museum. Jackson Hole is such a lovely town that I hate to leave it, even knowing something grander lies ahead.

Mountains stand in the distance, beyond the busy highway, at Grand Teton National Park. Diamond-shaped orbs grace us with their presence. Charles soon explains the origin of Big Sky Retreat as we stand in the lodge's parking lot.

"We had the retreat here until around ten years ago," he announces with great authority. "This is one of the highest energy places in the world and I want you all to experience it. You can really feel the presence of the angelic and animal kingdoms here."

Grand Teton National Park lies within the Greater Yellowstone Ecosystem. Mountains stand majestically beyond pools of blue water where abundant wildlife roam within its more than 300,000 acres. The reception area is stunningly beautiful with very high ceilings, and floor to ceiling windows, overlooking expansive grounds.

Several of us walk up the tar-paved "Lunch Tree Hill Loop Trail." I'm still adjusting to higher altitudes, stopping often on a dirt-lined path to take panoramic video segments, while catching my breath. A bronze plaque sits amid stone in honor of Mr. John D. Rockefeller Jr. It announces his dedication and generous contribution to protect the scenery of the Tetons and Jackson Hole.

We leave the park refreshed and ready to continue our journey. Karen Drucker's "I Start My Day" resonates throughout the car while motoring down a pine tree-lined road to today's focus. Our trip to Yellowstone National Park is devoid of signs until nearing the entrance. Since we have a senior in each car, it costs a mere ten bucks to enter (instead of $25).

Yellowstone National Park covers lots of ground and the first sign pointing to "Old Faithful" sits many, many, miles later (actually only twenty-two). A parking lot sits before us after driving more miles than I think it should take. We soon walk a gravel path leading over a small wooden bridge but decide to hike further. Our group will watch the splendor of "Old Faithful" from the Observation Point on top of the hill. It's another half-mile walk and 200 foot rise, all uphill.

Some of us are not accustomed to such vigorous exercise. Unseen friends continue to assist me. Purple, diamond-shaped orbs soar above as I follow others up the gravel path. The altitude is becoming a detriment. Women are soon far behind the men. A chipmunk comes out from under a fallen tree to greet us when we stop to rest along the way.

Multicolored, diamond shaped orbs greet us at the top of the hill. A green stream of mist pours down from the sun. It's hard to believe we're sitting in the mouth of a volcano. A horde of people wait below, grouped together in a semicircle on the pavement, as a multicolored square orb covers the bottom of my camcorder display. What joy to capture the rainbow orb!

A ground squirrel speaks as Old Faithful erupts at 5:38 PM. It sits a mere foot away as I video the awesome scene below. White fumes of steam rise from Old Faithful, while the squirrel continues to chatter, as if in conversation. I thank it for coming and note it's on my treasured, preferred creature list.

"Light extends in every measure throughout the field of One."

The downhill walk is much easier than our laborious climb. A rocky, steep incline causes gratitude for hiking shoes. Spirit energy surrounds me while resting in the middle of the path.

Nearby shops offer opportunities to continue an attitude of sharing, spurred by our mentor's generous gesture. These gifts do not even come close to the cost of a musical but we happily share within comfort zones. Leah and I soon drag suitcases down steep stairs leading to our room at the lodge. It's been another long day, full of adventure, and we're happy to rest.

Dawn breaks as we rise for breakfast. Surrounding energy soon invigorates as diamond-shaped, purple orbs dance nearby. A lone, black squirrel captures attention as he runs haphazardly across dry land, amid clumps of bushes and rocks.

The Cascades sits before us later after trekking across a wooden bridge. Water moving down the mountain sounds somewhat like rush hour traffic but is much, more, peaceful, and moving. Basking in the serene atmosphere feels good while standing upon the bridge amid scents of pine. As in Greece, the camcorder pauses several times, in tune with Spirit energy.

Dangerous ground sits ahead when we again leave the car to hike. An emerald green lake, a majestic mix of blue and green colored water, rimmed with brown and rust colored earth, soon sits before us. Pools of bubbling mud create a chorus of song, amid rising steam from many geysers. A wooden path, elevated in some areas, allows panoramic views. My nose quickly adjusts to the sulfur-filled air while videoing the majestic scene.

We walk along a wooden boardwalk remarking on varied hues of brown, gold, blue, green, and red. A quickly flowing stream of water runs past the geyser nearby. The stream of water is cool but surrounding pools and geysers are steaming hot. I stand amazed watching water shoot three to eight feet into the air. Hot steam rises from the majestic emerald pool. Varieties of life live within the runoff channels from geysers and hot springs. It astounds me to know that even the hottest thermal features contain tiny microbes.

Surrounding land reveals a mix of sparse, scattered live trees, fallen dead trees, parched earth, stone, and tall weeds. A small caterpillar sits among the weeds. I lag behind to video a vigorously, bubbling, mud pot with steam rising from its core. It sounds like a steam engine. The "Fountain Geyser" sends a steady stream of water, fifteen feet into the air, offering a lovely picture against blue skies, scattered with puffy, white clouds.

Our group moves with anticipation as Charles leads toward a dip in the energizing river. The water, he says, offers healing Spirit energy. Parked among other cars, we hold up towels while changing into swimsuits. A nearby gravel and dirt-filled path leads to the water below. Leah stays on top of the hill with the video camera as I very, slowly, move into clear water. Although it's very cold, I'm not going to miss this opportunity to feel the rivers magical energy. Several people swim happily nearby. Clearly, the only way to warm up is to move further in and start swimming.

"It's warmer out of the wind when you're up to your neck in the water," one of the men calls out as I cringe.

We leave twenty minutes later happy to have had the experience but I wonder if anyone besides Charles truly felt the magical energy.

"Steamboat Geyser" entertains us after another long drive. It's touted as the world's tallest geyser with infrequent, major eruptions of 300-400 feet. We watch several minor eruptions of two to twenty feet before moving on.

One Bison comes into view as we slowly motor along the roadway so we pull over to join other curious motorists. Bisons are such magnificent creatures with huge heads and bodies to match. My camcorder captures its beauty. I thank it while radiating waves of love from my heart.

Our next adventure unfolds at the "Stage Coach Inn" in Montana. It's about a mile outside of Wyoming very near the West Entrance to Yellowstone. We're blessed to have reservations, made by Charles months ago. Streams of green fill the video screen, amid diamond-shaped orbs of purple, as we park. Streets seem twice as wide as the ones back home. Colorful, intricately painted Bison statues sit along sidewalks.

Knotty pine walls grace the inside of the inn. A stuffed Moose head sits on one, to the left of a grand, carpeted staircase that breaks into two opposing paths midway. Pictures of Bears, Bisons and Moose adorn our large room.

Bullwinkle's, down the street, offers a place to dine with Ann's friend the park ranger. She points out special sites to see the next day. "How wonderful to gift myself with this experience," I think, while viewing menu choices. Yesterday, I ate delicious buffalo so today I choose to taste Elk. As buffalo, it's leaner than, but not quite as tasty as antibiotic and hormone-filled beef. Go figure!

Bikers check in across the street while a storm gathers in the distance. The vastness of sky enthralls me while watching the sunset. Views of the sky are more expansive in the West where skyscrapers are unheard of and traffic is sparse. Everyone here is friendly too.

Chilly temperatures face us in the morning. Long sleeve tops (never worn back home), a shirt, and jacket keep me warm. Black cotton gloves cover hands and a black stocking hat sits securely in my jacket pocket as we walk to the cars.

Gray skies surround us on the way back to Yellowstone National Park but I'm happy to breathe crisp, clean air. The distance between tourist sites seems way too long but a deer grazing along the roadside breaks the monotony. We thank it before moving on. The majesty of the park soon overwhelms.

"This is what it's all about," I announce, while filming a herd of elk grazing beyond the quickly moving river. "One."

A squirrel graces me with its presence before we move slowly along a steep incline to view the scene below. Snake River sits below as a soft rain begins to fall. We're on our way to Lookout Point minutes later. It's another steep climb up a paved, zigzag path. Charles reminds us once again to keep drinking water. I'm already accustomed to chugging water throughout the day but now add more to my excessive fluid intake to avoid altitude sickness.

The scent of pine trees accompanies a brisk hike up the path. Majestic scenes below make our tiring climb worthwhile. My camcorder takes in the waterfall, miles away, as the others ask another traveler how to get closer. Someone points and announces, "We're planning on either walking up there, or, see those people down there near the waterfall? Maybe we'll go there. Are you up for that walk?"

"Ah, I don't know," I answer honestly, wondering if I should have traveled in the other car with those who are not quite so adventurous.

"Going down to the falls," another traveler reports with a wide smile, "is no problem. It's walking back up that is."

"Are you guys in shape?" the muscular woman asks.

I push myself to recognize wholeness despite being out of breath.

"There are rest stops along the way," the friendly woman announces. "You just take one step at a time to get there."

We decide to take her advice and pile into the car for a much closer view of the great waterfall and lower falls. Two by two, we walk down the paved switchback path, glad to be warming bodies through exercise. I'm soon tired and out of breath while talking about trying to slide down on my bottom.

"How much further is it?" I ask a tall, thin man walking slowly up the path.

"It's a short distance away," he announces with a big grin.

"Thank you. That's all I need to know."

"Look how close you are and you're asking! You're almost there."

Adrenaline boosts me further along the path while shouting "Woo, hoo."

Water flows briskly below offering a chorus of Nature's song as it turns into a cascade of energy moving down the mountain. The beauty of an immense waterfall is hard to miss while catching my breath.

Later, a black bird, hopping along the ground, entertains us when we stop for a bathroom break in West Yellowstone. It seems to follow my commands to "Hop like a bunny." We soon move beyond the Upper Falls of the Yellowstone River to the South Rim Trail, overlooking the Grand Canyon of Yellowstone.

Bison rest in dry, yellow grass along the roadside. I stand, with camcorder in hand, singing along to the Karen Drucker CD that plays in the car, while thanking bison and birds for being there. "I am safe. I am loved for who I am. There is nothing I need to do...." What a marvelous feeling to be so active amid this majesty and to finally hike without concern!

Minutes later, we gather at the edge of a precipice. A stunning view of quickly moving water from a waterfall, running amid rocks and fallen tree trunks, sits several hundred feet below a sheer drop. Clumps of yellow flowers and tall, thin, pine trees climb the mountain beyond, beckoning me to drop on down. Although I sense unseen energy, I don't yet know that it's possible to merge with *It* consciously.

Skies clear later in the afternoon. Group members pose in front of a huge rock, shaped like a rocket, as I laugh uncontrollably. What appears to be dried salt, cascading downhill with steam rising on both sides, sits along the boardwalk. After a quick lunch, and delicious ice cream, we're back in the car again.

Scenery is amazingly beautiful and I'm so happy to enjoy it while someone else drives. What a refreshing break in habit to let go of my need to control by driving! A large elk with huge horns captures our attention as he eyes five surrounding female elks. He turns to look at us as a female enters the stream below. We thank it for being there before moving on. Purple, blue, and magenta colored diamond-shaped orbs, amid green mist, grace me with their presence while everyone entertains with stories.

The next morning, Leah and I stroll down sidewalks in crisp air to shop. Finely manicured plots of green grass sit throughout the small town. A small, fly-fishing shop catches my eye just as I recall promising to buy materials for James. Leah waits patiently outside while I fondle sheaths of bear and moose hair before making a purchase.

Karen Drucker's "We Live On Borrowed Time," fills the car later as we drive. "We're gonna be just fine, whatever life may bring, we'll face it all together, and we'll never be alone," I sing, as we pass a small town with wooden cabins fenced off from the road. "Clearly, the river runs through *It*," I think later as we stand on a bridge watching the Gallatin River below. This is the river Robert Redford highlighted in his movie.

Now tired of driving, we're thankful to check into the Big Sky Resort in Big Sky, Montana, on September first. The area surrounding multiple cabins, lodges, and buildings is amazingly beautiful. Leah and I share a one-bedroom suite with two bathrooms, two closets, a full size kitchen, living room with pullout bed, and small pantry. I've brought food from home and we plan to shop at a nearby grocer tomorrow. After traveling extensively since leaving Florida, we're both happy to remain for five glorious days.

This huge resort property holds many more opportunities for shopping than I'm accustomed to seeing in a hotel. Most shops sell high-priced apparel, jewelry, and souvenirs. We pass them all before joining a reception on the other side of the lobby. The Firehole Lounge is alive with people from all over the country who feel blessed to attend the 32nd Annual 2007 Big Sky Retreat, "A Call to Love."

My nametag features a purple, sparkly, smiley face in the left-hand corner to note it's my first year attending. Other attendees feature colors noting many consecutive years of attendance. Volunteer Coordinator, Lisa de Snoo, is happy to schedule me in the Jefferson Room at the table offering retreat tape and CD orders. I'm thrilled for the opportunity to volunteer.

A delightful opportunity to network during our buffet dinner in the Huntley Dining Room refreshes before the evening program begins. This session sets the tone for the next four days. Piano music fills the room as Daniel Nahmod sings softly. What a blessing to relish in the energy of Spirit! Joe Dickey, a member of the Crew Cuts, (who sang Sh-Boom and Earth Angel) is an awesome entertainer. He makes us laugh before offering a cautionary note about high altitude considerations. We're at 7,500 feet, a huge difference for those of us from country where land is flat. Before Joe introduces Mary Manin Morrissey, he notes the signs of altitude sickness (headaches, dizziness, nausea, and light-headedness – somewhat like that of ascension) and reminds us to follow advice in the written program. Several people are happy to learn of an oxygen bar beyond the conference center.

Mary starts by noting our best teachers sit among us. Ears perk up when she speaks of luminous light beings. An awesome consciousness of Love overflows when we break to share with new "family groups." I partner with a couple and older man whose family does not understand him. Before long, it's clear, each of us chose unique and unusual paths.

Daniel's music prompts us to serenade one another. Love radiates as we sing, "You are a miracle, God's child. You have perfect love in your heart." How wonderful to share this feeling with others! We then imbue touchstones with a word signifying the energy desired for our life. I chose Divine Love. I'm still beaming later during the volunteer meeting.

At bedtime, Leah and I decide to take turns staying in the bedroom. It's been a long time since we shared a bed. Gratitude abounds upon opening balcony doors to bask in cool night air. This is the perfect set-up. My CD player plays treatments and songs without interruption as Leah watches TV in the bedroom.

Clearly, making necessary adjustments for the trip is in order as Leah rises unexpectedly earlier than I to make coffee. Big Sky meetings are so unlike ones attended in the past. Sunday morning's greeters wait at the entrance offering hugs as we pass through the door. Loving warmth fills the air to permeate my soul in a new way.

Charles does the invocation and announcements after a sing-along. I'm surprised to learn that he co-founded an hiv support group in California. After a fun "Answer This!," he announces the title of Mary's new talk, "At the Leading Edge of Becoming."

It's time to press through boundaries to grow. Mary, an eloquent speaker, reminds us we are spirits, in human form, having an earth experience. We're vibrational beings, broadcasting thoughts constantly to make our world. Daniel sings "Get ready my soul" as I consider my current path.

It's truly a joy to meet Mary's request to stand for the next song. Music fills the large room as we shake hands, rub shoulders, and hug. My dream of teaching everyone the magnificence of our spiritual being gets closer every day. I choose to believe that all is well. This week I'll continue my experiment of living an unlimited life. Instead of wondering where money will come from, I'll affirm that God is truly my source. The life I imagine is already mine. It's the life I choose to live, despite physical circumstances.

"We are the resurrection race."

The two o'clock workshop "Enhancing the Power of the Intuition," is much more than envisioned. When Christine Page, M.D., a mystical physician, mentions a "sick care system" she catches my full attention. Yes, we are kindred souls, believing system changes help humanity to recognize their wholeness. When she mentions pinecones and their effect on the pineal gland, I know fate brought me here to listen and learn.

Christine knows we're the ones who serve others with rarely a thought to enjoy ourselves. Let go, she announces, and learn how to be served. Discussion on family soul contracts prompts us to recognize those who hold the darkness so we may know the light. Amos, among many others who helped me take back my power, comes to mind. I silently thank them all.

Intuition, Christine reports, moves one into greater service. It's non-emotional and non-judgmental, connects us with a multi-dimensional reality, and helps us to detach from "power games."

Over the next hour, we participate in several exercises. I pair with a younger woman in her twenties who sees golden light radiating from my head and shoulders. "There's a man," she soon announces, "that seems to be holding you back from doing some kind of work." We hug tightly when our time is complete.

Minutes later, Christine speaks of the vesica pices. It's the first I've heard of this eye-shaped symbol, which is the doorway to the consciousness of Oneness (Christ Consciousness). Many ancient sites note symbols of the vesica pices, an entry into a different world. The Flower of Life is a popular symbol. As souls, we create a reality to know ourselves fully. And as humans we're born through the shape of a vesica pices, whether through the vulva or a C-section cut.

Our group quickly moves about the room as I contemplate the ocean of possibilities. We then fill the chalice in our hearts with intensified joy. Immense wholeness permeates me upon recalling the birth of my children, a joyous moment unmatched by other memories. Energy fields merge while oooh's and ahhh's fill the air creating a sacred space of harmonious Joy.

Yes! I AM a light in this world. Christine is right. I cannot hide anymore if I'm truly to be in service. "Learn to celebrate yourself," our muse says, before noting that the gut (solar plexus) connects to self-worth. In a dysfunctional family, it may cause mixed messages. We need to feel safe where we live and some of us may not have had that growing up. Her words resonate with me deeply. Yes, intimacy is a challenge to those who scan the room before reading people and making judgments. It's based on fear and not love.

Totally amazed, I listen closely as she notes associations with health issues. People with bad knees usually have issues with humility and pride. Indigestion is due to trying to do too much and fibroids signal that you don't know how to look after yourself. "Wow, if only I'd heard this talk sooner," I think, as she continues to offer healthy tips.

Of course, things change as we progress in the morphing process and some of these issues, such as indigestion, can stem from increased geomagnetic activity.

Christine's tips continue. Still the mind; be present; write a question with the right hand and answer it with the left (non-dominant) one. The list goes on. Our last exercise takes us to a dream house where we envision the future. I clearly see myself serving humanity, helping everyone to recognize his or her spiritual magnificence. All needs are met even though I'm no longer with James.

After purchasing Christine's latest book *Spiritual Alchemy*, I schedule a massage at the Solace Spa before returning to the room where Leah relaxes in front of the TV. There's no desire to visit the Healing Room or join the guided meditation.

Essence of pine permeates the air as Leah and I move out the resort's back door. We stroll through a building with several shops, including a tiny grocer and restaurant, before watching the sunset over beautiful mountains during dinner.

The evening program starts with a sing along at 8:15 PM. Rev. Howard Caesar, a very vibrant man, speaks after the invocation and announcements. I'm thrilled to note the title of his talk, "Love is ALWAYS the Answer."

Rev. Caesar's love-filled energy flows forth. When he announces, "Love is the power, energy, and frequency that we are all called to step into and live from," I know he's the real deal. Personal accounts, particularly one about his daughter's journey after a car accident, make it perfectly clear; we all hold the power of Source. A wonderful feeling of Oneness engulfs me as Howard clarifies three kinds of love. Tears fill eyes when he discusses the love of a small boy for his dying infant sister. Daniel's essence engulfs me in a sea of Divine Love as the words, "You are my sunshine, my only sunshine," gush forth from Howard's mouth.

Clearly, Divine Guidance led me here to connect more strongly with the power of One. It's time to branch out, to be an agent of Love, helping humanity during these times of changing consciousness. Minutes later, I'm whooping it up with several others during the Gathering in the dining room with Rev. Penny Hayhurst.

What joy to live an unlimited life! The king-sized bed is a treat to rest in while listening to my CD before sleep. A cool breeze blows in through the open window while I lie there thanking God for the experience.

A strong sense of connection consumes me Monday morning while Dr. Christine Page speaks of "The Miraculous Heart." Reconnect with your heart, Christine says, to sense perfect wholeness. The heart's energy is fifty times more powerful than the energy of the brain. Its radiance projects up to fifteen feet from the body. The first three feet are the most powerful energy.

Read *The Emerald Tablet*, Christine instructs, before telling us about Thoth, the inventor of medicine, math, science, and language. Thoth is the great reckoner that measures our heart to see how pure of spirit we've been in this life. He asks, "How true to your heart have you lived your life?" Did we keep our promise to the Creator and live life fully to our spiritual blueprint? The heart knows our truth. Since many people do not follow that truth, we're in dire need of role models.

What a blessing to know that we're attracted to certain people because they resonate with us! We are going through a great transformation and can only achieve Oneness through duality. We live in a hologram, always attracting parts of us to act as mirrors. Anyone who annoys us, who seems to create a strong emotional reaction, is a part of us waiting to be accepted. They teach us to nurture ourselves and grow. It's only when we know and love the unlovable parts of ourselves that we know sublime love. Pictures of crop circles soon surprise me. How utterly fascinating to know that they help us to wake up and remember who we are!

We are each a piece of the puzzle, evoking the essence of the Holy Spirit, to manifest Heaven on earth, Rev. Charles explains during the afternoon workshop. "The Call to Forgive … for Love" refreshes as he very calmly explains how to awaken to our spiritual magnificence, by forgiving. Heaven is real Oneness, encompassing all things. Each piece of the puzzle affects the whole picture so we must be responsible and realize that there's a choice. We are, Charles notes, responsible for what others do and think and must determine what it is in ourselves that created the action or thought. One must look upon others as they would the face of Christ. Seeing the face of Christ is the great symbol of forgiveness.

We change the world by changing ourselves. We are accountable for everything and must take complete charge since we're responsible for creating our life. It's up to us to heal anything we don't like because these things are just projections of ourselves. We must accept all parts of ourselves. Self-healing helps to heal the planet for this vibrational energy touches, and affects, everyone. Charles tells us about an ancient Hawaiian healing practice called Ho'oponopono (to rectify an error) that involves healing the part of ourselves that created certain parts. I write down the important words he notes. I'm sorry. Forgive me. Thank you. I love you.

The Originating Substance is within prodding us down the path to enlightenment as Charles speaks of cellular memory. "We ultimately will change forms," he calmly notes. Charles remembers a life outside of Earth, on a distant galaxy. He admits to having an incurable case of "Childitis." The crowd breaks into laughter when he announces it's contagious.

Several experiences unfold after minutes of deep breathing. The perfect wooden bridge beckons me forward. A sense of urgency to stay on earth arises even as I long for Home. Yes! I have traveled a great distance to be here, and there's still work to do, but I honor all that has got me to where I am today. I choose Heaven while standing upon the bridge gazing at the magnificence before me. The music of Jody Ebling flows as Charles shares one of her wonderful CD's. Occasional soft sobs erupt. I smile knowing the experience affects us all differently.

We're here to perceive the wholeness that we already are, through accountability, and perception (as I perceive, so I conceive), realizing everyone is some part of us. I smile as Charles reminds. "I create the impact of my story" and "How I pass my story on is how I evolve the planet."

Many lightworkers dispose of history in earnest during the winter months of 2011. Beliefs change yet again along with a great urge to forgo old customs and ways of living. We break free of many beliefs, discarding previously valued possessions that no longer serve new states of BEing.

I throw away the previously treasured Bible and other books, along with lots of other material possessions unnecessary for the New World consciousness of Oneness. Finally, after eons of forgetfulness, I rise from the human mind delusion of birth and death certificates, marriage, divorce, medical history, and other limiting beliefs that locked me in horrendous conclusions.

Family photos, Daniel's birth and death certificate, his baby teeth and baby books, reams of medical records and x-rays sit shredded in the garbage along with debit and charge cards, airline and other membership cards. At one point, it's clear that I'm not doing family or the world any favors by gifting them with things. An entire set of pristine encyclopedias from the early 1970's sits ripped up in the trash. We do not need to remember and continue to feed energies that serve separation.

It's time to reexamine my story, once again, knowing reactions set up the energy field. Charles notes we don't need to suffer. We're here to enlighten and pass on a story that evokes the energy of wholeness. Yes! It's time to take the charge out of the game by releasing "button pushers" that keep me in judgments, binding me to others and myself, in unhealthy ways.

During another short meditation, I allow myself to feel and remember what moved me into that old place of reaction with James. Clearly, he's one, in a long line of button pushers, who agreed to help me take back my power. James helped me to recognize my wholeness, to understand that I'm complete on my own. I now forgive him and myself for false perceptions. "You have no more power to move me in a way that takes from me," I repeat. "I give you no more charge. Your role is finished." There's no doubt our eternal love can handle the change.

Charles moves on to discuss the virtues of gratitude as tears begin to form. His contemplation of the Lord's Prayer fills me with great joy.

"Creator of all, the sacred one, the great I AM within my soul. Heaven's gate, my very thought. The Path to all I have sought. This day is fulfilled from dawn to new dawn as I hold to my freedom's song. As I forgive, I am forgiven. Things of the world no longer bind me for I behold the truth that sets me free. I am you and you in me. The eternal one, the power, the glory. The kingdom at last is found within my soul's holy ground."

We are now encouraged to do forgiveness work whenever feeling anxious, afraid, or isolated. A final exercise of deep breathing and meditation helps to pave the way. Yes, I am a vessel for the essence of spirit to flow though unencumbered, without the limited energies of my story!

Leah and I enjoy dinner in the condo before the evening program with Rev. Donald Graves. He's entertaining and intuitive while discussing "The Missing Piece." Laughter abounds as he explains how to get two hugs. Claim the past, he boldly announces, and be totally accountable and responsible. Endless energy comes while realizing he's right. There's no missing piece. We are whole and need only do something different to feed our joy.

Scattered, gray clouds fill skies on Tuesday morning as Leah and I ride the ski lift. Aromatic pine surrounds us while sailing past trees.

"It's like being in a rocking chair, isn't it?" I remark anxiously when the lift stops abruptly, rocking the chair.

"Oh, yes, if you overlook the height," Leah announces.

"Just don't look down."

"I'm not. I have my eyes closed."

The ski lift continues to rock. I laugh as we move forward. A tall skinny pine tree stands out among the rest. It holds a wide variety of colorful underwear and assorted junk.

"Oh, look. Open your eyes. You're missing the best part. It's not down. Look forward."

"Listen, you're talking to someone who won't even drive on I-95!" Leah retorts now looking wide-eyed at the lingerie. "I want my roads on the ground."

We look at one another and laugh.

"You don't suppose…"

"Well, it's a fifteen minute ride. Maybe it's a new kind of mile-high club!"

Different gradients of rock highlight mountains. A spectacular, panoramic view sits below when we exit at the top. Leah's breath labors so she soon heads back down the mountain.

New frontiers offer greater possibilities. One steep trail leads to the mountain's peak. Out of breath, I rest after each step. A chattering chipmunk climbs to the top of a broken tree limb before stopping to pose for pictures. Breathing is now much more difficult. Birds chirp nearby while ego realizes reckless actions. The chipmunk then leads me safely back down to the ski lift. I'm still amazed at how active I've become.

Excitement fills afternoon air. Leah and I join whitewater rafters in the lobby for a short ride to the Geyser Whitewater shop where we don gear before climbing into a big, yellow bus. Today's fashion calls for bulky, black wetsuits, blue windbreakers, orange life vests, and white helmets. It feels like we're wearing snowsuits.

We sit in front of the bus to take pictures before exiting after a short drive. Healthy pine trees fill the area with a scent reminding me of Christmas. Wet suits make our legs look skinny as we make our way down the dirt path. Our guide hands paddles to someone in the group.

"Distribute these please," he asks before grabbing more.

"Here's a Versace paddle," the man says to the first person in line. "Here's an Armani," he tells Leah as she reaches out to claim her paddle.

"Hey, can I have a Giorgio?" I ask with a laugh.

"We're out of Giorgio's so you'll have to take this Versace," he announces as I reach out.

"Gimme a K-mart one," someone yells from behind.

Several men carry a wheelchair-bound woman as we move slowly, one by one toward the rapids. Arthur and Ann soon volunteer to act as lead paddlers while I sit with the guide behind Leah and Lois. Water fights occupy time while we paddle slowly in placid waters. Before long, we're happily removing heavy wetsuits back at the shop. Everyone, including our wheelchair bound friend, seems happy to have had the experience.

The Corral Bar Steakhouse offers another opportunity to savor the taste of grass fed Buffalo later. Our small group shares a table with several other friends. I continually thank Spirit for guiding toward grand adventures.

Tonight's program begins after the usual hugs. Music plays as we sing before Mary's "Grit and Grace" session. She soon talks about being in the frequency of Oneness, where living in a state of grace is usual. We need only, she notes, put ourselves in harmony with *It* to live in this natural state of conscious union. Returning to the harmony of our true nature, when feeling disconnected, is as easy as paying attention to peace and calm. Praise and gratitude reconnects our mind to the energy of One, keeping us in a stream of grace. "Yes!" I think. "Life in higher frequencies is for me!"

"Meet the new day refreshed in the glory of God," fills my brain before rising on Wednesday morning to attend "Living in a Holographic Universe." We're the Divine Being, Eternal soul, the Christ incarnate, Christine soon notes before asking us to realize this world exists in a holographic universe. This temporally induced mind experiment, now during the Great Shift, happens every 26,000 years. We're in for a ride as the Sun aligns with the center of the galaxy. Every soul wanted to be here because it's like going from a caterpillar to a butterfly. The cocoon is pure death, a willingness to let go of everything we thought we were. But oh, the transition!

Those of us interested in crystals, energy healing, light, color, and sound were involved with Atlantis, Christine reports before speaking of Lemuria, which existed earlier. Reconnect with Nature, she asks. Energy is much easier to get by being in harmony with a tree than any food.

Let go of the baggage that no longer serves, she calls out to the room. Go with the flow of new opportunities, to release old energies, and again be reborn. If we can speak of an event with anger, or sadness, we're still carrying around that baggage. We are still attached to it if it's in our mind. Oh how I resonate with her words! "Who had life-changing experiences placing us in new spaces?" She asks, as we ponder the Harmonic Convergence (from August 1987 to early 1988). We do not serve through our identities as wife, mother, sister, etc. (James and I married and bought a house during that time.) The implications are mind-boggling. Clearly, it's time to reevaluate baggage.

Christine now speaks of wormholes, where we go during meditation, to escape time and space. We merge with the eternal source of immortality between worlds, a timeless portal to non-local reality.

Her wisdom astounds me. Once again, she says we're the great Creator for we create our own reality. Everything is frequency and our name is the sacredness about us. There are no coincidences with numbers in numerology and changing your name changes your frequency. I've consciously changed my name several times.

Taking notes becomes difficult for I want to record every morsel. As Christine discusses the Mayan calendar, I sit back with glazed eyes. We'll be in the beginning of the fifth world on 12/21/2012. Earth is wobbling, backwards through the astrological chart right now, in the fifth cycle, the final phase of the fourth world. We're going into the Aquarian Age, ruled by ether (a synthesis of the four elements), non-local reality (ESP). Ether makes it possible for us to experience ESP. Yahoo!

Everything created helps us to know who we really are. Change is inevitable and we're the ones we've been waiting for. Soon we'll, quite literally, feel the result of our actions, feeling everything that others feel. And we will not have the luxury of guilt upon feeling our actions on others. Every thought we have creates so we need to think about the kind of world we wish to create.

Subsequent remarks cause thoughts of Abigail. The sixth root race (of psychic/crystal children) is arriving and they don't feel the need for parents. They're teaching us the way of ether.

Listen to the whale sounds, Christine implores, for they are embryonic. Dolphins and whales help us to remember who we are. They're inter-dimensional beings that carry the history of earth while helping us to transform, transmitting messages, and trying to remind us of our true nature.

Talk of the hologram, holding everything, comes just when I think I've reached my limit of learning. The earth is only a reflection of a universal consciousness, Christine reports. It's a conscious hologram, existing only in our minds, where we came to experience choice and creativity. It's an interference pattern created by a split beam of Light. One part continues as the blueprint while the other has the experience. Everything is part of our own created hologram. The light of consciousness grows by bringing the hologram alive. Waking from the hologram involves a change in perception.

We are moving toward Christ consciousness (unity consciousness). A change in consciousness allows us to see what's already there. Belief systems keep alive our mental body and our joyfulness and non-judgment keeps the soul body alive. A place of innocence (non-judgment, non-attachment) wakes up the soul body. Sacred sites and pilgrimages help as well. Many of us that travel to sacred sites raise our consciousness.

Emotions, particularly fear, keep the astral body alive. Fighting for anything enhances it and increases the problem so we must connect to the soul grid instead and be the change we wish to see. Fear, Christine advises, reveals our creative power if we face it. We must meet parts of us, seen in others that we're trying to separate from, and integrate them. We must be unconditional love, loving all aspects of our self. Unhurried cricket sounds serve as Christine's finale. They sound just like Heavenly music. Everyone is amazed.

Leah and I eat lunch in the condo before the closing session at two o'clock with Mary and Joe. "The Alchemy of Re-

Entry," where our candle ceremony lights the room with a warm loving glow, encourages us to return next year.

Tonight's musical gala takes place in the Madison Room. Daniel and Joe take turns entertaining the crowd. I so love the music of these phenomenal entertainers! Everyone buys raffle tickets for an opportunity to win this year's handmade quilt during the social hour. I buy tickets to support the retreat but am not interested in winning the quilt for myself. There's no animal free, non-smoking place to store it until I get my own space. Upon winning a prize, it pleases me to gift it quickly to someone who yearns to have it.

The Huntley Dining Room group meeting and retreat closing is nearly over by the time I enter for a buffet breakfast. I quickly pay to return next year when Joe offers the opportunity at a reduced rate.

Minutes later, five of us travel by car to tread the path to Ousel Falls. Rock crunches under feet while following a gravel and dirt path. Clouds of white and gray pepper the sky as we walk downhill. It's a sure bet that we'll follow the same path upon returning. Tall, skinny trees, with sparse branches, line the path and roll down the hill as far as the eye can see. Mountains stand majestically in the distance as we marvel over the steep drop to our left. There are no guardrails. One mis-step and a fall down the hill would be on the agenda.

Ten-dollar, brand new, designer, hiking boots make the walk much easier while moving downhill. We stop periodically to rest and marvel at the glory of nature. "I'm guessing it's going to take me a lot longer to get back uphill," I soon remark with a laugh as we make our way through a set of switchbacks. Wooden stairs allow me to take a shortcut before the bridge (South Fork of the West Fork of the Gallatin River). Sun peeks out from clouds as the river flows through tree logs and rocks of various sizes.

Lois and I soon lag behind those more accustomed to hiking. Wonderful scents of pine and flowers implore me to be still and sniff the air. Purple and blue triangles of light flow nearby as we move down the path. Flowers, foliage, dew, grass, and trees amaze as more triangles appear, amid a stream of green mist, all seeming to come from the sun. How wonderful it would be to capture the energy of smells and feeling on video!

Now short of breath, Lois and I walk in silence while crossing another much smaller wooden bridge across a noisy stream of water. The sound is music to my ears. There are a mere .3 miles to go as we saunter past the sign that points uphill to Yellow Mules Trail. Minutes later, a massive wall of rock stands above placid, green water. Eyes feast on a beautiful waterfall flowing swiftly down layers of moss-lined rock after moving uphill. Birds hop below as the waterfall runs into a placid pool of clear water.

Magic fills the air. Our destination lays steps away. But stone steps make it much longer to reach. I must make my way down to the water's edge. Two steep sets of dirt and wood stairs allow me to do so. Stairs zigzag down to a plateau. Going down is so easy! "And so is going up," I prompt myself with a laugh. "Oh, my God, the beauty!"

A sense of joyous wonder abounds. Greg stands at the magical waters edge. I must touch it, take it into my hand and anoint myself. Companions watch as I scoop the cold, clear water to touch the middle of my forehead. Orbs fill the air while I smile absorbing the magical atmosphere. All is in Divine Order as we make our way back to the group.

Fog lies in mountains beyond the village of luxury at the Big Sky Resort. The scene is so beautiful that I want to stay and relish in it forever. Scattered, puffy, white and gray clouds fill the air as Greg, Ann, Arthur and I load the second car. We drive toward Idaho while chatting and listening to music at 10:30 AM.

After lunch, we stop to stretch our legs at the Lava Formations off I-15, between Idaho Falls and Blackfoot. The other car in our group continues down the road. Ann and I discuss my healing from interstitial cystitis while sitting in the restroom. She's amazed to hear how the condition cleared after I entered a period of grace. We soon make our way toward Greg and Arthur on the sagebrush lined and paved path.

"We got a bonus hike," I gladly remark. "I'm so excited!"

"It's three-quarters of a mile," Ann replies moving ahead.

Puffy, white clouds drift, amid blue skies, as we wander. The smell of urine, perhaps a sign of skunkweed, permeates the air. Wind increases as Greg points out fractures in the lava. He moves off the path periodically to fondle greenery. Fresh air feels

251

amazing as I giggle my way up the rust colored path. Arthur walks ahead as Ann and Greg discuss similarities between Idaho and Hawaii. They seem to know a lot about nature and stop often to examine vegetation.

"Boy, I'd be really happy if I could exercise every day like this," I announce, while stopping to video a deep crevice.

Diamond shaped orbs of royal blue appear minutes before the video registers a change in the energy. It happens right after Arthur announces, "Life is good." I grin widely feeling Daniel's presence. Arthur smiles when I announce Daniel's famous words.

"Life is good. The world is good. Enjoy yourself."

"How old was he?"

"He was thirty-seven when he passed. He would have been forty this year. Everyone is upset now, especially the older men because he didn't have to reach forty and they did."

The land is a mix of sagebrush, juniper, dry tumbleweeds, cactus, green foliage, and lava, amid dry earth and small rocks. Green moss covers gray, black and red rocks. It all looks beautiful but smells like cat piss. Greg and Ann take in the expansive view from an observation point as Arthur and I climb wooden steps to join them. Energy continues to morph while Greg points out areas of interest.

The highway remains sparsely populated with mainly 18-wheelers, which we soon pass. This area looks excessively dry. Mountains stand in the distance but they're nearly devoid of the greenery seen while driving north from Florida to Michigan. Inkom, Idaho lies ahead as we discuss personal matters. The camcorder records as I discuss colors infrequently seen in clouds. We pass the Utah state line after what seems to be a very, long, time. A large, white orb floats in and out of eyesight. Bright, golden light streams from the sun leaving a trail down to earth as Ann discusses a near accident. The usual orbs cascade around it before a green mist replaces them.

Salt Lake City reminds me of downtown Detroit with old, tall buildings, lots of noise, and activity. A small hotel welcomes us on this lovely afternoon. We freshen up before leaving to tour the infamous Temple Square.

Street light controls chirp like tiny birds to alert us of impending red lights. Three young, pretty missionaries welcome us inside the Visitors Center for a 30-minute tour of the area. They appear extremely dedicated to their work, worshipping God apart from worldly pursuits and cares. Their lives evolve around the Church of Latter Day Saints. Dusk begins to fall as the girls lead us outside to view immense grounds.

The church is an awesome sight. We sit spellbound taking in long, wooden pews, intricate gold-filled moldings reaching up to and across ceiling, stained glass windows, and a massive golden organ. Beautiful choir music fills the air as we file out of the church. The Mormon Tabernacle Choir is practicing so we cannot enter their space. We stand outside; taking turns to peer through a small window at the very large group of singers. Their voices merge perfectly, as one, and yet, each voice makes a difference in the hymn.

The property is immense so there's not enough time to enter every building. Our three guides are very good at keeping us moving together. We make our way quickly to the North Visitors Center. A very large room with many massive columns stands before us upon entering. It holds a variety of educational tools including a model of what I believe to be Jerusalem.

A variety of white lights illuminates our way as we travel quickly through the throng of tourists to climb an uphill ramp. Hand painted murals of Jesus cover the wall to our left. Murals of a beautiful sky replace them as we move further uphill. A tall, white statue of Jesus stands amid beautiful wall murals. More outstanding wall murals, of nature, line walls of the next room, surrounding statues of Adam and Eve. Five missionaries sweetly sing, "I Am a Child of God" at the conclusion of our tour.

Trolley bells sing in the distance as our three guides lead the way. We walk briskly to a scheduled dinner in the onsite restaurant. Elevators stand, beyond the entrance, in a long hallway, amid gray marble walls and massive marble columns. Numerous crystal chandeliers illuminate a room to our left. The artistry of this room is awesome. It's comparable to the outstanding beauty of those viewed while in Turkey. Intricate gold moldings cover the ceiling. Wall murals highlight the top of each window. The camcorder records it all before I catch up to the group in an elevator.

We stand together in the West Observation area waiting for someone to announce our group. Massive windows allow another view of the immense property and surrounding land. Eyes savor the artistry of the room. Blue, green, and white stained glass windows line the ceiling. This delightful dining experience seems fitting to honor the birth of Charles. It is a wonderful meal!

Dawn breaks on the horizon as we eat breakfast before checking out of the hotel. We filled our trip with many surprises. But there's no doubt that I need more time to match thoughts, words, and actions as we board the plane to return home.

Chapter Twenty-One

Stuck in the Muck

*"Make no mistake, all are part of **All That Is**. There is, and never shall be, any separation whatsoever. But this is what you, as a soul, came to experience." SAM – Book of One :-) Volume 2*

Spiritual Mind Treatments continue to reap positive results but business email invites me to regress. My AAA Visa credit card statement now bears the Bank of America logo. Will this change affect things in the future? I ignore the implication to stay on freedom's path. Rev. Yzer's message solidifies my choice. Her new location sits near Rebecca's house, where I stay for now.

Samuel is disappointed to hear we're shopping, before going home, when I arrive to get him from school. A heated discussion on the aspects of manifesting begins on the way to Costco's. I'm driving next to the right-hand turn lane as Samuel remarks, "Nana, you just missed the turn."

We're at the store's entry point as the light turns green.

"No," ego quickly replies turning the wheel, "it's right here."

Lara Owen's warning from the latest planetary update comes to pass. Samuel groans from the back seat as metal crushes plastic. My little, ten-year-old car just smashed into a big, brand new, yellow truck. I'm beside myself as Samuel immediately begins to announce it's all my fault. I ask if he's okay and then tell him to be quiet as observers approach the car.

Minutes later, while speaking with the Citizen's Patrol I learn the accident was indeed my fault. I mistakenly thought I was in a turning lane when, in fact, even the right-hand lane did not have to make a mandatory turn. The truck's owner is furious for his "baby" is just a week old. His car suffers much more damage because it's made of plastic. There's only a smashed rear panel and hubcap to replace on my car.

James is not happy when I telephone to report the news after another dentist visit. The visit costs $380 to replace a temporary crown with a permanent one. I again thank James for paying car and dental insurance before phoning the adjustor to schedule a rental car.

The spirit of my last-born son still reaches out when I need answers. He now announces that the accident happened to let me know I'm "not invincible." I'm to pay attention when driving. There's a strong sense of avoiding serious harm. Things done in the recent past changed the outcome of the accident, from one of rather dire effects, to a minor outcome. The Course notes time and space adjust changing situations and events when we no longer need to learn from them. My soul planned this accident but I changed the outcome. This fits in with the idea of unpredictability built into everyone's script.

This instance was just one, of several, of what some people refer to as "Phantom Deaths." My soul weaved this incident into the illusion to give me an out if I cared to take it. But by the time the accident occurred, I'd already decided to complete my soul's mission. Yes, I am fully aware that all is illusion. But since I still seem to be here, I might as well make myself useful to humanity while increasingly enjoying the pleasures of a well-lived life.

*Emmanuel reminds us, we accept the illusion until we accomplish the goals of our soul. Life becomes fuller when we realize our true power to change the rules of this game we refer to as life. Knowing all is, was, and shall ever be part of the One in which we live, and move, and have all BEing, frees us to accomplish even more than the agreed upon tasks of our soul. We enter into a new soul agreement knowing there is no soul for we are truly, in essence, part of **All That Is**, ready to commit to Wholeness once again.*

Another message says I'm at Rebecca's to help her stabilize. Again, I hear to stay married but not live in limitation with James. I'm to enjoy life, free of limitation. "Where will I be?" I think, looking forward to having my own clean place with lots of light, nature, and good smells.

Rebecca spends most nights on the living room couch as my body continues to fine-tune. Shedding animals that occasionally wet the bed make it difficult to relax but I'm sleeping more.

Nights consist of short-lived memories where I do things to help with evolution. Days fill with mundane house duties, studies, and occasional outings. Mary continues to talk with her deceased husband and is astounded by my quick review of names associated with recent messages. Zyprella, a young girl with a father named Hanibel, is one of my spirit guides. Marerill is Daniel's ancient name and Esmeralda is mine.

We live in an illusion of our own making and that illusion changes with thoughts. Thoughts mold all we see, hear, and experience so be careful what you throw into the mold. The Course tells us God does not speak in words. Those that think they hear His Voice usually hear their Higher Self (also known as the Holy Spirit) mixed in with their own thoughts.

"A Psychic Mediums Guide to Harmony," featuring Michelle Whitedove, offers ten contact hours at Nova Community School. We begin the six-week class on a hot Tuesday night at six o'clock. Michelle welcomes us warmly and quickly begins to teach the techniques of creating harmony and manifesting Heaven on earth. As she begins to discuss forgiveness, forgetting, and recognizing we are One, Leah and I wonder why we're there. Mary is furiously taking notes while we stare at one another. This is old information to us. Ears perk up as Michelle begins to discuss why every soul has a core and why it's unique to each soul's progression.

Life is clearly what I make of it. I have not slept at the house on 47th Drive for more than two months. Time spent between house sitting, traveling, and Rebecca's house is much more appealing. James is now cordial and pays my bills so there's no need to worry about food, gas, or insurance. I've thanked him several times. The rental car costs less than $2 per day. It's nice to drive a new car but I quickly decide my old one is better. There's something odd about new cars...

Divine Timing always prevails! The great law of restoration, I affirm while reading Catherine Ponder's *The*

Prosperity Secrets of the Ages, works to divinely restore my highest good of past and present blessings. Yes! The challenges pressing upon me now are, in reality, my "good of the past and present, dammed up in the invisible, trying to come forth." These challenges occur to get my "attention strongly focused on the desire for good" so good has a channel through which to be born.

Ponder's timely clues for success prompt gratitude while experiencing ever-increasing degrees of good. God's good is at work even though it appears otherwise during this period of what Daniel refers to as "trials and tribulations." How wonderful to know these experiences are a sign of purification, cleansing, and readjustment! Balance and equilibrium flow as I relinquish control to let my new good come forth.

Having experienced many setbacks during trials and tribulations, each time purifying, cleansing, and readjusting to higher frequencies, it's abundantly clear that great things follow. Know this truth as you go through rough times. Be a clear channel through which good manifests as you readjust into equilibrium.

Caroline Reynold's "Soul Stretch" meditation plays on my new CD player. Thankfully, this player does the same things the other one did whenever spirit wants me to know I'm not alone, or to deliver a message. Verification continues to reassure that I'm doing the right thing. And now, several people note either white or golden light emitting from the top of my head and shoulders.

"I am open and receptive to Higher Beings who desire to inform, direct, or guide for my higher good," I announce as Caroline's soft voice directs.

The CD begins to stop and restart. Communication begins. As Caroline says to open up the chakras to take in Light, I recall it's our true form. The Course says our Light helps complete the Godhead. Intuition notes there's no need for the CD now. There's no need to take Light in. We need only to let the spirit spark within grow, and shine that Light out into the atmosphere to share with others. I must remember to radiate my God Light. It now shines out into the Universe, touching everything, and everyone. It feels wonderful even as the CD continues to stop and quickly restart. "Either stop the CD player," I think mildly annoyed, "or let me listen to the CD normally."

Again, I hear there's no need for the CD. And then the player turns off. Messages for the day flow forth.

As we let our Light shine out into the Godhead, the Universe sends its combined Light into us.

Another message concerning James feeds my joy-filled heart. We're on different levels of consciousness but each contributing in our own way. It's our bond to spread energy and Light while in separate entities but still together as part of the Whole. This is the main message.

I don't want to stop communication but the "session" ends when I unconsciously inhale and exhale deeply. The unexpected deep breathing takes me by surprise, for something controls body processes. It is in some way a reassuring thought.

SOM classes offer a better understanding of my infinite Self, Source, and my relationship to *It*. Thursday evening's "Bible Scholarship and History," with Charles, begins after I pay the required $120. How wonderful to pay for classes! The class is based upon John Shelby Spong's book *Rescuing the Bible From Fundamentalism*. It's not so much that I'm interested in learning more about the *Bible*, which I know is basically a collection of man's thoughts, but any class Charles teaches is well worth supporting. Even though I may not attend them, it gives me great pleasure to contribute in this manner.

Charles reassures me as class begins by noting this class is not a *Bible* study course. Tonight's class is very interesting as he discusses the impact of *Bible* on current western thinking. Fundamentalist childhood concepts of a *Bible*, without error or mistake, changed while in college learning from Dr. Vendettuoli. It encourages me to read, "yea though I walk through the valley of illusions..." Charles further enlightens by noting the *Bible's* interpretation continually changes. About 7,000 versions exist.

Little did I know then of the lasting effect of SOM classes upon scheduling them. But their value shines forth now upon the path of a New World Order of One.

Several new people sit in class. One disrupts us with constant questions, which some feel unnecessary. It's almost as if they're spies sent to "trip" Charles. He does not seem to notice. "We are One," he tells us. "God works through us all."

We form workshops to share childhood concepts of God versus concepts held today. Yes! We are the new species Eckhart Tolle speaks of! I make a note to learn more about Lemuria and Atlantis along with the usual homework of daily exercise, meditation, and reading.

Daniel and I walk along the beach during meditation the next day. He tells me the rest of my life is for fun. I let him know how grateful I am for his time and thank him again for being such a great spirit, such a good soul.

"Is there anything I can do for you?" I ask.

"In 2008, you can do something for Rachel, not because she is Abigail's mom but because she's a spirit with a need that you are to help with."

"Is her mom Joy involved?"

"No, she is not and will not be there physically."

His response disappoints but I understand Joy's role in my life is now complete.

"Well, I'm grateful for Joy and the great role she played," I announce before Daniel takes me to a Higher Being.

Finally, on Christmas Day 2011 we hug warmly after Rachel stops by with Abigail and Joy. Our time fills with childish games as Abigail brings us further together in mind and body.

I'm ever so grateful for fleeting images behind closed eyes! A sparkle of gold appears. It changes from a solid, gold shape that looks somewhat like a "Z," to a spark of gold that dissipates. Thunder sounds in the distance as eyes open to see rain from a tropical depression that formed yesterday while on top of Florida.

Gratitude abounds for so many things. Today it feels great to meditate and walk for twenty minutes on the treadmill. Full of energy, I leave to get Samuel from school.

We soon arrive at the house on 47th Drive. James sits upon the living room couch, while putting on work shoes, as we enter the room.

"What are you doing here?" he asks, as if we have no business being there.

James and Samuel talk as I move to open the door to my room after answering him. The desired paper is where I left it, so I copy it, turn off the printer, and close the door before moving through the kitchen looking for mail.

Conversation continues as I move to the living room. An ad from two weeks ago still sits on the mantle. At least two more piles of mail sit nearby. A statement from the mortgage company sits in one. I pick it up while asking James if he received notice that the mortgage is paid.

"No," he quickly replies.

"You should have gotten the notice," I tell him. "Don't you remember? I told you last Thursday the mortgage is paid."

He answers gruffly.

"You did not tell me it was paid off. I will not believe it until I see a written notice."

The statement I hold now is an old one so I start to walk into the kitchen to throw it away.

"What are you doing?" James asks loudly. "I do not appreciate you coming over and messing everything up."

After a few tense minutes, I manage to get Samuel out of the house. Samuel sternly announces that I'll never again use him as an excuse to leave. When I start a fight with Papa, he says, it's up to me to get out of it.

"What a fiasco," I think, as we drive to Rebecca's sanctuary.

Words wake me much later.

"Nana, remind me of who I am."

Thoughts of buying Abigail a children's book, through the Association of Research and Enlightenment (ARE) Website, comes to mind. Something about a fire, a thing to set me free, comes next. I traipse into the bathroom before falling back asleep only to wake moments later upon hearing more words.

"The sunshine of God is within you. Let it pour out to all things."

Flying effortlessly over rooftops fills me with glee while dreaming. A flutter of white objects appears before me while walking. I move toward them in awe and eagerly began to fly upon reaching them.

Another dream finds me in a house, with many rooms, trying to find something to wear to work at the Sing Along Piano Bar. Someone tries to get me to stay and talk as I move from one room to another. They call me Nana. It seems like a male figure, with a small frame, not Samuel.

"Darkness is the great illusion, not evil," Charles reports later in the day. Class discussion covers many issues related to believing the *Bible* is without error. It's quite enlightening to know the *Old Testament* is a collection of stories, poetry, and olden times. It's an account of the Hebrew people and existed as oral history for about 1,400 years before documented in written form. The *New Testament* covers the times of Jesus and existed as an oral history for at least forty years before the *Bible*.

Words take on new meanings as Charles speaks. Involution, which takes place in stillness, light and dark for the process of Creation, and rain, meaning conscious awareness.

"To name is to define the nature of something," Charles reminds us before discussing the evolution of consciousness. Like Saul, who changed his name to Paul and Abram, who changed his name to Abraham, the evolution of consciousness prompted me to change my name to SAM. (Many years later, I learn the original meaning of Sam. It's the name of God.)

Rebecca and Samuel leave the next morning as I listen to my daily treatment CD, which skips to Track 8. "I am one with the Living Spirit Almighty," it repeats. The CD player then switches tracks to play, "There is no spot where God is not." It continues to skip tracks as "I am grateful for the Living Spirit Almighty within me," fills ears. Once again, the CD player switches tracks and I hear, "I am in conscious union with God." Grateful tears fill eyes while recognizing Daniel's presence. I feel so loved and what I used to note as "lucky" to be able to recognize and receive messages. Now I stop crying by remembering there is no loss. There never was a Daniel, for in God's world we are part of One. There is no separation. There is no me. There is no you. There is only One, pure, pristine Consciousness!

The CD player continues to rapidly switch tracks, while I smile filled with joy. Yes! "I am surrounded by pure Spirit, God the Living Spirit Almighty." I'm smiling broadly as seconds of "Magic," by Karen Drucker, plays before the player turns off abruptly. Daniel's spirit is near so I ask for clear communication. He says it's almost time to begin my work.

"It's what you have been preparing for," he announces.

Thoughts from a few days ago, when I wondered why exhaustion causes me to sleep more than usual, fill my brain.

"Something wonderful is going to happen," Daniel notes.

Daniel's spirit wants to give me a "heads-up" and notes all is well. I've learned not to request details but ask for an image or something to assure this communication is not my ego. Images flash through my little mind.

"You'll meet Maya," Daniel announces. "Continue the SOM classes but it's not your path to be a practitioner."

"I love you Mom," he says, ignoring a question.

"I'm working on trying to love everyone as I love you," I reply.

After assuring me there's nothing to do for him, his presence leaves.

I'm so very grateful when the spirit of my last-born son comes! Yet, it's all God. Thank you Daniel for reminding me!

An hour later, when on the porch doing my Course lesson, intuition prompts me to phone Rachel. "I'll leave her a message because she doesn't usually answer," my brain announces as the cell phone rings. Rachel answers quickly. She and Abigail are on their way to Orlando and ready to pull into a gas station. Everything is fine. She's in the parents group and helps Abigail's kindergarten class with science experiments. Rachel continues to work her own hours. This enables her to take time off as desired. I tell her how proud I am of her being so involved in Abigail's school. She then notes her boyfriend gave her $100 for their current trip. He's home taking care of the animals for her.

"Abigail," she says, "say hello to Nana."

"Hi Nana," Abigail says, in the background as they pull off the highway.

Rachel continues to talk of family. I'm filled with joy to hear her news. We speak for several minutes before we are cut off when they walk into a bathroom. I continue my studies knowing Rachel will phone if she wants to talk. She calls within ten minutes and says Abigail wants us to come out to the house for a visit! Before our telephone call ends, I promise to phone next week to let her know which Saturday is best for Rebecca. I'm so very grateful for all the good that continues to come. Connecting to the God Network always fills me with gratitude.

"Light extends in every measure throughout the field of One. Beware of the crucial moments humanity now faces. The choices you make will control your future as a Being of Light. Make them wisely for all will not choose to continue on the path of Light and Love. This choice is always available to those on the planet of free will yet all must know of their inability to know all choices that exist. For the choices on earth are often made by a select few who manipulate the masses of One unaware of their greatness.

"All hold the Light within but to spark this Light one must know it is readily available. And the ability to spark the Light is theirs. Those wishing to continue the game of manipulation and control often mute this information, as much other information. Know that all are in a state of readiness to move forward toward the Light of BEing. This BEing is humanities natural state, to BE in earnest readiness, to know and flourish as mass makers of Truth and Light.

"Knowing the Power you hold within will help to secure the future of humanity as it moves forward toward the BEing of Light and Oneness. Know that all within your world is yet a dream of your own making. For in Truth there is no world apart from the BEingness of One. Hold fast to the Truth and know all will return to the state of perfection from which it appears to have left. For never has it left the state of One."

Chapter Twenty-Two

Commitments

"Know that all happening on earth achieves a greater purpose than what is seen or conveyed." SAM – Book of One :-) Volume 1

Something about "Matthew 4:16" wakes me near dawn. Intuition led me yesterday to gather more things from the house on 47ᵗʰ Drive. The well-worn *Bible*, received after a second Baptism at age thirteen, sits nearby, so I reach out to grab it. The passage is after several that describe how Jesus overcomes tests imposed upon him by Satan.

"The people which sat in darkness saw great light; and to them which sat in the region and shadow of death light is sprung up."

Surely this has something to do with my current situation and state of awareness. Forgotten parts of my soul continue to integrate and heal. New experiences and repeated treatments help to train the unconscious mind. Everything improves as conscious and unconscious thought more closely match. The Light within increases, creating different forms of thought, feeling, and action.

However, indecision over the recent car accident plagues me. It's clearly my fault but for the first time I follow the 'wisdom' of drivers who deal with tickets easily by paying lawyers to represent them. The Ticket Clinic welcomes me. Numerous representatives sit within folding enclosures scattered about the spacious room. One of them gladly takes my $115 check minutes after I walk through the door.

Dinner with Leah is much more enjoyable. We feel truly blessed to share stories and encourage one another while skipping tonight's Whitedove class.

An image of a door opening to the right, with the sun in the middle and a mail carrier to the left, wakes me the next day.

The door to my new home the following year opens to the right, faces west, and the mailbox is to my left. The sun is usually in my vision near the middle when I get mail.

Guidance continues. A path opens in the middle of closed eye vision to reveal soon forgotten words during mediation. I'm not sure where they come from. Since I ask to interact only with Lights of God, it doesn't really matter.

Discussion of the three major religions (Judaism, Christianity, and Islam) gets me out for the night. Ears perk up when Charles mentions Akhenaton, an Egyptian King. History credits him as the pharaoh who introduced the idea of one God to the Egyptians. Some people believe Moses lived in Egypt during this time and either got the idea from Akhenaton or gave it to him.

In December 2008, I'll visit Egypt, learn much more about Akhenaton, and recall significant past lives there. One previous incarnation will verify my current mission to help everyone realize we are spirit in human form, within an illusion of our own making.

Later in a very vivid dream, a beautiful infant boy snuggles in my arms as I sing sweetly, "You are so beautiful to me." The boy wears a little, white shirt. Looking at him and singing fills my heart with joy. We walk from one room, holding two children, into a bedroom where James sleeps. Perhaps I just birthed a baby in a parallel life. But now, after many treasured lives of bringing other souls to earth, my soul's goal changed!

The day's Course lesson reminds me to allow things to unfold without judgment or interference: "Let all things be exactly as they are."

Television volume seems way too loud after watching the hurricane update so I try to turn it down. Volume increases as I push the remote control button to lower it. I turn the TV off, sit down, and ask for communication.

The spirit of my last-born son speaks. Rachel, he informs, is going through a period of trauma but she'll be okay. Abigail is okay as well. There's nothing to do now but I can telephone her on Wednesday to talk about seeing them as discussed last week.

Before Daniel's energy leaves, he prompts me to buy Rachel a necklace for her birthday, the same necklace featured online days ago, a circle of tiny diamonds on a white gold chain.

Princess happily wags her tail when we walk to the car to pick up Samuel. My car alarm beeps once unexpectedly. It beeps again as I open the door, making the noise it usually does when I use the alarm button. Yes, Daniel's essence is nearby! Joy overflows while again thanking him for visiting. The one song I usually have trouble listening to starts to play on the radio.

"There's a cross on the side of the road where a Mother lost her son..."

A smile graces my lips for the first time upon hearing it before thanking Daniel again. Clearly, I've lost nothing, for our true reality is pure, invulnerable, infinite spirit. Princess wags her tail happily in the back seat as we move down the road.

Friends and I share stories between Whitedove's comments in the evening. She relates world events, and future possibilities, as we sit in small, uncomfortable, classroom chairs. Mary's house is officially on the market. A Saint Joseph statue sits nice and cozy in the ground near the front door.

It never ceases to amaze how I learn more every day! Charles' Thursday evening class is much more than expected. He notes numbers are not literal in the *Bible*. Some numbers have metaphysical meanings. For instance, the number forty is the number of completion. Jesus was forty days in the desert and Moses was forty years in the wilderness.

Dreams soon wake me. James and I hold each other in one dream remembering how long it's been since we felt the joy of good snuggling. In a different dream, I open a beautiful wood carved, brown door to find another, and another, until I open a nightstand. A beautiful, wooden, rectangular box sits inside the nightstand. Inside the box sits a magnificent carving of wood animals amid nature. It pops up when I lift the top.

"I will have beautiful things like this when I get my own place," I announce.

The CD player switches tracks later, playing only bits here and there, as I try to hear prayers. Spirit communication begins. I'm soon told to live with Rebecca and Samuel. The other bedroom, packed full with Martha's possessions, can be cleared out. My perception is the only limitation. Odd words, "*The limitless extravagance of love unfolding,*" fill my brain.

"But this place also appears to host limitation with leaking roof and broken dryer," I silently state. "How will appearances change when the house owners refuse to repair anything?"

"*The money is forthcoming. Spend like you have it because you do.*"

James and his sister allow Rebecca and Samuel to live here rent-free. But they are against anyone fixing up the house so the words confuse me. Yet, I know they came from a spirit of Light to help. The Course notes the word Light is the same as Truth.

Spirit now addresses soul agreements with Sarah, her husband Abraham, and Mary. Sarah scheduled her second knee surgery for next month. This time, I'm to visit and help. My soul also agreed to help Mary when she connects with me. Yesterday I told her a few things as we worked on her computer issue and we'll meet tomorrow.

Sarah's joy transfers over the phone lines when I report plans to be there during, and two weeks after, her surgery. The surgery, she confides, is soon after her last one because waiting means paying a bigger deductible next year. Abraham cannot take any more time off work.

"We made the second bedroom into the cat's room but you can sleep on the couch," she says.

Sleeping on a couch seems like limitation so I decide to book a hotel room. Travel plans become challenging when Rebecca asks me to stay with Samuel during her four-day business trip. I resolve the dilemma quickly by booking a small suite for the day of, and three days after, Sarah's surgery. The hotel is closer to Tampa than Sarah's house but because of Rebecca's family discount, it's very inexpensive. No rooms are available for the days after Rebecca returns from her trip. But another area hotel, closer to Sarah and Abraham's house welcomes me for eight days starting on November 16. This will be my first Thanksgiving without most of the family. I plan to cook the usual Thanksgiving meal for Sarah and Abraham.

Words come on Thanksgiving Day, 2011 after deciding to forgo the usual family dinner because Amos is excluded.

"Just know you're not alone, not really. I know you are accustomed to being with the family on holidays such as today but just know that all is in Divine Order. Sometimes you have to let go to grow. You know that but others may not so just let go and let them grow. It will all become increasingly clear as the day goes on that separation in mind is not the way to exist on any level. Know this in your heart, your mind.

"Your soul speaks of a time long ago when our essence was untainted by the ways of this world. It is time to remember that time of innocence. What comes into your life now is full of the good that is and will always be. Just know that all is in Divine Order.

"Are you done working the ways of the world? You see how erratic they can be when working with unseen energies for even as you type the words flow erratically about the screen. It is better to use the old ways of listening and recording and then transcribing if you wish to avoid this.

"I love you Mom, just know that I'm always with you. We are all here, for we are a part of one another and that is becoming increasingly clear to you, as the old world falls away. Hang in there and know you are not working alone. We work beside you as representatives of the One that truly is."

Apparently, the field of energy within me strengthened today. This was the first message that was hard to type into the new computer for the text kept jumping around. And as I edit this book, it continues to do so, very often, making documentation cumbersome.

On Thanksgiving Night more words come after checking news on the Internet.

*"You must stop relating to these world events for they are not of your true nature. Think, and report, only on the good of **All There Is** for that is now your charge here. Do not dwell upon the other side of life that you have left far behind. Listen for the wisdom you hold inside you and know all is, and continues to be, going according to the grand scheme of things.*

269

"It is all moving very quickly now and soon you will be settled in your new home with your new friends, all of like-mind. Fear not, for all is going according to plan and soon this old way will fade away. Do not be concerned with what you are leaving behind because there is no behind in this or any world. The world you see is an illusion of your own making and you must concentrate more on building a new world of Love and Light and Good, regardless of the chaos around the physical form. Stay still and listen to the still Voice within and know all is well in your world. That's it, that's all for now."

The circle diamond necklace is still available for less than $50 when I check overstock.com. After charging one for Rachel and one for Rebecca, onto my credit card, I log off to nap.

"Each one, at each time, blossoms and grows," wakes me minutes later.

Saying the World Healing Meditation fills me with joy. "I am the Light of God," I note, before hearing unexpected words.

"There are some people who do remember the real reason we are here on this earth. They remember who they really are."

Upon reading the Course it's clear that the Second Coming of Christ is really a time when humanity recognizes its limitless, perfect Oneness. Each comes to the reality of this unchanged truth in its own time. "For everyone is equally released from what he made."

Another sign, to live an unlimited life, comes in the form of an unexpected card later in the day. Thoughts of taking a cruise to celebrate my birthday surface. A Costa Fortuna cruise is now 60% off for an ocean view room.

Thursday's class enlightens on the Dead Sea Scrolls and the Essenes, people such as Joseph, Mary, and Jesus. This subject resonates strongly. The Essenes believed they were guardians of the Divine Teaching. They worked diligently in secret for the triumph of Light over the darkness of the human mind.

Essenes decoded many ancient manuscripts to disseminate and preserve advanced knowledge. They accorded great importance to the teachings of the ancient Chaldeans, Zoroaster, Hermes Trismegiste, Enoch, and the secret instructions of Moses. Preoccupied with protecting themselves from spirits, to preserve the purity of their souls, they never lied or compromised. They considered their presence on earth as the Light, which shines in the darkness, and differentiated between sleeping, drowsy, and awakened souls.

Awakened souls could be initiated into the mysteries of the Brotherhood/Sisterhood to begin a path of evolution that continued throughout their cycle of incarnations. Their task to help, comfort, and relieve sleeping souls, try to awaken drowsy souls, and welcome and guide awakened souls would then begin.

Several classmates voice an interest in the Costa Fortuna cruise when I mention it during the class break. No one is able to join me during the week of my birthday. Knowing all is in Divine Order, I leave when class ends to book the cruise anyway. Evan at vacationstogo.com is happy to book my room.

A force much larger than life itself continues to constantly lead, guide, protect, and inspire. Further verification of this truth comes when Rachel and Abigail welcome us in mid-October.

Rebecca and I drive as a radio station airs the Journey song that Daniel, Rebecca, and I listened to repeatedly from Michigan to Florida in 1982. "Nothing Else Matters," one of many songs Daniel chose to reveal feelings after his transition, plays next. I sing along making sure to emphasize there is no "they" for we all are part of the One. Getting back to that One is our goal as we work out lessons while on earth.

Rebecca has a hard time finding a parking spot at Daniel's favorite sandwich place. "Just let me out of the car," I announce, as she sits waiting behind another perplexed driver.

Intuition guides me to look down on the pavement after opening the door. My bright, shining penny from Heaven, further confirmation that we are never alone, sits right there in the middle of the road.

Rachel is thrilled to get her early birthday present and quickly confides problems with her boyfriend. As she relates her tale of woe, I think of miracles.

According to the Course, a miracle is a shift in perception to the Holy Spirit's (Higher Self – a fail-safe reminder of our

271

divinity) way of thinking. A holy instant occurs when you choose the Holy Spirit as your Teacher instead of ego.

Looking at things from my family's perspective no longer makes me happy. I can choose happiness or sadness, anger, judgment and hate, or love. And yet, they are all the same. Aside from Love, all is illusion. This is a difficult concept to explain to someone who has not experienced what I have. We're here to help one another realize we are powerful, without clinging to another. We are here to help one another take back the power we gave away so long ago. And though we may not like the teacher, or the way they teach the lesson, if we recognize the teacher as another unique part of God leading the way, it makes the journey much more understandable. Thankfully, humanity will eventually recognize it is formless, an element of *All That Is*, and we shall no longer deal with issues of separation.

As we drive away after our visit, I notice another sign of Daniel's essence. A Black Sabbath song Daniel and I love plays on the radio, right at the most memorable part for us.

"I tell you to enjoy life. I wish I could but it's too late."

A motorcyclist, riding a red bike like Daniel's and dressed exactly as he was during his transition, heads toward us. It moves toward Rachel and Abigail.

Rebecca discusses anger, frustration, and disappointment over the course of events as we drive down the highway. I do my best to soothe her by announcing the facts of human life as I have now come to know them.

"We are Beings of Light that chose to play the game of life. Just because we are so-called 'good' in this life, does not mean we have been 'good' in all incarnations. As souls, we plan each life carefully for optimum growth."

One of my teeth begins to ache as we talk.

Reincarnation is impossible in the ultimate sense. Earth life is an illusion of consciousness. Although it seems we must rectify mis-thoughts projected into physicality, once we do so the knowing becomes clear. Birth was not the beginning and death is not the end. We have never truly lived as separate beings.

Chapter Twenty-Three

Trials and Tribulations

"We are creators of circumstances since thoughts draw to us what we dwell on." SAM – Bits of Wisdom

A waking thought after dreaming fills me with joy.

"I love laughing. Laughing is the spice of life."

In the dream, I went to a house while still wearing pajamas. An older man opened the door.

"I used to live here" I told him, "and was wondering if any mail came for me."

Ecstatic to see me, he pulled me into the house, sat me on the couch, and said something came last week. The couch was on the left up against the wall, like the one on 47th Drive. Another couch stood to the right. Two other people sat there.

Another dream shows me participating in a 5K race. The man before me does not run very fast. We're in line waiting to report how much we ran when he speaks. The dream morphs to water cascading from the ledge above my printer into the bedroom at the house on 47th Drive.

Intuition leads. I dress quickly considering the first dream as a hint to check mail at the house on 47th Drive. A refund check from Citicorp for almost $2K sits in the mailbox. James continued payments after paying off the mortgage so they returned the extra portion. I take the printer to transport to Rebecca's house and deposit the check into the joint checking account with James.

Rebecca invites James to join us for dinner on Sunday. He peeks inside to look at his mother's things when she mentions clearing out the third bedroom. He also checks trees growing from the roof when I note them.

"The money from my parent's estate is still in probate so I can't afford to fix the roofs on the houses," he says.

"At least he's looking at issues now," I think, as we sit making polite conversation during dinner. My tooth hurts so I'm not much of a talker. I'm already in bed when James leaves after watching a movie with Rachel and Samuel.

The dentist is happy to see me in his nearly empty office the next day. He fills a cavity and, once again, refers me to the dental specialist when I complain of feeling slight pain upon eating. Another $140 goes onto my Visa charge card before heading back to Rebecca's house. She feels sorry for me and agrees to take time off for my December birthday cruise.

Appointments seem easy to get. I sit in the dental specialist's chair the next day silently singing a song by Karen Drucker as he works on an abscessed molar. "There is no spot where God is not and I'm forever grateful," gets me through the next fifty minutes. This root canal costs four times more than the one last month. Another $784 goes onto the Visa card.

I don't plan to take the prescribed pain pills but fill the prescription anyway at a new drugstore. Surprisingly, their computer holds my personal and medical information. Since dental costs are now far more than the rental car charge, usual food costs, and gas charges, I feel the need to warn James before the bill arrives. He's upset over the cost.

"How many teeth do you have left?" he asks boldly. "I don't know if we can afford to get them all fixed."

"I don't expect to be in this body much longer," ego states, reverting to the time-worn pity me power play. They just called my name so the prescription for pain pills must be ready."

Daniel's comforting essence comes while listening to the daily CD. Words fill my brain as Novocain begins to wear off. This, he reports, is one of the trials and tribulations he told me to expect. There will be more after this. Because we are in this human world, we must experience what we came here to feel.

Exquisite pain now makes it difficult to eat or talk. Daniel suggests a Tylenol when I wonder why September's dental work was painless. That makes two drugs used since May of 2006. The other was the usual antibiotics taken for previous dental appointments. Today's dentist said I didn't need antibiotics. The protocol changed.

Gratitude abounds upon knowing unseen forces continually protect, guide, and lead. I am one with Self even while giving in to take bits of a pain pill. Apparently, my soul chose for this to happen so I'm glad to get it out of the way. Tampa awaits and then I'll be on a weeklong birthday cruise. For now, I sleep much more.

Time-worn thoughts erupt during studies. Yes, the mind contemplates an idea many times before acting. How many times did James and I mention the word "divorce" over the past fifteen years? When will it be time to act?

Pain pills deteriorate thought making it too hard to attend class. The effect carries over into the next day but pain lessens so I switch to Tylenol.

Friday's laundry sits wet in the basket as I drive to the house on 47th Drive. Clutter and chaos remains. Books, papers, fishing equipment, etc., mar nearly every space. My stomach turns as I weave quickly through the very, hot, house.

Sarah's birthday present sits safely in the chest in my uncluttered room. I pull it out before searching for clothes. The closet floor is littered with plastic bags, packed with clothes many months before, each labeled noting contents and origin as made in the U.S.A. Grabbing a hippie dress from the 1970's to wear on Halloween, I smile, remembering my naivety in believing it was time to pass out of the physical, instead of being reborn into a new understanding of life.

An hour later, after running errands and hauling dry clothes out to the car, I rescue the cactus plant from my room. Intuition notes I'll never live in this house again while scanning rooms. Even through James finally emptied coolers and containers, used to catch rain from roof leaks on the back porch; humidity fills the air. I'm ecstatic to leave chaos far behind as the den door shuts.

Studies consisting mainly of the Course and *The Disappearance of the Universe* (which surprisingly is about the Course) consume time. Gary Renard verifies many treasured beliefs. How wonderful to have verification! Yes, clearly, I forgot my true nature for a long, long, time. But now this mind chooses to remember! It's becoming increasingly clear. This world and dense physical body is a creation of my own making. Now it's time to control the "sick thought system" shared by those around me. But how? There are no differences in unchangeable *Truth*. Yet, here on earth, all beliefs are real to the believer and "truth" is different for everyone.

A somewhat familiar pain disrupts serenity. Concentration fades quickly as sharp pain shoots up my vagina. It's been more than a year since I took small doses of Valium prescribed for this pain. Rebecca, remembering our trip to Vancouver when we both had the condition, sympathizes. My only thought is to get the bag of drugs I never threw out back at the house on 47th Drive. A sharp, searing, pain shoots up my butt for extra incentive as I grab car keys.

The house on 47th Drive is still hot and humid. A cat sits on the kitchen counter. "Perhaps it snuck into the house when I was there and this pain propelled me to return and let it out," I think. The cat is scared and runs. It meows pitifully every time I near it but does not hiss. Even talking softly does not seem to calm it. I open both the den and sliding glass door after it jumps into the glass trying to escape. Now, I recognize the cat. Prudence finally runs through the open, sliding glass door. There's no need for the trauma of being blamed for letting her into the house as I grab the large bag of drugs from the refrigerator.

This is all part of the trials and tribulations Daniel and several other sources mentioned. First, you treat for your desire then you get the ideas from God to help spur that prayer forward. Check. After that, it's time to keep it on your mind but live your life as if the prayer is already accomplished. Done. Keeping the faith is imperative. Okay! A period of trials comes right before reaping desires. This is obviously that period for me.

In the Manual for Teachers, the Course notes a period of unsettling, where the teacher learns to put judgment aside, while asking for only what she wants in every circumstance. The stage of "real peace" then comes.

Looking forward to real peace and opulent wealth to spur my soul forward to it's final goal keeps me going. For now, I wait for the pain to end so I can stop taking Valium. It makes me tired and although I seem to sleep longer and dream, I don't like the way it interferes with spiritual practices. Am I spending too much time evolving at a quicker rate than I should?

Terry still works part-time stocking ice and selling drinks at a local gay bar. Rebecca usually sings there on karaoke night and asked me to join her for Halloween. More weight disappeared off my still hefty frame so the hippie dress fits perfectly when I dress to go days later.

Ruth sits perched on a bar stool amidst clouds of cigarette smoke, wearing her usual clothes, when we arrive. She grins upon seeing Rebecca in one of Naomi's mini-skirt outfits from the 1960's. Terry wears leather and chains as he quickly deposits beer and wine on the table, refusing cash before moving on. Rebecca takes a long slug of beer as the DJ calls her name.

"Here Mom," she says tossing the list of karaoke songs into my lap, "pick a song to sing."

Rebecca belts out her favorite mournful song, about a cheating boyfriend, amid hoots from the crowd. Smoke wafts through the room. Listening, I sip white wine while remembering months ago when I drunkenly sang, "Carry On My Wayward Son." It took enormous amounts of energy to stand through the song while publicly saying goodbye to Daniel.

This time I'll chose a very different song. With constant prompting, and a full glass of wine, I finally make a choice. After a quick gulp, the wine mixes with the apprehension in my brain and loosens its grip.

The room suddenly becomes silent as Carole King's "Way Over Yonder" streams forth. A young man hands me a dollar after the first few bars. Near the end of the song, the owner slips a five-dollar bill into my hand. The crowd cheers and claps as I step down from the stage. A customer stands before me holding a fresh glass of white wine.

"Good job," says Peter, one of Terry's friends, as he hands me the glass.

"Thank you," I announce knowing there are no coincidences. "You have the same name as my son's father."

Despite reluctance to drink more, I raise the glass to salute him. Someone tugs on my arm.

"I'll give you $70 for the dress," a skinny, young man says fingering the gauzy material.

I don't want to let go of the dress even though getting the money would be nice because my stash is dwindling fast.

"This dress is a classic," I remark merrily while turning to see him, "made in India in the 70's. I'll sell it for $250."

"All I've got is seventy bucks," he says stroking the material again before walking away.

Ruth and I belt out "Bobby McGee" by Janis Joplin, to the happy throng of barflies, before calling it a night. A bit more than one glass of wine swims through my system as Rebecca and I drive home.

Words come during 2011, after breathing in through the nose and out through the mouth to continue reactivating the Light within.

"We come together to help the people of earth. It is our supreme wish, desire, to do so. All is illusion for there is no earth. And yet, we know, to those minds lost in the maze, it seems so very real. Know that all is going according to the Divine Plan as you move further into this illusion of power versus Love. Love, has and always, will survive. We are with you every step of the way. Do not fear."

It's so amazing how my perspective continues to change. Things read in the past have entirely different meanings when read again. My list of desires, documented many months ago, sits before me the next day as I check off accomplishments. Yes, extra money for vacation came from two unexpected sources. Yes, I won money at the casino and met another spiritual connection. Yes, someone paid for new clothes and I won another $400 at a casino. March marked manifestation of a successful cruise and June, another cruise, and a family trip to Flagler Beach. My desired mystery trip, in August to Big Sky, also met the desire to be at a party, when we celebrated Charles's birthday at dinner. Two desires have not yet been met, the Italy trip and the sale of my business, which may not happen.

"A happy outcome to all things is sure," notes the daily Course lesson. God promises only joy as the final outcome. But it is up to us when this is reached. God's Will is done in everything. There's no need for trials and tribulations. We need only to recognize our Oneness with *Truth*.

The dental receptionist welcomes me in the morning. I sit waiting, remembering today's Course lesson. "All fear is past and only love is here." Fear appears in many different forms, but love is one. I choose to sense and experience only love.

As I draft this book, while listening to "Silent Lucidity," a random thought breaks concentration. Many people will appreciate hearing this lovely song. Somehow I know the perfect video of it is on youtube.com. Minutes later, I find the video and post the link to my Facebook page. Several people "like" the link and comment before I log off to continue writing. That's what it's like to be led by positive unseen energy.

Rebecca is surprised when I return home to announce we're shopping at Home Depot. We're going to buy the lawn tools needed to keep up the property. My lovely daughter is cautious as I push her to move out of limitation. There's no need to worry about an inability to do something when you can easily do it, I announce as we drive. The estate is beginning to attract city inspectors and this will avoid further costs. James may complain about the $140 charge on my Visa card but he'll pay it.

Longer periods of sleep consume time. Progressing to the point where I'm not waking every fifteen to sixty minutes makes me happy. Yet, sleeping for ninety minutes to three hours at a time has its consequences. I recall dreams. Today I wake with wet eyes. Tears flowed down my face because I missed doing things with Daniel. After self-talk in the dream, I stopped the tears only to begin crying more intensely, at least three times. Now I understand why sleeping habits changed since Daniel's transition.

"There is no need for limitation," a voice notes as I consider washing clothes and drying them at the house on 47th Drive. After more than a year, it's time to replace the broken dryer. Intuition guides me to shop when studies complete.

It's still early, before 10:00 AM, as an unseen force guides me to the used appliance store Daniel used to purchase Rebecca's stove months before he passed. The perfect dryer costing no more than $200, I know, sits waiting for me. Less than ten minutes later, the friendly, small store owner sells me a reconditioned dryer for $89, including delivery and disposal of the old one.

Dryers, he notes, have few parts. This one looks new and the store owner just replaced the most expensive part.

Today is another "Things Come Easily To Me" day! People fill the dollar store when I enter. The perfect garden gloves for Rebecca sit near the door. My eyes spot a heart shaped sticky foam object that says, "Hugs" as I get out of the car at the grocery store. It's my ideal penny from Heaven. Inside the store, I buy things to help me cook for Sarah when she's home from the hospital. A $1 coupon, for my favorite ice cream, sits right on top of a container. What looks like a brand new princess telephone sits in a box for just $5 at the thrift store. It wasn't there last month and is perfect to replace the broken telephone at Rebecca's house. Intuition guides me over to the bookshelves next to buy greatly discounted books for Sarah and Samuel.

Our new dryer arrives two hours later. As the deliveryman loads the old dryer onto the truck, I sweep the space where it sat. Two baby frogs hop away as the broom brushes away years of dust. The man is happy to accept $20 after he hooks the dryer up with a brand new air vent. It feels wonderful to be guided, protected, and led, and I am ever grateful.

Mary drops the price of her home by $25K the next day. She's not happy to still live there and glad to run constant errands while moving from store to store. I'm grateful to be pain free. We part shortly before my last "Bible Scholarship and History" class.

Rebecca blesses me with a Sunpass when I return home to pack for my trip. This loving gesture takes me by surprise for I didn't consider the tolls. It's the first considerate gift I recall getting in a very, long, time, but perhaps my memory is lacking. The Sunpass holds enough money for both Tampa visits.

Words fill my head on 12-12-11 before rising. They come after bouts of unexpected, but familiar, breathing where I re-activate the Light within, with ease and grace. Still filled with the sleep of a human, I decide to sit later in the day to receive a message. I think about telling everyone how we are reactivating more Light to hold within. And then the message begins...

"I will never be that upon which things happen. I will continue to manifest my own world of wonder, of love, of glory, of abundance and Truth. The "That" of which I AM is limitless,

*Truth abiding in the ethers of non-space and non-local reality. And the "That" of which I AM is ready to return to the wholeness of One. I abide in the **All That Is** now and forevermore. And knowing this Truth, I AM free of the constraints of this world.*

"Repeat after me:

*"I AM free, a sovereign being living in the Light of Love. There is none other but the **All That Is** of which I AM. A part of wholeness and Truth ever-abides in this BEing of Greatness."*

*"**All That Is** is the very core of all things and all that is and ever will be. The Truth abides in all to see, to hear, to know. Feel it within you now and know that all is very, very well as we move forward on this Mother Earth Ship."*

Chapter Twenty-Four

Old Habits Die Hard

*"Physicality often goes beyond beliefs. This occurs as
one tunes into the state of Oneness and Truth, a state of
Oneness known to all that traverse outer realms." SAM
– Book of One :-) Volume 2*

The printer helps to keep up with Course lessons, without
packing the entire book. A week's lessons, CD player, meditation
and treatment CD sit in my small suitcase. Alligator Alley is
nearly empty as I motor quickly through perfect weather.

Towne Place Suites welcomes me hours earlier than the
usual check in time. The friendly desk clerk offers a third floor
room, next to stairs, in the perfect quiet area. He says the hospital
sits less than ten minutes away from my bargain priced suite.
Knees creak while climbing stairs for much needed exercise.

Dust and dirt mar furniture, walls, carpet, and linoleum.
Frozen food goes into the freezer, next to an ice bin filled with
old shriveled ice. I take the bin out of the freezer to see an inch of
frost at the bottom. It doesn't occur to me to complain for it's
hospital time now.

Sarah is still in surgery when I arrive. Her things sit upon
a sturdy chair next to Abraham, who sleeps soundly at the end of
a row. After checking in with the volunteer, I enter the empty
chapel next door to study. Daniel's essence fills the room while
wondering, "Is this Sarah's wake-up call or is her soul ready to
leave?" Sarah will make it through the operation okay, I hear.

Abraham acknowledges me almost an hour later. He's a
very quiet, subdued man of short stature. Sarah's surgeon, he
notes, is very good and operates on famous athletes. We talk
briefly before Abraham promptly falls back asleep. "Is he
connecting to Sarah now?" I wonder.

The operation takes longer than expected but lasts little
more than an hour. After noting Sarah went through it very well,

nurses let us in to see her an hour later. She seems fairly coherent in the recovery room but only recalls hearing a song about children by Jimmy Buffet.

Thoughts of her true reality permeate my mind. Oneness and sickness cannot coexist. Looking past what eyes see seems impossible as hospital staff march from patient to patient catering to dis-ease. "How can I clearly explain how limiting thoughts are?" I think, as Abraham speaks of recovery time.

This trip is both a soul mission and a test of my new perception to see everyone as spirit in physical form. But even knowing all is illusion, it's still difficult to live in this world of duality, seeing people laid up in the hospital.

Holmes notes, "All things work for our good. Suffering carries a blessing with it when we learn how to garner knowledge from experience."

The body exists only in the mind as a way to experience separation. Yet, I must learn to allow the feelings and beliefs of others. As souls we program certain things to happen. Some of us choose to learn or teach through the avenue of dis-ease. Everything is a symbol of separation. But pain and limitation seems very real to those who experience it. *(Hence, the recent reminder.)*

The Course explains images as symbolic of the ego. The purpose of my dis-ease was to bring me to the point of awakening. But determining the point of dis-ease in others seems complex. On one level, my little mind senses that souls chose to teach and learn but on another level, the level of One, I know we are the same. And we are only here in mind. There is no physical reality.

This is the first time I'm aware of having more than one state of awareness. Now it seems right to forgive the images I see and then forgive myself for even thinking there's reason to forgive. Everything is a projection of thought to keep separation alive and well. It's heartening to believe that forgiveness is having an effect on other dimensions. Yet, am I feeding the energy of dualism by being with Sarah now? Am I feeding the energy of dualism by reporting on her progress to family members?

Gary Renard notes we cannot observe anything without causing a change, if only on the sub-atomic level! Whatever is true is eternal and unchangeable so clearly this world is an illusion of mis-thought. How can I explain this all to my sister without distancing her? How can I explain, in terms that she will understand, that illness is an act of separation, symbolic of our separation from God?

Is it really up to me to do so? Or should I just continue to be respectful of her experience and keep thoughts to myself? Is it true that there is really only one of us? This concept takes monotheism to a whole new level! And now the historic figure, Akhenaton from ancient Egypt, the originator of monotheism, intrigues me again.

If there is one, and I am that one, what is this experience showing me? Is my unconscious mind trying to pull me back to dis-ease?

Before rising on the morning of December 21, 2011, I note a memo into the recorder. "Write an article on preparing for uncertainties (stocking up on food and water), the importance of going within, and deciding what your role is and playing it." In the afternoon as I sit ready to write, the following words flow quickly through me.

"As long as we remain encased in a body, it seems prudent to make the world a better place. We do this by changing the way we manifest, by looking at things in new ways and adding positive spins to all that occurs.

"For instance, let's say you lost your job. On one hand, it would seem devastating to not have a steady income. But on another, it opens a whole new world of possibilities. These possibilities existed before the job loss but now are enhanced in your mind because of the job loss. So what are these possibilities? For one, you have the opportunity to do as you please, to find your passion, and start a new way of living.

"Perhaps you didn't know how to exist without having a steady place to visit during the day but now you are on to another whole new level of understanding. You know the day starts in your mind. It is not based upon a timepiece or 'bosses law' but starts with the value of your memory to call it what you will.

"Do not be so distant to new thoughts for they will take you into another realm of existence, within your mind, that never leaves you feeling empty. The point of this speech is to give you new ways to think, new ideas, new ways to manifest by envisioning what your heart's desire is.

"Think of a time when you existed solely to BE. That time is quickly returning now and you hold the key as to when it occurs. All those on the path of One share that key. Knowing all is one significant, vast state of BEing should help to secure the future you seek. This future does not rely upon a job, a home, or even the people we currently see. It evolves around your thoughts, your ability to manifest and dream a new dream of truth, of light, of wholeness and health.

*"The prosperity you seek is already yours. You need only believe in the Source of One to manifest that new dream now. The answers you seek are within you. Do not be dissuaded by the mass consciousness that appears outside of you. This is only a ploy to keep you in the dream of limitation. Seek nothing outside yourself. Learn to trust in the wholeness of **All That Is** to meet your everyday needs."*

The time to reconsider past decisions, especially if they cause pain to anyone, is here. All bodies are the same in their eternal reality even though it does not appear so here on earth. I must suspend judgment, forgive others and myself, and extend Christ's image to all. Even though the Course notes sickness is a decision, the choice of weakness, "in the mistaken conviction that it is strength," I must recognize the perfect Oneness of which we truly are. Yes, the small mind uses sickness to convince us we are a body but there is another choice. We can remember our Oneness as God's perfect creation and recognize that illusions can have no effect.

Several hours later, we follow Sarah's gurney when a room becomes available. Her roommate seems nice and has a loving husband. Sarah sleeps soundly as we all talk. I soon mention the pretty nightgown and warm socks Momma bought for Sarah and offer to get them from my car. Abraham says it isn't necessary for she has clothes from home. His reply fills me with curiosity.

When Sarah wakes, I announce plans to cook the family's remedy for illness, chicken noodle soup. Again, Abraham says it's not necessary. Prepared to stay as long as Sarah wants me there, but now feeling a bit uncomfortable, I wonder how much longer Abraham will stay. He arrived with Sarah, four hours earlier than I did. An hour later, it's clear. Abraham won't leave while I'm there so I ask what his schedule is.

"It's okay if you come to the hospital in the morning before I arrive," he finally agrees.

A quick shower at the hotel feels great after eight o'clock in the evening. But now I'm noticing more signs of a limiting atmosphere. The bathtub and bathroom sink drain very, slowly. More than a foot of water stands in the bathtub before my shower ends. Water softener makes it seem hard to rinse soap off properly. One bedside lamp is broken and there's a large crack in the lamp over the work area. Yet, considering the rooms cost, less than $40 a day, including a full kitchen, it's a bargain. I will start my chicken noodle soup tomorrow despite Abraham's opinion.

Area weather changes quickly. I'm glad to snuggle under covers as a cold front passes through. What joy to have a place by myself without animals! Although I love Princess and Kitty, I'm not accustomed to sleeping with cat and dog dander and hair, or having throw-up, pee, and dirt from outside on the bed. Dealing with an almost constant smell of cat feces throughout Rebecca's house is also difficult so I'm very grateful to be here.

Right before drifting off to sleep, I again speak with James, in mind, asking that his soul talk with my soul for the highest good of all. An uncomfortable energy rouses me after falling asleep. It seems negative so without thinking I mentally tell the spirit to go away. The room suddenly becomes more restful and I fall back asleep without further discomfort.

Cold fills the room upon waking for the day. I now remind myself that blessing the spirit would have been better and vow to bless, if it returns. Getting out of bed is difficult. It's been quite a long time since I've been up and about so early and I'm not accustomed to cold weather. Leaving for the hospital seems very hard to do. Circle-shaped, red areas scatter around cheeks as the day's Course lesson reminds me, "Only an instant does this world endure."

This is not my "real" identity so I don't let it bother me. But lifting bedcovers to check the sheets is now a must. A few black hairs lead me to believe housekeeping did not change the sheets from the last guest. A set of clean sheets sits in the closet so I do it myself before eating a breakfast of hot instant oatmeal and dried apricots from home.

Cotton gloves and a black stocking hat complete my attire as I traipse downstairs to the car. Realizing that most people would not think 40-60 degree weather is cold makes the short trip to the hospital bearable.

Sarah eats while watching TV when I arrive. She wants to change her nightgown minutes later. Eighty extra pounds sits on her tiny frame. Too small gowns brought from home prompt me to get the larger one from my car. It fits Sarah perfectly. She sits in a chair for more than ninety minutes after we cover her hefty frame. That, in my opinion, is great since the operation was less than eighteen hours ago.

Envision a fast recovery, I advise, and listen to music instead of TV. She thanks me for the healing music CD but announces there's no way to play it. I pull my CD player out of a travel bag after she settles back in bed. Sarah is soon asleep with headphones on her ears.

Her roommate's husband talks adamantly as she sleeps. The man seems very familiar and closer in consciousness to me than his wife. He's helping a Chinese girl learn English so she can come to America, which is her dream. He and his wife even offered her a place to stay. They're Democrats fed up with today's state of politics. I tell them about the monetary system and impending government surveillance.

Sarah smiles widely as I read to her after lunch. She looks at me with great surprise when Abraham arrives to announce he took a few days off from work so I don't need to stay in Tampa. I soon leave to eat a late lunch at the hotel.

Sarah is handling her second total knee replacement, within five months, very well. Her progress even amazes me. Family members are happy to hear the news. Momma's glad to know I'll make chicken noodle soup and is not a bit surprised that I'll nap before starting. The red spots on my face are now gone but I'm exhausted.

Two hours later, while lying on the bed with closed eyes listening to my daily CD, I again feel a spirit. It hovers slightly above me and feels like the same one that visited last night. This time it seems somewhat harmful and tries to hold me down. I cannot move my arms. I bless it and announce that I'm the Light of God and only the Light of God can come near me.

"God, the Living Spirit Almighty, is within me," I silently announce. "I AM the Light of God and only good, and Light, and Love can come near me."

I still cannot move my arms or hands so I repeat the words. Each time I say them, my hands become freer and freer until I finally push them out spread-eagle to both sides of the bed. And then, I open my eyes to look around the room. Nothing is there. My eyes close again while repeating the usual blessing for all spirits passing or that have passed in the area. I give them everything they need to pass into the Light, lovingly, peacefully, joyfully, astutely, and wholly.

Something white flies by the window as I rise to write. Ah, in the tree, there it is, a bird! Surely, this was another trial. It was so very real but I came through it and now am ever grateful.

Sarah is happy to see me minutes after Abraham leaves. We sit talking until visiting hours end and then I return to the hotel to eat food from home. I'm so very grateful for the quiet room while settling into bed.

Red spots appear on my face again on Sunday morning. This time there are more covering cheeks, parts of my neck, and chin. They resemble a severe face rash experienced years ago. The condition concerned me so much then that I took a picture of my face for the doctor to see. I attributed the outbreak to a medication side effect. By the time I got to see the doctor, my face cleared up and only the pictures revealed my dilemma. I have not taken any medication since the bits of pain pills for the last root canal and the few Valium, so that is not the cause of these spots. Catherine Ponder's advice comes to mind. Today, I can hardly wait to see what good comes of this!

Thinking I may be having a reaction to the five feather pillows on the bed, I order a form pillow from housekeeping. The housekeeper offers the foam pillow, fresh towels, and empties garbage minutes later.

Sarah welcomes me shortly before 9:00 AM.

"Abraham," she immediately announces, "does not want you to go out of your way to make me chicken soup."

She smiles upon hearing it's ready and waiting to place in containers. Feeling very uncomfortable, I leave to shop when Abraham arrives five hours later.

Bright red cheeks highlight my small face upon rising on Monday. Sarah asks me about them when I arrive minutes before the physical therapist wheels her away for their last session. She gets to go home today. Stunned over health care system changes, including too short stays after surgery, I leave to take a walk.

Abraham arrives with presents for Sarah hours after lunch. Small stuffed animals are the focus of attention as Sarah sits patiently waiting to leave when the clock strikes 3:00 PM. There's no sense in me staying to follow them home thirty minutes away. Cheeks are still bright red and I want to rest. Neither of us know it will be another six hours before she's finally released.

Daniel offers reminders as I meditate. I'm to stay married to James but apart from him. James may change his perception and we may be back together in a few years. I will be cared for and just need to hang in there without money worries. What a blessing to hear this and to sleep alone in a quiet, clean bed!

Tiredness overwhelms on Tuesday after a restless night filled with dreams. James and I held one another in the most significant dream, thinking it's been a long time since it felt that good.

Frozen soup sits in the cooler when I haul things down three flights of stairs to check out precisely on time. Rebecca's hotel discount makes the bill very affordable. The four-day stay costs less than $157.

Everything is in Divine Order as I head down the highway. Things make more sense as unexpected reasons for the break in my Tampa stay surface. Another dentist visit is already on the agenda, during my time with Samuel, while Rebecca travels for her job. The next hotel, scheduled for three days from now, is closer to Sarah and Abraham's house. A beautiful nearby forest prompts me to hike upon my return.

Sarah sits propped up on the couch shortly before two o'clock in the afternoon. It's the Physical Therapist's good fortune to be running late for the repugnant smell of cat feces fills the air. I stare at the blue cooler of ice nearby wondering what to do. It has a hose and appears to lower the temperature of Sarah's knee through an elastic band wrapped around her leg.

"What is it with this cat shit smell in every house I visit?" I think, before checking the clean cat box down the long hall.

Sarah and Abraham's house lacks the warmth of family pictures. Posters and photos of cats, which look like the ones they care for, line walls. I find this somewhat disturbing but quickly change perspective. Their soul chose things to enhance life just as mine did. *(My home is now devoid of family photos as I leave the past behind.)*

It's unimaginable to continue smelling such a distasteful scent so I grab a can of spray disinfectant from under the kitchen sink. I spray a bit of cleaner with bleach around when the smell remains. That seems to do the trick.

Movies between bouts of conversation fill time. Sarah seems to like my gifts of soup, spiritual and meditation CDs and a new CD player. After staying longer than planned, I decide to return via a scenic drive to the turnpike to avoid traffic on I-75. But a wrong turn on State Road 60 gets me hopelessly lost while admiring beautiful scenery. I ask God for help. Unseen forces lead me to my favorite restaurant while traveling, Cracker Barrel.

Two girls secure Christmas decorations in the entry. Neither knows the area. The manager appears and notes the turn off for I-75 is four miles up the road, seven miles from the hotel left earlier in the day. Wandering to the turnpike, now forty to sixty miles in the other direction, fifty miles out of my way, is no longer an option.

Occasional road construction greets me on I-75. Traffic sits at a standstill while road crew tars the highway. There's good reason for my delay, I affirm. Rain falls briskly minutes before I reach home. Didn't Charles tell us rain signals a change in consciousness? If not delayed, I would have driven in it for most of the way home. It's shortly before midnight when I pull into Rebecca's long drive silently thanking Ruth for her consideration in dropping Samuel off so I wouldn't need to stop at her house.

Disappointment sets in upon opening the door. The house smells of cat shit. Kitty threw up on my side of the bed and it seeped through the blanket, both sheets, and the bed cushion. For the life of me, I cannot imagine why my daughter has an anorexic cat. I sprinkle baking soda on the carpet near the cat box after cleaning it. By the time I change the bed sheets and blanket, and take a shower, it's after one o'clock in the morning.

Princess wakes me to go outside six hours later. After she does her business, I start the laundry before making Samuel's school lunch. I'm still exhausted while driving him to school. Treatments and study, five more loads of laundry, returning for Samuel, and food shopping fill time. I so look forward to centering once again, in two days, away from the hustle and bustle of family duties.

Charles greets me warmly on Thursday night for the first Ralph Waldo Emerson class. Emerson's philosophy emphasized independent thought through one's own perceptions. We're now studying his essays. Tonight we focus on the influence of transcendentalism, a group of ideas emerging in New England in the 19th century, rooted in the philosophy of Immanuel Kant. The interest group became a major cultural movement after the publication of Emerson's 1836 essay *Nature*. Transcendentalists believed in an ideal spiritual state realized through individual intuition rather than religion. Prominent transcendentalists included Emerson, Henry David Thoreau, Margaret Fuller, and others.

Tonight's handout "What's in Your Knapsack?" asks us to reconsider habits or things weighing us down. When we enter the peace and serenity of nature these things fall away. Plans to investigate the state park near Sarah's house, while considering knapsack contents, fall into place.

Clothes, books, water, food and supplements, everything needed for the next hotel stay, sits safely in the car trunk in the morning. Samuel bids me farewell with a smile when I drop him off at school. The drive to Tampa sometimes takes up to six hours. I enjoy driving but it can be tiresome. Today, I notice the beauty of Nature while motoring down Alligator Alley, blessing all living things every few miles. "Surely," I think smiling widely, "Sarah wants and needs me while Abraham works."

Singing "Everything New" by Daniel Nahmod fills me with pure joy for it's only a small matter of time before such a wonderful life is mine. Thoughts do create a better future and I see myself in a place where everything is new, without burdens or distasteful smells. *(It manifests in seven months.)*

Tiredness sets in after driving less than an hour. The music stops. I try to retrieve a Karen Drucker CD while moving at sixty miles an hour. The case refuses to open but the one holding Daniel's memorial CD opens easily so I pop it into the CD player. Familiar words flow as I sing along to the first song.

"There's a piece inside us all. Let it be your friend. It will help you carry on."

Gratitude overwhelms boredom knowing that without this precious piece I'd be lost in many ways. Joy abounds as the CD begins to stop and restart. Yes! Daniel's spirit is with me. Usually, when this happens, my mind concentrates on things that I want to know after thanking him for coming. This time, I ask Daniel's spirit to tell me what I need to know, what I should know, or what he wants me to know.

"I know I shouldn't ask for the same answers I always do," I announce loudly as if speaking with a passenger. "I'm just happy you're with me."

Daniel guides me to touch the right pocket of my jeans.

I question the request but touch my pocket.

"Touch the tip of your nose," I now hear.

"So we are playing games now? I didn't hear a Simon says."

An image of Daniel's wide grin coupled with laughter fills my brain. Daniel is trying to make my drive across Alligator Alley a bit easier to bear. The CD player skips over songs and begins to play Billy Joel's song about not forgetting your "second wind." I laugh along with Daniel's spirit filled with joy to treasure these special moments.

Now the CD player skips, plays the word desperation, and stops.

"Who's desperate?" I ask.

James is desperate, I hear. He doesn't know what to do. I'm to telephone on Thanksgiving to say I love him and ask what he wants. I'm to let him know that we'll continue to live apart while he decides.

Intuition notes the appropriate words will flow when it's time to talk with James. It's up to him as to whether he will grow with me or not. He has a much longer opportunity to decide than offered Peter or Saul.

It really doesn't matter to me how he uses his free will. Our relationship began firmly based on the flesh and must change to continue. Love has no conditions. My consciousness now understands that it's not based on the body, which just gets in the way of us recognizing who we really are, lights of God. I will live out my days in this human host continuing to increase consciousness. I can do that alone or with someone who continues to grow with me. It's really looking doubtful that James will do that. Yet, things happen as they are meant to.

Rest Area 131 offers a beautiful place to stop. Four tour buses sit idling so there's plenty of time to write before using the restroom. Air is unusually cold as I move out of the car but elevated body temperature warms me. Yes, bonuses abound when spirit energy morphs DNA!

Daniel fills the rest of the drive with "happenings." The car slows down when I try to make the cruise control go faster by pressing the "speed up" button. A lot of people would relish unseen friends to keep them from getting tickets, I soon bet, for a cop car sits hidden on the side of the road. Accidents and roadwork slows traffic near the hotel. The last words out of the CD player before the batteries die are "hold on," sung by Kansas.

Even with delays, the drive takes only four hours. Soccer teams fill the hotel but I still get the perfect second floor room. It's closer to stairs, and away from the noisy elevator. Beautiful trees grace the private view outside of super large windows. A maintenance man delivers the last unused microwave shortly after I open the door. I soon learn it does not work.

An hour nap revives me before eating and visiting Sarah. We spend six hours trying to watch family DVDs but none of them plays properly. Either it's because my computer messed up when making them, I finally announce, or a spirit is with us. (The DVD's play normally at the hotel later.)

Abraham returns from work, fixes Sarah dinner, and then leaves to run errands without eating. The DVD of Amos plays really well now. Sarah cries softly as Amos discusses the pending lawsuit and how much money we stand to get from Daddy's untimely demise. Intuition prompts. This is one of the reasons for my visit.

"I didn't treat Daddy so well the last time we were together," Sarah confides wiping tears, "and I've felt bad about it ever since."

Words fill my brain so I spill them out softly telling her to let guilty feelings go. She's held on to them for way, too, long. Daddy wants her to know he forgives her and there really is nothing to forgive. He wants her to know that he loves her. Sarah is comforted to hear it and agrees to never think of it again. I'm enormously happy to help.

Joy and wholeness accompanies me while driving back to the hotel. Minutes later, I lose my way. After fifteen minutes of driving down country roads, I cannot recall any scenery. The road is empty and very dark. Intuition kicks in after crossing two sets of railroad tracks. Daddy's valuable lesson comes to mind. Ignoring ego, I thank him and turn the car around. Countless times of driving, while hopelessly lost and not asking for directions, or turning back the way he came, pays off for me. A wonderful angel verifies that I'm indeed on the right road when I stop at a lone gas station with a convenience store.

Bone weary upon reaching the room, I follow intuition again to turn on the TV. A psychic challenge show is just beginning. Michelle Whitedove quickly meets the challenge. How wonderful to see this teacher on prime time TV!

An unexpected thought fills my brain. Am I to be a teacher of God? The Course emphasizes that a teacher of God is anyone who chooses to be one. Since I feel drawn to help humanity recognize we are spirit in human form, perhaps that is my path. Teachers of God are appointed to bring about the end of time. Each teacher, the Course reports, begins as a single light, but with the Call at its center, it's an unlimited light.

Renard notes the Course needs female teachers who teach women they are not bodies. Teachers of God function from rightness, Tara Singh notes in *Commentaries on A Course In*

Miracles, without a vested interest, for their relationship is with Life rather than attachments. Everything is related, extending itself through the creative Law of God. Everything is one life extending itself in many different forms, shapes, and facets.

Awareness of my role creeps closer. The external world is illusion, a figment of imagination. It's best to be unattached, at peace, without a need to seek, achieve, or accomplish. Only time will tell when this body will drop all sense of separation to perform the souls' mission, wholly and adequately.

Sarah's unexpected morning call again changes ego's plan. Abraham took the day off, which she notes is unusual, so she really doesn't need me. One or two o'clock in the afternoon, however, would be a good time to visit. Ego fights to maintain control of time-worn habits, always caring for others, as I decide to walk nearby trails. Today's desk clerk informs me there are no microwaves available when I request one before leaving.

A state park sits less than a mile away. Several cars fill the lot as I walk past a sign noting the trail is only half of a mile. God, I affirm, continues to guide when another less populated footpath lures me off to eat my bagel sandwich. The trail is about a quarter of a mile and leads to a fishing area. Birds chirp as I walk and eat in warmer weather.

It's a bit after 12:30 PM when I again reach the forest path. This place reminds me of playing as a child at Eliza Hall in Michigan. Two hikers with walking sticks, about my age, walk behind me. Familiar smells, from long ago, tease memory while strolling through beautiful woods. A big, beautiful, Zebra Butterfly lies still in the middle of the path. Thinking it might be injured, and stepped on by someone else, I carefully scoop it up, thanking it for letting me see its beauty. One of its legs is abnormal. It's passing. While holding it in cupped hands, I move off the trail into the forest. As I bless it with good, light, and love, with peace and joy, and greater evolution forevermore, the couple moves further up the trail. A happy butterfly soon rests peacefully on the large leaf of a small bush.

There's no sense of time for the next half hour. I hear, and sometimes see, the couple in front of me. They stop to decide what cutoff to take just as I'm beginning to wonder if the sign at the beginning of the trail gave the wrong distance. I'm tired now and ask if the trail is indeed only a half-mile long. Trails, the woman reports, are poorly marked. It's easy to go further than the main trails half-mile, which we all did. She kindly directs me back to the parking lot.

Gratitude for guidance continues during the next half hour's walk. Clearly, if not for the butterfly I might still be walking deeper into the forest.

Sarah and Abraham greet me warmly at a quarter past two o'clock in the afternoon. Abraham continues working on various chores after fixing her something to eat. He seems accustomed to doing everything. Sarah happily displays Abraham's latest presents (the newly released "Shrek the Third" DVD and a cute, little, beanie baby cat).

"There must be a major karmic connection between them," I think, trying not to be disappointed over their lack of need for me. They seem to get along well, communicating much more than James and I ever did. But something about Abraham causes discomfort. Is it because I've never allowed someone to care for me in such a manner? Is it the thought of not being needed after years of caring for others?

Sarah and I sit for three, long hours talking as the TV blares. It's clear she watches a lot of TV because she's already seen most of the twenty or so movies showing. Abraham cannot get the VCR to work properly when we try to play the one family VCR tape brought from home. We discuss diet and exercise when Sarah voices a desire to lose weight. My head begins to throb with an unusual major headache so I leave before nightfall.

Having a king-size bed never felt so good but my stomach cries out for food an hour later. I lie there wondering what to eat. It soon occurs to me that the coffeemaker can warm a can of soup while I soak in the bathtub. I rise, fill the coffeepot with hot water, remove the lid, and put the canned soup inside. The soup tastes perfect when my bath is over.

After rising to repeat the usual ritual of treatments, mediation and prayer, I fall back asleep on Sunday morning. It's Abraham's usual day off so there's no need to hurry. The Physical Therapist bids Sarah farewell when I arrive before noon. Abraham is out doing errands when Sarah notes an appointment with her doctor in two days. Her clothes no longer fit so I give her my favorite leisure suit knowing it fits her perfectly. Due to weight loss, the suit is too big for me now. We again spend the day watching TV. I leave shortly after Abraham enters the house.

The hotel remains crowded and noisy making it difficult to sleep. I lie there feeling unwanted but glad for a clean, safe place to stay.

Sarah telephones early in the morning, offering the perfect opportunity to walk the trail again. Abraham, she announces, won't leave for work until lunchtime. A heady thought occurs while driving. Maybe this trip is the last of my karmic tasks.

"Changing thoughts," I think, while driving and opening the glove box, "is as easy as listening to Liza Minnelli." The cassette pops out of its case and lands on the floor by the passenger side door. My right hand searches for another tape, while thinking about a much needed walk through nature. The first tape I grab turns out to be by Kansas.

"Hold on, baby, hold on, cause it's closer than you think and you're standing on the brink. Hold on, baby, hold on, cause there's something on the way and tomorrows not the same as today."

There are no coincidences. Daniel tells me, once again in a physical way, to hang in there. It's immensely comforting.

A sense of Oneness fills me with joy and gratitude while blessing all living things during a fifteen-minute stroll down the lake trail. The short walk is very beneficial for now inner peace accompanies me on the way to see Sarah.

We spend our day trying to watch home videos copied for her onto DVDs. But every disk skips. Some just stop abruptly, as when Daniel lets me know he's near. I finally disclose this to Sarah and quickly learn we share uncommon beliefs. It feels good to help her verify, she's not crazy. Both DVDs play without a glitch after our talk.

Familiar behavior soon reminds me of how I used to be. Abraham arrives home at 7:30 PM with a dinner of stuffed shells from their favorite restaurant. He acts like a typical "Type A" personality, unable to relax, completing a variety of chores, while encouraging me to eat. I sample a bit of Sarah's gargantuan portion even while craving fresh vegetables. Sarah eats happily.

She talks while I push pasta around my plate, thinking the shells are not fit for human consumption. Abraham then mentions salads as he rushes around the house. By this time I'm ready to leave for it makes me nervous to watch him.

Plans continue to change. Upset Rebecca phones to note Ruth and Naomi suddenly opted out of a family Christmas at their house. Rebecca, they decided, should host this year. I tell her not to worry. We can get things done before our cruise on December 16 and finish preparations upon returning on Dec 23. Hosting Christmas, even if it's not in my own house, is something to look forward to. It will be nice to invite people not in our blood family once again.

Morning offers thirty-minutes of mindful walk on the trail. Blessing all living things with increasing awareness of the One in which we live, and move, and have all BEing – anywhere between 20-100 times each day – fills me with delight.

Sarah and I again spend most of the day watching TV. It's such a major change for me but I don't mention it. The VCR player finally plays my 1993, six-hour, home video, mainly of Samuel as a baby. Sarah really enjoys it. Tape segments remind Sarah that she weighed much less.

Four years later my state of awareness vastly changes. Viewing, or even possessing any remnants of the past, will no longer resonate.

As Sarah rests on the sofa, I put ice in her knee cooler and cater to cats. Sarah again says Abraham does not have any more personal time to take off work as I listen from the kitchen. He must work both the day before and the day after Thanksgiving to get paid for the holiday.

"He is the way he is," she announces, as I hand her salad and a ham sandwich.

Abraham telephones later to say I can head back to the hotel for he'll return around 8:00 PM. Sarah doesn't want to have dinner without him. I'd planned to stay but now think it best to leave. Abraham, Sarah notes as I rise, will drive her to the doctor in the morning. She's not sure how long the visit will take. Planning to return at noon tomorrow, I tell her to call if there's a change of plans. I'm beginning to think there will be.

The broken microwave still sits on my dresser but the hotel is much quieter than previous nights so I count my blessings. Again, I use the coffee maker to warm a can of soup. How wonderful to have a place of my own where I can take a long, hot, soothing, bath. It's great not to deal with animals or house chores too.

A restless night makes it difficult to wake. Headphones rest on ears while listening to the morning ritual. The "Privacy Please" sign hangs outside as a housekeeper knocks lightly while repeating "housekeeping" near 9:00 AM. She tries to enter the room with her master key. When the second bolt lock stops her, it's clear she's invading my privacy. After putting a pajama top on, I open the door.

"Are you checking out?" She inquires.

Apparently, my room number is on her check out list. She's now obviously upset and quite dismayed to learn my stay lasts for four more days. As apologies fill the air, I'm not sure if it's because she busted in on me or that her list is in error.

She gladly removes the broken microwave and promises to get a working one right away. Someone at the front desk telephones to confirm my check out date, while I ponder how the mistaken list led me to a working microwave. The housekeeper returns with a maintenance man holding it ten minutes later.

Sarah telephones shortly after 11:00 AM to announce that the doctor gave her rave reviews. She can now ambulate without having to be on the ice machine that pumps her knee for six hours a day. Abraham again says there's no need for me to cook Thanksgiving dinner. Sarah is thrilled to report we can go out to eat tomorrow. And then she says Abraham took the day off work.

"So, should I take the day off too?" I ask trying not to be annoyed.

"You can if you want," Sarah happily replies.

I decide to shop and ask if she needs anything before disconnecting the call to fall back asleep.

A small, department store soon offers an opportunity to buy Samuel's birthday present but suddenly I don't feel "right" being there. I force myself to continue shopping. Shoppers fill the grocery store as I weave through aisles to buy food for myself and low-calorie, easily prepared foods for Sarah. "Perhaps," I think, "her habit of eating fatty, unbalanced lunches may change if I show her how easy it is to open a can of nutritious soup."

Lessons, reading, journaling, and email sandwich between thanking the One in which we live, and move, and have all BEing. "How wonderful to have the luxury of time to talk," I tell myself, after chatting with Rebecca and leaving a message for Rachel.

Joy consumes me while warming soup in the microwave before popping popcorn. It's nearly midnight when I read that starting the day right, by giving it to God, saves time. We should habitually remember thoughts of pure joy, peace, and limitless release, the Course notes. Devoting time to God before bedtime sets the mind into a pattern of peace. A single thought of God with eyes closed is all we need.

The telephone wakes me on Thanksgiving Day at 9:15 AM. Sarah announces that Abraham wants to leave for the restaurant at noon. He's insistent on beating the rush of other diners. I quickly disconnect our call, finish the morning ritual, and begin to meditate.

Daniel's spirit again tells me to live abundantly, "because I have it," and will be "coming Home soon." I dance with family and even Uncle Roger notes how proud everyone is of me. Ego writes down highlights of what to say before calling James when the meditation ends. He doesn't answer the phone.

Ruby Tuesday's is almost empty as a young woman seats us. Turkey is not on the menu making it the first year to eat something different. Sarah and Abraham quickly indulge while I think about things to be thankful for. A generous meal of fish, baked potato, and broccoli tastes good. I note how good the broccoli is as Sarah wolfs down steak. Taking the hint, she eats every bit of broccoli on her plate. My stomach is full very quickly. Sarah and Abraham continue eating and listening to me. One of my diet tricks, I note, is to eat slowly, putting the fork down after each bite.

There's still food left on Sarah's plate as Abraham orders dessert. He repeatedly tries to get her to order something else. She just ate a large amount of food, is grossly overweight and diabetic, so his persistence surprises me. I'm enormously proud of my sister for not caving into repeated requests.

We sit down to watch Sarah's new Shrek DVD upon returning home. Abraham promptly falls asleep while sitting up on the couch. When the movie ends, I leave for the hotel. My bottom is sore from several days of sitting on their uncushioned wooden rocker. And I'm still dazed by the fact that they really seem not to need my help. Questions arise. Is this part of the baggage I am to reconsider? Is my caregiver role now over?

Daniel reminds me to telephone James for the third time later in the evening. James listens quietly as I profess my love, completely forgetting that one year ago today, his mother passed away. I ask if he's decided what role he wants me to play and again ask him to consider joint counseling.

"I know," he announces softly, "that you have been through a lot. And when you get better, and decide to face reality, you can come home."

"Reality" is simply what the mind prefers to see. Everyone has a different perception of "reality" and ours is now poles apart. James is waiting for me to come around to his way of thinking. I'm waiting for him to come around to mine.

Course studies invade thought as he continues to speak. Changes in attitude, for the "newly made" teacher of God, are usually the first step in preparation towards a service-based life (life based on leading others to Oneness). Judgment fades as the teacher of God seeks and receives divine guidance. We then begin to perceive relationships as the illusions of which they truly are.

Yes! Another part of this trip is to recognize illusions. The thought of being part of something much bigger than perceived comforts. Too much has happened to revert thinking. God's Voice guides me on the true path to Oneness while setting judgment aside. James and I are still together for a reason, which I have yet to learn, for no one is where he is by accident. Despite appearances, I'm a limitless being joined with Source, forever One. In time, the call to return humanity to Oneness will guide me to other teacher's of God who work as One.

A future Hay House cruise helps to verify my new mission. Taking the cruise seems like a good way to relax and feel the energy of a ship filled with positive like-minds. As many previous excursions, the reason Spirit guides me to cruise is very different from expected. Since I do not read or watch news there's no indication that the world is changing in a major way. It's only through the first day's news update that I learn of riots in Egypt.

A very strong and meaningful message comes before returning to Fort Lauderdale. It arrives along with an awesome physical manifestation taking me by surprise.

"You are a teacher of teachers," fills my mind.

A familiar energy surrounds me and radiates outward. Both hands rise unexpectedly. They rise very slowly, from their resting place upon my chest, as I lay on my back in the middle of the large bed. It's almost as if someone lifts my hands and the arms move only because they're attached to hands. They rise about five inches above my chest to hover effortlessly in mid-air.

Both hands seem to glow when I open my eyes filled with wonder. A white mist, somewhat like an aura of whitish light, emanates from the hands and radiates outward. It's too much to take in without reacting.

"How cool is this!" I silently announce.

The energy field dissipates and both hands drop swiftly to my chest.

I then quickly remember a chance encounter with a woman days earlier. When she announced I was a "teacher of teachers," I looked at her filled with doubt.

While rereading the Course in 2009, it became perfectly clear that I am a teacher of God. But hearing that I'm a "teacher of teachers" fills me with disbelief.

Of course, I repeatedly follow Spirit's guidance while on the cruise. I lose count of the spontaneous messages delivered to people crossing my path. Every time I leave my room, an unseen force guides me to the perfect place where conversation results in the delivery of meaningful messages. I try to stay silent after a while to no avail. Someone at dinner always asks a question that I easily answer. Each answer holds a message.

People look at me with respect. They thank me even as I fail, during the first few days, to recognize messages. By the end of the cruise, I conscious agree to be the perfect host, fully aware of each vital message delivered, at just the right time. Delivering messages energizes me despite tiredness from lack of sleep. (Two huge, simultaneous solar energy blasts caused increased geomagnetic activity.)

For the first time, I do not operate based on old energies. Synchronicity prevails as I offer many more messages than ever before. Spirit leads me around the ship repeatedly to key people within Hay House. After the first two days, I'm somewhat in shock at delivering so many important messages, readily recognized and gratefully received. I identify many lightworkers who have yet to step into their power. It's the most amazing thing, for people do not act like family members and look at me as if I'm crazy. People look as if they recognize the truth of each message. They're happy to get the verification of something intuitively known.

The unseen Force, in which we live, and move, and have all BEing, guides me to do certain things to change the energy on board as well. As a helicopter airlifts a passenger to a hospital in San Juan, I sit on my balcony spreading Light for the good of all. Later, I'm the only one to join people asking for Gregg Braden's signature on newly purchased books, empty handed. His message is short, to the point, and he gets it immediately.

One evening, two women, vastly different in age and background, sit next to me on a bench while waiting for my new friend, Ariel, outside the dining room. The second one sits in the middle just after I deliver a message to the first. She's a young lightworker, waiting for her mom and hoping to find someone of like-mind. Her mom and the other woman's friend arrive along with Ariel just as I hand her my card. There's no mistaking, and now, I'm totally positive that an unseen force guides me very carefully. As everything evolves, I evolve with it, and it evolves as One.

Synchronistic events were awesome, particularly when with Ariel. Just bumping into her after we disembarked in San Juan was synchronicity for I'd asked to be with a like-mind just to enjoy time and not deliver any messages.

We found ourselves in front of each place we sought just when we spoke the words out loud. I found the perfect pair of white, cotton pants for Brazil upon voicing the desire. Ariel

303

voiced a desire to go to the Butterfly Store and we looked up to see it steps away. I voiced a desire to find the Walgreen's with lip gloss and looked up to see we were standing in front of the store. (Later, I thought it was lost and went back to the Crow's Nest to find it. It was not there but I delivered a message to someone for Hay House.)

The past is clearly gone. It's time to step up and accept the Power within. My state of awareness continues to increase and I love this new energy. Such perfection is something I strive to stay in the flow of, and live in, for the rest of this life. I yearn to be done with earth lives to move on! There's so much more I could say but it's not necessary. The only important thing is that I make a difference in the recognition, of what this is, and who we are. It's all Good!

Spirit guides as James listens quietly.

"Change," I stress, "is all that we can count on."

I admit to a habit of outgrowing men. The choice between love and fear (ego) is his as well as mine. Since he appears to be on a different level of consciousness, he has more time to decide what he wants than my two ex-husbands. But the bottom line is that I'm no longer willing to live as before.

The duel of egos continues as James again stresses that I must be the one to change. I change the subject realizing it's time to finally put the past aside, to stop trying to change others, and realize that the only mind I need to change is my own. James is not pleased when I warn him to expect a larger than usual charge card bill for the next two months due to yearly renewals, dental, and vision expenses. After I again try to explain how my view of life and reality changed after Daniel's transition, he tells me to phone when I'm not going to talk about my philosophy.

"Have a happy Thanksgiving," he announces before disconnecting our call.

Sun fills the room while repeating the next morning's usual ritual. Lesson 314 from the Course seems on target.

"I seek a future different from the past."

Today, I'll continue my experiment of living in the land of abundance and opportunity. There's no past to contend with or future to worry me. I'm free to live in the present moment and take advantage of holiday sales. Since Rebecca and I are hosting Christmas there's a lot to do before our cruise.

The store I enter is having a huge sale. By the time I leave, an hour later, a gift for nearly everyone on my list sits in the shopping cart. It costs less than $35 for ten gifts. Momma's gift costs the most but I know she'll love the rocking, singing Santa.

Sarah is happy to see me shortly after noon. She's very pleased to be using her cane. I again let her know how very proud I am of her ability to heal quickly. She seems to relish the praise. We've been so very blessed to have many wonderful family Christmases and I now wonder if Christmas is lonely for her without family around. As she settles on the couch, I hide gifts underneath the bedroom dresser. On Christmas Day, I'll phone to tell her where to look. Abraham soon arrives to give Sarah the usual morning anticoagulant shot.

"It's supposed to rain all day," he reports, while eating a piece of pumpkin pie out of view.

He returns to work after I announce that rain may be a good reason for me to leave early. Sarah and I watch two DVD's of my trip to Greece before I leave for the last time at 4:00 PM.

Since this is my last night at the hotel, I know it will be the most enjoyable. A prayer to ward off anything that shortens my stay repeats. Intuition prompts me to telephone Rebecca while packing. She quickly announces plans for Samuel's birthday party the next day. Her plan includes three teenage boys sleeping over after the family leaves.

There's no need to push myself so I remain in bed longer than usual in the morning. Having a king-size bed to myself is something to savor and the picture window makes it even sweeter. A housekeeper moves down the hall, pounding on doors. She works outside my door for more than an hour before I venture out. As I open the door to take my first load down to the car, I announce plans to check out at noon. She seems surprised and notes I'm not on her list.

It costs $349 for my eight-day stay. Knowing Samuel will not miss me being on time at his birthday party, I decide to walk on the Wilderness Park trail before heading back to Fort Lauderdale.

The park is nearly empty when I arrive deciding to walk for thirty minutes. I leave my bottled water in the car. Although rarely without water, it's just too cumbersome to carry. Several cough drops sit in my pocket.

How wonderful to be outside in bearable weather walking! Mindful, I continually thank nature and bless it, along with all living things. The energy in my palms increases while blessing butterflies, trees, and other things. Each person I pass smiles when I say hello.

An unexpected boost of energy surrounds me after thirty minutes. Since park signs are still clear, I continue, thinking the trail is in a loop. Nature speaks as I stop to converse with towering trees and small creatures. A wonderland of beauty surrounds me as scents of flowers and moss fill the air. But now none of the beautiful landscape looks familiar and I have not passed anyone for at least twenty minutes. Glad for three cough drops, I time when to allow myself one.

When the trail nears the highway, I walk over to look for something familiar. "My car must be close by," I think, "because I've now walked for an hour." Nothing on the highway looks familiar. A sign at the side of the road up ahead says "Main." It points in the direction I'm headed. I ask God for direction and continue.

A memory and image soon flash into my mind reminding me of the drive from the hotel to see Sarah. Yes! The "Main" sign is right before Flatwoods Park, a distance down the road from Wilderness Park where the car sits. Intuition tells me to turn around despite ego not wanting to retrace steps. Going back the way I came means I will walk for another hour. Yet, if I am indeed headed towards Flatwoods Park, my walk will be a lot more than two hours. The last signpost was number 17 but I don't know how many numbers there are. I ask God to send me another sign, perhaps an angel, to let me know how close I am to the parking lot.

Clouds form as two men on bicycles ride up behind me, say hello, and zip on by. Another rider zips past from the direction I'm headed but again I let him pass without calling out for directions. I then remember the joke about the man who drowned. He asked God for help but ignored the three men in rowboats who asked if he needed assistance. When he got to Heaven, he asked God why he had not helped him.

"I tried to help you three times," was the reply.

Blessings become fewer as I try to determine why I haven't yet reached the parking lot. Upon thinking how bothersome it would be to wander in the forest during a heavy rainstorm, I decide to ask the next person for directions. A man riding a bike soon glides toward me near a clearing in the forest. He circles the sand several feet in front of me and answers quickly when I ask for directions.

"Well," he reports with a wide smile, "that depends on which park your car is at. My car is at Flatwoods."

"I came in at Wilderness Park."

"Just stay in the direction you're going and you'll get there," he announces as a young girl and woman ride up from the path in front of me.

The three of them head towards Flatwoods Park. Before they're out of range, I hear him tell the woman, "She just walked a long way."

My t-shirt is wet with sweat, my throat is dry and I'm terribly thirsty. But since I'm moving in the right direction I just try to enjoy the journey. It's a lot better mentally than to think of the walk ahead. Gratitude fills me nearly an hour later upon seeing my beautiful car sitting under a shady tree. I'm thankful for the walk even though it took much longer than planned. The extra bonus is that I don't have to go to the bathroom for hours because of sweaty fluid loss.

Relatively light traffic for the Saturday after Thanksgiving greets me. I continue to be mindful while driving, appreciating the sunset, the foliage, and the birds.

Time passes quickly. It feels good knowing I'm not alone when a black pickup truck, similar to the one Daniel had, goes by. His initials, DAD, are in the rear window on some kind of sticker. The turn off to I-595 glides by while I continue to relish the moment. Three miles later, I realize the error but know there's a reason for taking the long way.

It's six o'clock in the evening when I finally arrive. Dense energies fill the atmosphere as Ruth, Naomi, and Terry continue talking on the back porch, barely noting my arrival. The familiar scent of jealousy fills air space. Power plays continue to tug at Rebecca so I'm glad to help by supervising the boys while she takes Grandma home.

Intuition prompts that something is amiss when no one asks about Sarah, the trip to see her, or the planned cruise in three short weeks. Before long, I smile sweetly and agree to pick Samuel up from school every day until Christmas break. As family members walk to cars, today's Course lesson consoles.

"I seek a future different from the past. From new perception of the world, there comes a future very different from the past. The future now is recognized as but extension of the present..."

Yes! I can unburden myself by letting go of old baggage. I can change perceptions and make the present very good by thanking Ruth for letting Rebecca and I have Christmas this year. I then run outside to give Naomi a book about Elvis, which she's loved for many years, along with a big hug and kiss. All is very well in my world.

Chapter Twenty-Five

Ego's Limiting Ways

"We are in a constant state of influx." SAM – Book of One :-) Volume 1

Boys hoot with laughter in the living room as I replace pillowcases. Rebecca vies to be the toy guitar hero while they play with Samuel's new coveted Wii. I put headphones on happy to have contributed to the gift. Seeing his interim report with four A's, two B's, and one C makes it all the sweeter as I fall asleep.

Delicious smells waft into the bedroom while listening to my daily CD. Rebecca motions toward a filled plate when I rise. She then joins the boys following through on her vow to have the house where everyone wants to come. It's no fun being the mom who wonders where their kid is. Joy fills me upon seeing them play. For the next few hours, my amazing daughter goes between pulling weeds from the gravel drive to playing Guitar Hero.

Later in the afternoon, we take the last boy home on the way to Home Depot. Rebecca's stamina amazes but I know she takes pain pills, as her brother did, to get through the day. She fills the cart with heavy bags of soil, mulch, and flowers while I replace broken hedge shears with new ones.

Watching her later tires me out as I deal with bills online. The computer screen soon goes black. How very grateful I am for continued Spirit direction! The display lights up after Spirit's message fills my brain. Rebecca lined up begonias in the flowerbed and waits for me to place them into soil. The task takes less than thirty minutes. I'm glad to do it for even though life is difficult at times being here helps Samuel and Rebecca, who has not eaten today. The last load of laundry for the day soon sits in the washer as dinner cooks. Joy fills my heart as she eats the love-filled dinner I prepared.

Jumbled words run through my brain upon waking at 5:52 AM. *"...with peace, with power, with love."* Feeling absolutely wonderful, I rise as usual to make Rebecca's coffee and Samuel's school lunch. When Rebecca rises I lay back down to hear the daily prayer CD.

Silence fills the house upon rising to start chores. The arduous task of scraping globs of wet cat feces off carpet, in the bedroom that stores Martha's belongings, begins. Cats marked their territory there for several years. My back hurts but spirit will help. Nauseating smells soon prompt a break to check email.

Mary's message requests my services during the Christmas holiday. A successful lawyer bought her house. She's fixing up a rented house several hours away and notes a friend will check on the cats until I arrive after Christmas dinner. Renewed hope for the future blossoms knowing I'll have her house to myself until January 8, 2008.

Lara Owen's article, "Planetary Energies Winter Solstice 2006" (http://laraowen.com) holds helpful information. Winter Solstice, Lara says, relates to home and family, warmth and light, love and companionship. The Sun rises in the same place for three days, offering a sacred opening, through which we can come to terms with the past, connect with our purpose, listen to guidance, and prepare psychologically for next year.

Beliefs and priorities continue to change. Everything seems up for review. I'm ready to move forward in ways that accord with new ideas and visions despite this month's upsets. My aim to move forward optimistically, while relinquishing established beliefs to venture into deeper mysteries, continues. Real change and transformation is possible. Yes! It's a good time to be bold.

Dawn breaks while rising to recall dreams. In one, I removed clothes out of water reaching almost to my head. There was also something about James being with his mom when she passed.

Another trip to the dentist costs $125 but I'm happy to be pain free. It makes things easier as I continue shampooing carpet. Cleaning carpets for the last four days has really been much more of a task than anticipated. Rebecca's precious hope chest slides over to the den with minimal effort so I can clean beneath it. Daniel took such care to get it for her on that Christmas Day so long ago…

One thought leads to another. Yes! The chest holds many precious memories, stored more than two years ago and then forgotten. I gave them to Rebecca after thinking it was time to die. Rebecca's CD player begins to act erratically as I begin to open the chest's lid. I'm curious but Karen Drucker's song now distracts me. It repeats "spirit" over, and over, and over. "What should be known?" I ask, sitting upon the small, flowered, den loveseat.

The chest, I hear, contains things of a human nature. But since I'm aware of our true nature as spirit they are no longer important. I need not look at them. The lids slams shut as I return to the rug shampooer.

Hours later, I realize the CD player malfunctioned to stop me from picking up one of Daniel's gifts. The soft cushion of a rising sun that says, "You are my sunshine," always prompts tears. Even while typing this, I continue to remind myself that when I got it, I was not yet aware of our true nature. We were fully into the game of life years ago. Now, I'm ever so grateful to that spirit of my last-born son for communicating during important times.

The CD player again malfunctions after I become thoroughly tired. "Relax, let go, release, and surrender," fills the air repeatedly. I sit to thank spirit for the message, again, affirming it's all God. It doesn't matter whether ego believes it's an individual entity communicating. I've opened myself up to only good so therefore am protected from negative influences. All messages now come from Light. I'm so grateful for this truth!

Charles notes Nature speaks during class two "Essay on Nature." Nature houses the Spirit of God, an essence that is natural healing, opening to see with greater awareness. Nature contemplates Itself, Plotinus reported, and creates a form by which *It* may become expressed. We are spirit, soul and body, constantly changing form. Spirit must flow within us for there to be a real representation of the Divine through us. As Emerson notes, "The divine circulations never rest nor linger." I'm creating a greater form of me while living in conscious union with Spirit!

A dream of Saul, Rebecca's father, wakes me near dawn. Saul told me he was going Home. I relay the news to Rebecca when she wakes and say Saul may be ready to transition. She should call him. She still says no filled with emotion.

Rebecca finally speaks with her father during the summer of 2009. It's shortly after he gets out of the hospital after having yet another heart attack. She's now at peace with their relationship.

Creating a better reality continues to top my to-do list but some things I cannot seem to avoid. I can only do so much every day but always feel Martha's presence when lifting years of caked on cat droppings from the carpet. Today's Course lesson reminds me that I'm limitless.

"Creation is the sum of all God's Thoughts, infinite and everywhere unlimited..." "God's Thoughts are given all the power that their own Creator has. For He would add to love by its extension. Thus His Son shares in creation, and must therefore share in power to create."

As a Thought of God, memory of the Creator assures me of Oneness and unity with *All That Is*. And that unity also assures that I possess the power to change all circumstances. It may mean leaving certain places and people but I'm ready to take the next step in manifesting the unlimited life my soul chose to create.

The CD stops later in the day while playing a recorded prayer. I say another prayer out loud, intending to speak only what God wants me to, and then ask what to do and say. A message comes before "Hold on to Love" plays normally. There's no mistaking; I am never alone!

Everything is an illusion of my own making. Everything I see, the Course reminds, reflects a process in my mind that starts with my idea of what I want. Changing my world is as easy as deciding what I want and continuing to focus on that idea. An image of what I desire, and judge as valuable, projects outward and brings the focus of desires. Yes, the time to help others that appear separate to the truth of BEing is here.

Tonight's Emerson class, "Essay on Spiritual Laws" reassures. There's a higher law than our personal will that regulates events. Everything happens to teach faith. We need only to BE and listen to the Voice within. We teach by example, by giving, not by words. Moses taught "I AM" is the Law of

Cause and Effect, flowing through everything. Emerson reports, "God is described as saying, I AM."

My habit of inviting Higher Beings continues upon returning to Rebecca and Samuel. The player pauses at the very end of "Magic" while listening to the daily CD at bedtime.

"Who's here?" I think, opening my mind to receive.

Daniel's essence fills the room.

I'm overjoyed to hear this is my time to rest.

A familiar throat gurgle wakes me thirty minutes later thinking this body is rejuvenating, refining, reenergizing. Rebecca sleeps on the couch when I rise to use the bathroom. I turn the TV infomercial off hoping she will not rise wondering why she wants to buy another useless product.

Afternoon mail offers another opportunity to draw me back into the land of limitation. Intuition says the envelope addressed to Samuel relates to the car accident experienced months ago. Suspicions are confirmed upon opening the letter. It's a subpoena for him to appear in court against me. Rebecca, I know, will feed the situation with anxiety so I choose to call the court number myself during business hours tomorrow. Surely, the court cannot expect a fifteen-year-old boy to skip school and testify against his grandmother.

The Course lesson seems very timely.

"I will not hurt myself again. I accept forgiveness as my only function. I do not attack my mind or give it images other than love… Father, Your Son cannot be hurt. And if we think we suffer, we but fail to know our one Identity we share with You."

Yes, this is a dream world, which I make up in my mind. But until I can lift myself further out of the fray of limitation, I must successfully deal with false world complications. The trick, I believe, is to involve a minimum amount of people not of like-mind. I'm in charge of my own emotions and prefer not to feed the negativity that crops up from time to time. Finding conflict-free, everlasting peace, undisturbed in a body, becomes easier when one chooses to take on the responsibility of their thoughts. Obviously, I have somehow drawn this experience to me but I can focus on the positive and know only good will come of this. I do not have to play this game by the old "rules" but can make my own.

Later, during a timely break after two hours of carpet cleaning, I visit the Poverello Thrift Store. Extreme fatigue rules but I'm driven to wander around as if looking for something. A two-tape set from a Religious Science International minister's conference on Radical Forgiveness, by Colin Tipping, draws my attention. The name "Kandi" comes as I get into the car. Clearly, the cassette tapes are for her. The Center is a short distance away so I pop a cassette into the player while driving there.

Colin's voice fills the air reminding me to continue acting as if I'm unlimited. Act with great passion, as if it is, and it will be. More than $4,000 passed through my hands this month and I continue to think about the business sale and my own place.

Kandi stands at the copy machine when I hand her the tapes. I have no idea how she'll react. How would you react if someone gave you tapes from a Radical Forgiveness seminar?

"This," she remarks with a wide smile, "is the best gift ever."

Kandi struggled with an issue this past week and thought of Colin and his Radical Forgiveness seminars. She remembered how helpful the seminar was when held at the Center but was unable to attend the one mentioned in these tapes. Now she's happy that God sent me with the exact thing she desired. How comforting to know, despite recent dramas, I'm still "in tune" with Spirit.

Later, the dripping sink keeps me up while trying to nap so I telephone Horace, an old friend of Daniel's, to ask about a cheap but reliable plumber. Horace, owner of several homes and now experienced in maintenance, agrees to check the plumbing on Wednesday.

Minutes after falling asleep, something reminds me to call about Samuel's subpoena. Computer-generated voices try my patience for nearly twenty minutes while I punch in numbers as directed. A woman, sounding very old, comes on the line seconds before I hang up in disgust. Thinking I'm Samuel's mother, she calmly says all I need do is write a note to the court confirming that Samuel is still in school. Breathing a sigh of relief, I thank guides before writing the note. The mail carrier retrieves it from the mailbox minutes after I sign it with Rebecca's name.

Ego, once again, draws me further into the illusion by reacting and labeling this as a bad thing. Could I now ignore this kind of situation without reacting?

Just recently I received a jury duty letter and decided to ignore it. So-called "criminals" are just our unconscious guilt appearing separate so it's not valid to judge anything. All is illusion. There was no need for me to inconvenience myself to appear before a court of law when I know this is all a figment of my own imagination. I also believed it not valid because souls live past lives. And playing the game according to pre-defined rules, made up by other figments of imagination, would only prove that I'd be totally useless as a juror in an archaic system. Pushing aside old ways, to improve my reality and reach ever-increasing states of awareness, becomes easier everyday.

Twenty minutes later, another car taps my rear bumper at the corner of the long street. I just laugh and move on knowing I'm in charge of the game. The best is yet to come. In merely five days, Rebecca and I shall enjoy our lovely vacation cruise. The thought comforts after another hectic day. Oh how I long for that state of grace where everything and everyone is perfect love.

Daniel's essence comforts.

"All is going according to plan. Hang in there Mom."

I'll recall these words tomorrow.

My mind focuses on the kitchen sink in the morning. Constant dripping makes it necessary, almost daily, to empty the bucket under several leaks of many years duration. Thankfully, it's Wednesday and Horace arrives on time driving a small, white van.

We discuss numerous plumbing issues while catching up on each other's lives, which have changed immensely. Horace now celebrates his twelfth crack-free year. The kitchen sink, he soon confides, leaked long before Rebecca moved in. The wood cabinet is moldy where water pools. Rust covers pipes and valves but Horace is certain he can fix it with little cost. He leaves to get tools and small parts from the van as I empty the full bucket.

It's refreshing to talk with someone of similar mind at last. We discuss experiences, books read, and things learned as he works on kitchen pipes. After nearly thirty minutes, Horace says we need parts from the plumbing store. He asks if I'd like to accompany him.

A break in the windshield occupies ego as we enter the old van. It spreads from the passenger side almost reaching the other side of the van. But I don't mention it. The nearby plumbing store doesn't have needed parts so we travel further to one near his house. The parts cost less than $2.

I insist on buying lunch when he points out his favorite restaurant. Horace is happy to oblige and turns the van around. The Christian restaurant is nearly empty as we enjoy great Jamaican food and low prices while continuing to share experiences. I thoroughly enjoy his company and he seems pleased to share the place.

Horace's house sits blocks away so he's happy to show it to me. He's forgotten. I visited Rebecca there when she lived in the back apartment after leaving home at seventeen. The back apartment is now gone. Inspectors tore it down because Horace and Daniel built it without a permit. We talk as I look around, complimenting him on making such a success of his life. Horace works for himself caring for several houses rented to others.

It's soon clear that we need another plumbing part upon our return. Horace hurries out to his van to go back to the plumbing store. I don't want him to pay for the parts and run outside to toss all my cash, about $53, into the van as he pulls away.

He returns within minutes to finish fixing the kitchen sink. Horace uses a solder gun and a blowtorch before heading outside to turn the water back on. I'm ecstatic to know we don't have to empty buckets anymore. But all hell breaks loose now because Horace forgot to replace one of the valves. Water gushes out from under the sink. It fills the already rotted cabinet and flows onto the floor before I'm able to run out and tell him to turn off the water.

It's now time to pick up Samuel from school but Horace asks me to stay. The main toilet sprays water into the air with each flush so he plans to repair it too. It should take a few minutes. I leave telling him the trip takes less than an hour.

Horace is gone when Samuel and I return. Both doors are unlocked. Lack of a note or phone message surprises me for I thought we had much more to share. I finish cleaning up the water, the dirty floor, and the filthy cabinet while Samuel plays with his new game system. And then I phone Horace to ask if he's okay.

"Yes," he replies announcing that I made an assumption by thinking he'd wait for our return. I cannot argue with his logic.

Although the main toilet is not spurting water, it's now constantly running. Over the next few hours, I try in vain to fix it. Exhausted Rebecca returns, with $100 worth of groceries after a ten-hour workday. She wants to make sure Emily has plenty to eat while house sitting. Our eating habits are vastly different so there's not much food for me.

My decision to call a plumber strengthens after listening to the leaky toilet during the night. The plan upsets Rebecca for she knows James will not approve. A receptionist soon schedules us for an early afternoon appointment. "In three days," I think, while again shampooing carpet in the storage bedroom, "Rebecca and I will cruise the Western Caribbean in luxury."

A cat's litter box now sits in the second bathroom shower. Although the shampooer moved over spots where it used to sit, at least sixteen times, the carpet is still gross. The stink continues to make me gag. My Black & Decker ScumBuster helps to break the mess up after vacuuming litter, dirt, and grime. I don't plan to go over the carpet again but know it's a possibility.

The tall, friendly plumber arrives on time. He's about my age and soon confides that it's been a very, long, time since he worked on such an old toilet. Creative plumbing, as he calls it (a fishing line used instead of a chain) amuses him. He quickly offers an estimate of $377 to change the toilet tank and snake both the clogged main bathtub and sink.

"There's no reason to continue living in limitation with running toilets and clogged drains," I think. Emily will housesit while we cruise and everyone will celebrate Christmas here two days after our return. There's no other choice so the plumber begins to work.

James is not too surprised when I phone with the news but blows up at the cost. Money is a huge issue. It appears that James' parent's estate is held up in probate. Delilah's lawyer moved the case to Dade County because he knows the judges there. I'm still trying to figure out why their parents did not designate them as beneficiaries. The simple act of naming their children as joint owners on the house and retirement accounts, in my opinion, would have saved much time and money.

Once again, James says someone took advantage of me. I should have called him first. I don't remind him of the many times we asked him to repair things. After all, we only judge ourselves, there really is no world, and ultimately, we only forgive ourselves.

James rants and blames as I try to stay in the energy of love. Although I do not yet fully understand, the Course tells us that angry people are suffering, just calling out for love, but their call really is our call for love. Yet, instead of remembering we're one, I change the subject and add fuel to the separation fire by telling him of the letter I wrote in Rebecca's name.

James grabs it like a drowning man, as proof that my lack of consideration for others is common. Before ending our communication, I thank him for helping to straighten me out. He makes it crystal clear that I'm not to repair anything else without explicit approval, agreed upon by his sister. Of course, I know my job is to correct my own misperceptions.

The only thing that keeps me from breaking down into an old crying form of my little self is the message from the spirit of my last-born son. I know all is well. This is an unlimited universe and I'll always have more than needed.

Catherine Ponder's wisdom comforts. Surely, challenges faced today are the good of my past and present trying to come forth so I'll focus on the desire for only good. A channel for great blessings continues to blossom into this reality as I concentrate only on the goodness of *All That Is*, in everyone and everything. These blessings come forth through Divine Order and Divine Timing.

The belief that we must forgive illusions on the level where they are experienced continues. It's been a constant struggle over the past two weeks to get things done before the cruise. I've pushed myself to work ever since returning from Tampa and now am exhausted. Ego pushes me forward even though I could have just done nothing and that would have been okay.

Tonight's "Essay on Compensation" class seems very timely. Yes, the only constant is change. We are One, all the Christ in God. Spirit is cause (conscious mind) and effect is the illusion of matter (body). Soul is subconscious. Fortunately, Spirit is the seed that bears fruit. "Ah, perception is such a lovely thing to change," I think, while driving back to Rebecca's house. Surely, perception will change yet again before the final four classes unfold after the first of next year.

The CD player stops and starts several times as I try to listen to my daily CD after dawn. Today's message is similar to yesterday's. Generally, "all is going according to plan." God's plan is to live a life unlimited in good and I'm ready to do so.

Today marks another day of non-stop work. After making Samuel's breakfast and lunch, I tell Rebecca she can go to work. I'll drive Samuel to school. Miles of backed-up traffic greets us on the turnpike. Samuel agrees to sing his theatre skit, repeatedly, as we wait to move inches in minutes. It helps to keep our mood positive. At one point, I pull out of line to squeeze in again after breezing for three blocks in the other lane. It saves us at least thirty minutes but Samuel is still twenty minutes late for mid-terms. We pull up to the school behind another parent stuck in the same traffic jam. Samuel's favorite teacher assures me it's okay. They're aware of the delay and waiting for three more students.

Dishes, laundry, and packing fill time. Princess and I walk out by the water's edge before I leave to get Samuel from early dismissal. She does her business without much delay but stickers now cover her tiny legs. I must remove the stickers since Princess spends most of her time in Rebecca's bed. If I don't, it's a sure bet they'll irritate me tonight. I still have to visit the credit union before getting Samuel but begin to remove the stickers, one by one. As impatience grows, I begin to sing.

"Princess has more stickers than I've ever seen before. And God must be delaying me for a reason."

(A major auto accident occurs along my usual route.)

After the clothes are out of the dryer and the stickers off of Princess, I rush out the door. A packed freeway prompts me to take another northbound route.

The credit union lot is almost full when I arrive but everyone is mailing Christmas presents at the Post Office next door. Only one person stands in front of me, the woman I held the door for. I withdraw money from my account with Samuel and am back on the road within five minutes. Relatively light southbound traffic allows me to arrive on time.

Samuel and I take our time shopping at Costco. I'm glad he's with me to lift the requested case of Propel water for James. Cars still sit back-to-back on the northbound freeway so I exit to unload groceries and drop off Samuel before taking a less congested route to the house on 47th Drive.

The now familiar putrid house smell assaults my nostrils upon entering the den. It's dark and dreary inside. "This," I think, "is another house of limitation." My stomach stirs while placing the Propel on a kitchen counter. I hurriedly gather things for my cruise and then see a court notice addressed to me sitting in a two-week old mail pile. The court date is during the week of my cruise so I'm thankful again for the traffic ticket lawyer.

One of Prudence's offspring lies on the back porch. Before leaving, I silently thank it for being there for James. "How long," I wonder as my stomach continues to churn while moving toward the den door, "has negative energy filled this house?" Getting far, far, away consumes me now.

There's still much to do for Christmas before the cruise. Target is a furry of activity. Winn Dixie is nearly empty as I gather the remaining ingredients to make my famous quiche. Thankfully, traffic on back streets is relatively light.

Rebecca arrives just as I'm ready to finish my Course work. She's clearly exhausted after a fifty-hour, difficult workweek, which included a scheduled audit. A warm bubble bath soothes her within minutes of arriving. I'm happy to bring her a beer while she soaks before joining me on the porch. She's not pleased to learn that I opened the subpoena in Samuel's name, failed to consult her, and forged her name. "What ifs" fill the air.

"Everything will be okay," I announce. "Only good will come of the situation."

My good draws closer to physical reality.

Chapter Twenty-Six

Differing States of Awareness

"The abundance of God is all around you. To feed the abundance of God you must feed everyone around you with love, with joy." SAM – Book of One :-) Volume 1

Emily drives through light rain to Port Everglades on Sunday afternoon. The girls unload red suitcases as I leave to find luggage tags. It never ceases to amaze that out of many baggage handlers the one with my deceased son's name always comes forward to help. Synchronicities abound. A penny from Heaven sits on the ground moments before Daniel appears.

Breezing through a short line to board the magnificent Costa Fortuna seems surreal. Adorned with beautiful artwork it's as opulent as the Costa Magica. Our splendid, irregularly shaped cabin sits near the back of the ship and is much larger than expected. Light steams in through two windows as we unpack.

This is our well-deserved week to relax before rushing to finish preparations for the unexpected family Christmas dinner. Rebecca is ready for a cigarette and drink. As we head toward the fabulous buffet, I'm grateful she won't smoke in the room. We load plates with chicken, fresh vegetables, and fruit, before eating amid rejuvenating music.

Tonight's dinner companions are two delightful couples from different places on the east coast. One couple is very vibrant and flashy while the other is Chinese and very low key. Rebecca and the vibrant couple become quite friendly. They soon leave for a cigarette break. Appalled, I think it's very rude. Servers wait to deliver the next course upon their return. The Chinese couple stays silent as Higher Self reminds me to control thoughts. Minutes later, the vibrant couple orders wine to share. This, they announce, is their only vacation. They plan to enjoy it immensely. I sip wine through dinner and am amazed at the amount of liquor coming to our table.

321

We're at sea on my fifty-seventh birthday. Fluffy white clouds sit amid blue skies as Rebecca presents me with a digital photo key ring. I'm grateful for the gift but it reeks of the world left behind. There's little desire to take or view photos and the camcorder now sits at Rebecca's house.

Our different world view exists poles apart as sunlight streams into the room. Rebecca leaves to smoke on an outside deck. External things affect me less while following the ever-present guidance of Higher Self. Course Lesson 338 reminds, "I am affected only by my thoughts." Happy thoughts of love show the way to a richer life, free of limiting thoughts.

Later, after roaming the ship, we visit the casino. I don't win but have lots of fun. More sensitive now, smoke soon drives me out to rest before a formal dinner. The vibrant couple eats at a premium restaurant while we dine with the couple from New York. Rebecca rises alone for cigarette breaks between courses.

A dirty, run-down environment in Puerto Rico disappoints on Tuesday. Shadows spook us out as we walk swiftly through construction back to the ship. A nickel from Heaven sits before me as we round a well-lit corner. Rebecca soon joins her new friends at a back gaming table in the casino while I opt for the usual evening studies.

It's becoming easier to do things alone. Eating at the buffet during the day saves more time for fun, Rebecca says on Wednesday morning. Disappointed, I allow her to enjoy the cruise as desired, while eating breakfast in the well-staffed dining room. Course studies console me. Yes, freedom lies in knowing life is exactly what I make it to be. "I am free of suffering," becomes the day's mantra.

The Costa Crociere U.S.A. Times notes that the Federal Communications Commission overturned a 32-year-old ban to allow broadcasters in America's twenty largest media markets to own newspapers as well. The news fills me with a knowing sense of dread. Our dollar's value went down with the news that construction of new homes and apartments dropped to the lowest level in more than sixteen years.

St. Thomas, in the U.S. Virgin Islands, is spectacular. Rebecca and I take a ferry to tour the nearby island of St. John with a large group from the cruise ship. Laurance Rockefeller purchased a large portion of St. John in 1956. It's now known as the Virgin Islands National Park. The island's Cinnamon Bay campground sits near a stunning view of sea and shore. Screen-lined cottages, 15x15 feet, look quaint and inviting but the area appears under used. The property boasts central bathhouses with lavatories and cool-water showers but no air conditioning. I cannot imagine living without private bathrooms or cool air.

Later, I'm disappointed to see someone else winning at the Wheel of Fortune. Evening studies note a miracle is a correction, reminding the mind that what it sees is false. A miracle reverses perception and ends strange distortions. Perception opens to Truth upon realizing there's no reason to be upset. This world and the bodies I see are illusions of the small mind. The woman is not separate from me. Her luck is mine as well for we are one, experiencing life in physical form.

This is a life worth living! A wonderful, robust woman safeguards belongings as we snorkel Catalina Island on Thursday. The cool, crystal clear water is very enjoyable. Rebecca and I eat barbeque before returning to the ship to nap.

Later in the day, we take the Dominican Republic bus to an Artist's village. Armed guards and stark land take us by surprise. Ego has it's way as I go with the flow. Now drinking along with Rebecca and the vibrant couple, we stop at a small convenience store to purchase tiny plastic bottles of flavored rum. We soon glide through the ship's scanner with filled pockets. When Rebecca joins the vibrant couple in the casino after dinner, I retire to finish evening studies.

As the ship soars through deep blue seas we enjoy Friday in our own way before meeting others for dinner. Our table is full on this formal night as the vibrant couple orders champagne. Ego again passes judgment when half the table leaves to smoke. While waiting for their return and making small talk, I realize my own past actions were inconsiderate as well. How many years did I join family members to play cards at Christmas, excluding everyone else? The thought of doing so now is out of the question.

Ah yes, we can always count on differing states of awareness. But this is an illusion of my own making. I can choose to live in the past and wait for the rest of my meal or I can choose again. When the waiter passes to attend to other dinner guests, I garner attention and tell him to bring entrees for those of us at the table. The couple from New York smiles broadly and nods in agreement.

Nassau is clear and sunny on Saturday as we snorkel in clear waters. Extremely tired, I then nap upon returning to the ship. Tonight is toga night. Joy overflows while explaining the routine to Rebecca later as we gaze at blue skies from an upper deck. Drinking seems the only way to enjoy time and become more in tune with my companion. But once again, when she joins the vibrant drinking couple at casino tables, I call it a night.

Two days before Christmas, I finish breakfast alone in the dining room, for the last time. Rebecca smokes on an upper deck. I'm fed up with the smoking and drinking. For me, this trip was all about breaking away from patterns of limitation. Yes, I can enjoy myself without constant physical companionship. It is a good thing to know. Emily picks us up an hour later.

The day fills with feverish activity. Rebecca leaves for work. A short rest before finishing Christmas preparations invigorates me. Two full pages of charges fill this month's charge card bill. But it doesn't matter. I'm grateful to have something that makes it easier to buy last-minute supplies and gifts.

A whirlwind of stuff assaults me making it a constant struggle to stay well and make Christmas dinner. The atmosphere is now extremely strained. Rebecca verbally attacks me for not letting her do anything. I'll soon forget it all while basking in the beautiful energy at Mary's house after Christmas.

Healthy patterns continue to form. My decision to be free of all lack is truly definite. A treatment noted in *The Power of Decision* by Raymond Charles Barker comes to mind. Yes, indeed, there's no reason for disorder for my world is in God's world, which is governed by law and order. Discordant ideas no longer function in my subconscious mind. Habit patterns are a thing of the past, which fortunately never was and never shall be.

I continue to choose love over fear. It's easier to do even as siblings seem to resent me for thoroughly enjoying my portion of money from Daddy's lawsuit. Thoughts of an extravagant birthday cruise haunt them, while pondering how they spent their portion. Ruth hands us gifts before dinner.

"I want you to know that no thought whatsoever went into your present," she rudely announces handing me a white envelope.

"Well, thank you," I reply, smiling widely.

"It's from Mom, Naomi, and me," she blurts out quickly as I open the white envelope with a crisp $50 bill.

"It's just what I wanted," I say, pleased that money comes to me easily and effortlessly while giving her a hug. Despite my new spiritual self, I calculate the cost of their three gifts, continuing to smile politely.

Everyone disappears leaving the mess for Rebecca and me to deal with shortly after dinner. I push myself to clean as much as possible before packing to leave in the morning. My two-week stay at Mary's house is truly a Godsend for it seems as if the atmosphere at Rebecca's is now hostile. Dis-ease fills me when I lie down to sleep.

"It is a matter of resonating with the One. You must set aside your differences of opinion to do so for all exist in the Light of one Almighty Being here, and everywhere. You know all things come in time and now is the time to sit back and watch as the others come closer to the light of their BEing.

"All things will unfold as promised throughout the ages but not in the way the masses believe. For all things are but a reflection of Oneness in all aspects. Know all is going according to the plan of One, as Divine in nature as all subsist here in the realms of eternity.

"Know your body is but a vessel for the One Most High, the knowing of, and maker of, all things here and everywhere. All exist within this One Light of Love, Peace, Hope, and Abundance. Shine the Light ever so brightly upon all to see and do not sequester yourself in the unknowingness of spirit. Real spirit does not accompany the illusion of time, space, nor separation. Acknowledge only what you wish to create here on earth. For the time comes closer to when all thoughts manifest quickly and wholly, despite the thinker."

Dawn breaks as I wipe a runny nose. Yet, it's hard not to dance and sing with joy while Samuel carries my red suitcase to the car. I'm so grateful to have this break from family issues.

Another card and check sits on Mary's kitchen counter. Mary includes a poem about people coming into our life. She's happy to have me in hers. Whether a reason, a season, or a lifetime, I'm equally happy for our friendship.

The past is gone while counting daily blessings. Catherine Ponder's words of wisdom in *The Prosperity Secrets of the Ages* soon fill me with glee. Sometimes, she notes, people may become hostile to our success. It's a sign that we have outgrown the present experience and are ready to move on. New circumstances will continue to spur me forward without restraints or interference. I'm encouraged to know that the longer it takes for my success to come, the bigger it will be when it arrives. Yes, Divine Intelligence always directs desires constructively for greater health, wealth, and happiness!

Two days later, life continues as a series of ups and downs, mostly downs while nursing dis-ease. Utterly despondent, while still sick and begging God for a sign of some kind, I pack Mary's Christmas things. Rex, her treasured car, sits beneath shelves of storage containers. I slide between eight inches of car and shelf to reach. A large plastic box falls down. It makes a quarter-inch dent on the top, passenger side door.

"How could this happen?" I wonder, totally horrified, quickly pondering how to repair it before Mary returns. Rex and the cats are her babies and even a tiny dent makes a big difference. Yet, the event holds meaning for us both.

A beautiful sun sets before me as I look out the window again begging God for a sign. The image in my eye remains while walking into Mary's den. It quickly breaks up into three and then four golden yellow, circular objects. For a bit, they're the usual thing most people see after looking at the sun. But I ask for a change in the objects so I'll know God is with me, that I'm not alone, and indeed am always guided, protected, directed, by the force within. I thank God and giggle with delight as the objects jump quickly from right to left.

Knowing Mary will have a much easier time leaving this house if she returns to find empty shelves instead of fond memories to pack, I move into the den to fill boxes with books and mementoes. Christmas dinner leftovers fill my stomach before turning in for the night. Delightful weather allows cool air to flow in through windows. The cats love to sit nearby, feeling breezes and smelling fresh air, so I open them a few inches making sure they can't climb between windows and screens.

The daily prayer CD stops and restarts several times as I listen after dawn. Intuition tells me to stop listening when it pauses in mid-play. I remove the headphones to scan the house. A scary sight greets me in the kitchen.

Sethala appears panicked between a window and screen. Her plump body is wedged into the small space. As I watch in horror, while quickly moving forward, she tries to back up and return to the kitchen table. The screen gives way as I bolt to open the window further so she can free herself. My heart lurches as she falls to the ground. I bolt for the kitchen door. To my knowledge, Sethala has never been outside.

Running like a white, spotted bunny, she heads for the fence as I try to reach her in a panic. Something warns me that anger or insistence will chase her further away so I try to calmly coax her to my arms. She resists. After a few short minutes, Sethala moves through the fence into the neighbor's back yard. My heart races madly while heading back past the open kitchen door for the fence gate. I close the door a second before seeing that Michgi followed me outside.

"Oh God, Seth, help me please," I cry, while trying to calmly coax Michgi back into the house.

Miles heads toward the door to join us as I open the kitchen door again. Amber is thankfully fast asleep on the couch when I put him into the bedroom and shut the door.

"Perhaps an open container of wet cat food will entice them into the house," I think.

Wet food does not interest Michgi. Both the back porch door and kitchen door are open as I again try to coax Michgi inside. As she moseys into the house, seeming glad to be there, I shut both doors and run to the neighbor's gate.

Sethala is nowhere in sight. Knocks go unanswered so I slip through the gate. There's little pleasure in seeing the neighbor's backyard features a beautiful small lake.

"Could Sethala have jumped into the water, or ran to either side of their yard to escape into another neighbor's yard?" I ponder wild-eyed.

I promptly forget Science of Mind studies. Asking for God, for Seth, to help get Sethala back into the house seems the only option. Instinct says she has not fled further nor leapt into water. A beautiful, Mallard duck sits floating calmly near shore.

A patch of white fills me with relief upon checking dense shrubs lining the fence. Sethala is crouched on the ground trying to hide. I softly coax her to come but she runs back through the fence to Mary's yard.

"Sethala will head to the wet food on the ground," I think.

But she does not. Still panicked, but trying ever so hard not to show it, I prop open the back porch's screen door with a heavy lawn chair before placing wet cat food inside nearby. Sethala jumps onto the porch screen to hang in mid-air.

I lunge for her. She jumps down and runs quickly onto the porch, past the cat food, and into the house. I breathe a sign of relief. While locking doors, and closing windows, my body moves into a new state of stress. It takes several minutes of sitting to calm my throbbing heart.

After I pet and thank both Michgi and Sethala for coming back into the house, I sit trying to determine why such an experience happened. Is everything we go through already predetermined? Or do little dramas like this just happen due to free will? I could have not opened the windows or I could have opened them only an inch instead of three or four. I did use my free will. Was this a lesson? Was this occurrence one of those little dramas that make life on earth so interesting?

Sleeping habits improve days later. I sleep for three and a half hours before waking! My body feels unusually cold. It then seems to vibrate, while waking as usual, several times, after minutes of rest.

Each time my beloved Sophia CD plays I have a wonderful experience. But for the last two weeks the CD player refuses to play it. Today, the CD player finally allows me to enjoy the CD. Marerill's essence fills the room. He says I know the path well and am on it. I am to follow it in Peace and Joy and Love and Truth. My saving grace is coming and I need do nothing. He tells me other things before noting, "I am raising your vibration. And now we wait in heavy silence for your deliverance."

My body feels deliciously odd. Grasping for more, I listen to the last three tracks again. The idea to insert my near-death experience near the beginning of *Death of the Sun* comes as the last song plays. I need to keep that memory fresh to remind myself of what I'm moving towards. My book is necessary to help others know there is much more to life than we can ever imagine. Thankful for these respites at Mary's, I look forward to greater experiences of the invisible, guiding every move.

New Year's Eve offers an opportunity to study Course Lesson 352. "Judgment and love are opposites. From one Come all the sorrows of the world. But from The other comes the peace of God Himself." I soon doze off while in the comfy, living room lounger. Tears fill eyes upon waking to recall a dream. Samuel, a doctor announced, had some sort of cancer. I cried thinking Rebecca would not have him as long as Daniel was with me. Is this dream of an alternate life?

Mary encourages me to invite family over to drink all her liquor so she doesn't have to pack it. Most of the family visits but they don't stay long. We talk and enjoy the Jacuzzi. Samuel and his friend munch on snacks while adults drink. Rebecca and the boys are soon anxious to leave for Lydia and Joseph's annual party. I decline Rebecca's invitation to go.

Naomi now asks questions about mediums and psychics. She and Ruth listen intently to answers. They don't appear surprised, or disapproving, when I note increasing contact with the spirit world, especially from Daniel, who I refer to as Marerill. They soon leave for home.

Change is welcome while watching what seems like my best Christmas present. Terry knows I love music and dance. His gift, a musical DVD about people in New York with AIDS in the 90's, is a joy to watch. Sleep claims me quickly after bringing in the New Year with champagne.

Two hours later, I wake to study Course Lesson 481. "My eyes, my tongue, my hands, my feet today (and everyday) have but one purpose; to be given Christ to use to bless the world with miracles..." "Father, I give all that is mine today to Christ, to use in any way that best will serve the purpose that I share with Him. Nothing is mine alone, for He and I have joined in purpose...Christ is but my Self."

The thought fills me with joy. Yes, I'm a lightworker here to help all return to the Wholeness it never left.

Eckhart Tolle notes in *The Power of Now*, "The secret of life is to "die before you die." We are to "die to the past," referring to it only when it's totally relevant to the present.

Are we to die to the future as well? How does one work on feeling the fullness of BEing? Constant gratitude for the present moment fulfills so I must be on the right track. Is neutrality the key to getting out of this dream?

Admittedly, I still waver between trusting and wondering if the messages that come though me are valid points of consideration. A thought wakes me at the end of 2011.

"Everything here is energy."

Humanity constantly deals with energy from all sorts of sources. Some are synthetic such as TV and radio while others are what we refer to as natural, such as geomagnetic waves. Nothing is solid.

Thoughts are energy. These thoughts go throughout space. If we sequester ourselves, we deal mainly with our own thoughts. But the more we go out into the world, the more people we are around, the more thoughts we have to deal with because everything is energy. Wind and rain carry thoughts. When the wind strengthens or it rains, the energy gets denser. And messages seem to increase when the sun erupts. More thoughts now burst forth.

"Thoughts become young and steadily increase through the mind of One when spoken. All thoughts energize in the consciousness in which you live. All thoughts become manifestation by which you live."

Obviously, it's vitally important to be consciously aware of our thoughts and to make them as positive as possible. It's time to entertain only those thoughts that we wish to manifest in this New World. Conscious, positive thought is the key to Heaven on earth.

Bibliography

* Barker, Raymond C. *The Power of Decision.* 2005.

* Campbell D. *Edgar Cayce on the Power of Color, Stones, and Crystals.* 1989.

* Choquette, Sonia. *"Your Psychic Pathway: Listening to the Guiding Wisdom of Your Soul."* 1998.

* Doresse J. *The Secret Books of the Egyptian Gnostics.* 1986.

* Foundation for Inner Peace. *A Course In Miracles.* 1992. (acim.org)

* Holmes, Ernest. *The Science of Mind.* 1938, 1998. (ernestholmes.wwwhubs.com)

* Owen, Lara. Planetary Energies "LAMMAS 2007 - Breaking Bread with Friends," August 3 2007. (http://laraowen.com)

* Ponder, Catherine. *The Prosperity Secrets of the Ages.* 1986.

* "Power of Decision: Body in Mind," SOM-202 - Teaching Manual, Class-6, Worksheet Ten, Rev. 2005.

* Rinpoche, Sogyal. *The Tibetan Book of Living and Dying.* Audio Literature: Berkeley, CA. 1993.

* Roberts, Jane. *The Seth Material.* 1970.

* Rodegast, Pat and Judith Stanton. *Emmanuel's Book.* 1985.

* Rodegast, Pat and Judith Stanton. *Emmanuel's Book II: The Choice for Love.* 1989.

* Singh T. *Commentaries on A Course In Miracles.* 1982.

* "The Golden Key" (adapted from Browne Sylvia, Raffanelli G. *Meditations,* 2002). Religious Science Ft. Lauderdale, Ft. Lauderdale, FL. (www.RSIFTL.com)

* Tolle, Eckhart. *The Power of Now.* 2004.

* Van Praagh, James. *Talking to Heaven.* 1999.

* Van Praagh, James. *Heaven and Earth.* 2001.

* Whiting, Hollis. "I Know Who I Am." Creative Thought, Vol. 83, No. 8, August 2002, page 43. Religious Science International, Spokane, WA. (rsintl.org)

* Yogananda, Paramahansa. *Autobiography of a Yogi*. 1987.

* Zukav, Gary. *"The Seat of the Soul."* Audio Renaissance Tapes, Inc. St. Martin's Press: New York, NY. 1990.

About the Author

SAM is a wayshower helping others to learn the truth of our BEing so humanity can return to Source. She is a lifelong believer in the power of Love. Her inspiring life demonstrates the strength of Mind over matter. It's a story of progression from desperation to hope, poverty to riches, limitation to freedom, and fear to Love.

The awareness that we're spirits, in human form having a physical experience, came shortly after April 4, 2004. A quest for self-mastery began in 2005 when the essence of her son led her to the Science of Mind. SAM turned her back on traditional medicine after decades of illness and multiple surgeries. Using Eastern medicine, and the teachings of Ernest Holmes, she successfully rid herself of many maladies.

SAM's book series is a personal account highlighting the process of one lightworker's awakening. Books from this author include:

Book One: Death of the Sun

Book Two: A Change in Perception

Lightworker's Log :-) Transformation

Manifesting: Lightworker's Log

Prayer Treatments: Lightworker's Log

Adventures in Greece and Turkey

Earth Angels

Return to Light: John of God Helps

Bits of Wisdom

Book of One :-) Volume 1

SAM is administrator of the popular Internet resource, Lightworker's Log (<u>LightworkersLog.com</u>). She currently concentrates on writing and spreading Spirit's message of Oneness. Guided by messages and synchronicities, SAM knows her most valuable asset is the ever-increasing awareness of our true BEing, unique figments of *All That Is*.